Arab Soccer in a Jewish State

Over the last two decades, soccer has become a major institution within the popular culture of the Arab-Palestinian citizens of Israel, who have attained disproportionate success in this field. Given their marginalization from many areas of Israeli society, as well as the ongoing Israeli–Palestinian conflict, such a prominent Arab presence highlights the tension between their Israeli citizenship and their belonging to the Palestinian people. Bringing together sociological, anthropological and historical approaches, Tamir Sorek examines how soccer can potentially be utilized by ethnic and national minorities as a field of social protest, a stage for demonstrating distinctive identity, or as a channel for social and political integration. Relying on a rich combination of quantitative and qualitative methods, he argues that equality in the soccer sphere legitimizes contemporary inequality between Jews and Arabs in Israel and pursues wider arguments about the role of sport in ethno-national conflicts.

TAMIR SOREK is an Assistant Professor of Sociology and Israel Studies at the University of Florida.

Cambridge Cultural Social Studies

Series editors: JEFFREY C. ALEXANDER, *Department of Sociology, Yale University, and* STEVEN SEIDMAN, *Department of Sociology, University at Albany, State University of New York.*

Titles in the series

(list continues at end of book)

Arab Soccer in a Jewish State

The Integrative Enclave

Tamir Sorek

CAMBRIDGE UNIVERSITY PRESS
Cambridge, New York, Melbourne, Madrid, Cape Town, Singapore,
São Paulo

Cambridge University Press
The Edinburgh Building, Cambridge CB2 8RU, UK

Published in the United States of America by Cambridge University Press,
New York

www.cambridge.org
Information on this title: www.cambridge.org/9780521870481

First published 2007

Printed in the United Kingdom at the University Press, Cambridge

A catalogue record for this book is available from the British Library

ISBN 978-0-521-87048-1 hardback

In memory of my beloved brother Alon (1985–2006)

Contents

List of tables

List of figures

x

Preface and acknowledgments

As a child in a Kibbutz in the western Galilee, and a mediocre player on our very mediocre soccer team, I sometimes participated in regional soccer competitions against teams which represented Arab towns and villages. These competitions were among the rare opportunities for us, the Jewish youth from the Kibbutz, to meet Arab youth, who despite their numerical predominance in the Galilee, were almost invisible for us. My memories from these encounters include sentiments of alert and worry; I always felt that for our Arab rivals, it was much more than a game, as if they were trying by any means to prove something to us, or to themselves.

Holding a very superficial and selective knowledge about the social history of the landscape of my childhood, as well as about the political dynamics of Arab–Jewish relations in Israel, I did not yet have the tools to decipher the political complexity of these encounters. Years later, as a graduate student at the Department of Sociology and Anthropology at the Hebrew University, equipped with much more historical and political knowledge, as well as theoretical perspectives and methodological tools, I had the opportunity to investigate in a scholarly way Arab–Jewish soccer encounters and study the tension I felt as a teenager. Between 1998 and 2001, I conducted a doctoral study on Arab soccer in Israel, which constitutes the core of this book. This long journey, which began as an attempt to study "the other," has taught me as well much about "my" side in the Israeli–Palestinian conflict and even about the ways that the boundaries between "them" and "us" have been constructed.

I began the study during a relatively optimistic period in Jewish–Arab and Israeli–Palestinian relations. Since then, we experienced the crisis of October 2000 when Arab demonstrators were killed by Israeli police, and four years of the second Intifada during which more than 3,000

Palestinians and 1,000 Israelis lost their lives. It is in this context in particular that many good people consider soccer to be an island of sanity and tolerance in a stormy sea of enmity. This book is not intended to pull the rug out from under this conviction, but it does shed light on the less popularly known and less discussed aspects of soccer in Israel, as well as on the complex (and not always innocent) role which soccer plays in the relations between the Jewish majority and the Arab–Palestinian minority.

Parts of this book have been previously published as articles in journals and edited volumes. Some of the main arguments appeared first in my article "Arab Football in Israel as an Integrative Enclave," in *Ethnic and Racial Studies*, 26 (3), 2003, as well as in "Arab Soccer in a Jewish State," in *Jews, Sports and the Rites of Citizenship*, edited by Jack Kugelmass University of Illinois Press, 2006. Chapters 2 and 3 are an extension and elaboration of my article "Palestinian Nationalism has Left the Field – A Shortened History of Arab Soccer in Israel," which appeared in *International Journal of Middle East Studies*, 35 (3) 2003. An earlier version of chapter 7 appeared as an article, "The Islamic Soccer League in Israel: Setting Moral Boundaries by Taming the Wild," *Identities – Global Studies in Culture and Power*, 9 (4), 2002. Chapter 8 is based on my article, "Between Football and Martyrdom – the Bi-Focal Localism of a Palestinian Town in Israel," *British Journal of Sociology*, 56 (4) 2005.

Throughout the years of working on this book I enjoyed the support of a number of institutions that financed the study, as well as many colleagues and friends who helped with good will and talent. First, thanks to my two thesis advisers who believed in the project from its inception: Baruch Kimmerling, whose sociological *Weltanschauung* served as my main source of inspiration, believed and supported, encouraged and challenged; and Danny Rabinowitz, whose original anthropological viewpoint is obvious throughout this book. I wish also to express my gratitude to the Israel Foundation Trustees and to the Shain Center for Research in the Social Sciences at the Hebrew University of Jerusalem for research grants which facilitated gathering of data, and to the Eshkol Institute for a sustenance grant. A special and warm thanks to the Meyerhoff Center for Jewish Studies at the University of Maryland, where, during my stay as a research fellow in 2000–2002, I wrote much of the original dissertation. The former center director, Marsha Rozenblit, provided generous support with much good will. The Department of Near Eastern Studies at Cornell University, where I spent three years from 2003 to 2006, was a warm academic home. Special thanks to the then Department Chair, Ross Brann, who secured funding for translation which enabled me to publish this book in a relatively short time.

I would like also to thank my research assistants who worked with me during the study: Suha Ibrahim, Najwan Ighbariya, Sammy Khatib, Iyad Mahamid, Ṭaleb Mukari, Ṣallah Muhsin, Afnan Muṣarwa, Vivian Siagha, Hiba Zidan, and Ṭareq Zu'abi. Rami Shala'aṭa, my research assistant, who also became a good friend, was very helpful in interpreting for me many of the subtle nuances in his town, Sakhnin. Nabil Khaṭṭab from Bristol University, who was then a graduate student and my colleague at the Hebrew University, was very helpful in building the questionnaires for the survey and in designing the sample. Also deserving of thanks are David Malka of the Sports Authority at the Ministry of Education, Ronit Nirel of the Department of Statistics at the Hebrew University, the sports reporters, Wa'el Hakrush and 'Abd al-Salam Shalabi, and a very special thanks to the devoted soccer fan 'Awni Shahin. Many thanks also to Kadish Goldberg, who assisted me with translating significant parts of the Hebrew version into English, and to Alexei Waters whose skills in language editing were very important in improving the linguistic style of the text. I would like to thank as well the photographer Shlomi Bernthal who provided the cover image of this book.

Thanks also to the hundreds of interviewees – soccer fans, journalists, functionaries – most of whom I did not know personally, but without whose cheerful compliance I could not have presented you with this book. In order to preserve the anonymity of the fans, their names appearing in the book are fictitious. Functionaries interviewed by virtue of their positions, however, appear with their original names.

Many of my colleagues and friends gave of their time and talents to read the manuscript at various stages of its development and enlightened me with their observations. Ramzi Suleiman, Moshe Zimmerman, and Kobi Metzer, read an earlier version of the manuscript in Hebrew and made significant contributions with their valuable comments. Allan Bairner and Paul Silverstein reviewed the English version and their insights were very helpful in upgrading and polishing the final product. I wish also to thank Nabih Bashir, Eyal Ben-Ari, Amir Ben-Porat, Ruti Kadish-Brener, Laleh Khalili, Etan Kohlberg, Daniel Maman, Shira Robinson, Sezet Rohana, Zeev Rosenhek, Guy Stecklov, Michael Shalev, Ishay Shneydor, Nurit Stadler, Shawkat Toorawa, and Ibtisam Tarabiya, who read and commented on parts of the manuscript.

Finally, I am grateful to my wife Michelle, who has been a wonderful emotional and intellectual partner. I benefitted from her comments, insights, and editorial suggestions, and she deserves special thanks for her support.

1

Introduction

The Maccabi Kafr Kana soccer team is one of several hundred Arab soccer clubs that take part in the Israeli Football Association (IFA). At the end of the 1995/6 season, after climbing to the second division, the team went on a tour to Jordan. The tour's highlight was supposed to be a game against the al-Wihdat soccer team, which represents the Palestinian refugee camp near Amman and bears its name. In Jordan, al-Wihdat is identified with Palestinian nationalism and the Palestinian struggle, and this particular sportive encounter was intended to emphasize the shared identity of Palestinians from both banks of the Jordan river. A few minutes before the scheduled start of the game, al-Wihdat's managers appealed to Kafr Kana's manager and sponsor, Fayṣal Khatib, with an unusual request in the world of sports: to exclude his three Jewish players from the match, or at least to ensure that no Hebrew would be used during the game.

Khatib rejected this request firmly, arguing that in his view his team consists of only soccer players, and that he never distinguishes between Arabs and Jews. In addition, he pointed out that the Jewish players on the team do not speak Arabic, and could therefore communicate with the coach only in Hebrew. In the end, after a long debate and a delay of several days, the game took place as a mini soccer match in a closed hall and without a crowd. In that game, Maccabi Kafr Kana beat the famous Palestinian team 3:2. Three different players who did not speak or understand Arabic scored the goals for Kafr Kana ...

Soccer and dilemmas of national identification

The Kafr Kana–al-Wihdat incident illustrates the well-known complexity of the social location of the Arab-Palestinian minority in Israel. This term refers to one million Arabs, about 16 percent of Israeli citizens, and includes those Palestinians who were not uprooted during the 1948 war and subsequent expulsions, and have remained under Israeli rule. The participation of Arabs from Israel in a sportive encounter in Jordan stemmed from a sense of the shared identity of Kafr Kana residents and the Palestinian refugees in al-Wihdat, some of them originally from Kafr Kana itself. However, the encounters that were allowed to occur following the Oslo accords in 1993 and the Israeli–Jordanian peace treaty in 1994 have taught both sides that long-term socio-political processes have shaped divergent social identifications and political orientations.

In spite of this, it would still be impetuous to explain the confrontation between Palestinians from both sides of the Jordan river as evidence of the alienation of Arabs in Israel from their identity as Palestinians. Similarly, the solidarity shown by the Kafr Kana management with the Jewish players does not prove that integration into the Jewish Israeli majority has become a realistic option for the Palestinian citizens of Israel. The source of that incident is the paradoxical role that soccer plays for the Palestinians in Israel: an *integrative enclave*. The integrative enclave is a social sphere that is ruled by a liberal-integrative discourse of citizenship – in sharp contrast to the ethnic discourse that governs the Israeli public sphere in general. It is a sphere which permits a limited and well-bounded inclusion in Israeli citizenship. This study is concerned with explaining the emergence of soccer as an integrative enclave and in tracking the ways it has been constructed as such.

As Palestinians by their ethno-national identification and Israelis by citizenship, the Palestinians in Israel face persistent predicaments regarding their socio-political location and self-presentation for several inter-related reasons. First, historically, Israel as a Jewish state was established in 1948 on the ruins of the local Palestinian society – and this historical association is the major anchor of the Palestinians' collective memory and national identity. This zero-sum game narrative makes the holding of both self-identifications, Palestinian and Israeli, extremely challenging; therefore, diverse strategies have been developed to solve the dissonance (Bishara 1999).

Second, the Palestinians in Israel face contradictory expectations by Israeli Jews and by Palestinians outside Israel. Rabinowitz (2001) characterizes the Palestinians in Israel as a "trapped minority": ". . . a segment of a larger group spread across at least two states. Citizens of a state hegemonized by others, its members are alienated from political power. Unable to influence the definition of public goods or enjoy them, its members are at the same time marginal within their mother nation abroad" (Rabinowitz 2001: 1). As such, the status of a trapped minority contradicts the standardized symbolic structure of national identity (Anderson 1991; Weitman 1973), which is intolerant of ambiguities and incongruity between ethno-national affiliation and political boundaries. While their Arab-Palestinian identity places them in the position of "an enemy within" for the Jewish majority, they are simultaneously considered suspicious – "Israelified Arabs" – by Palestinians outside Israel.

Third, but no less important, as Arab citizens in a state that defines itself as Jewish, they suffer from diverse forms of prolonged discriminatory policies in diverse spheres (Benziman and Mansour 1992; Dichter and Ghanem 2003). They are systematically excluded from the major political, economic, and social centers of power in the state, their culture and language hold an inferior status in Israeli public life, and they are alienated from the exclusivist Jewish–Zionist symbols of the state. At the same time, they do not see any realistic political alternative to the current situation. A viable Palestinian state does not exist, and a return of the Palestinian refugees which will transform the demographic balance in their favor is unlikely to occur. In addition, with all the above-mentioned deficiencies they still enjoy more political freedom and economic opportunities than any other Palestinian group (refugees and Palestinians in the West Bank and the Gaza Strip) and even than most Arab citizens in neighboring countries. These contradictions further complicate questions of belonging and identification.

Nevertheless, in spite of these contradictions, it does not seem that Arabs in Israel collectively abandoned being active players in either of these two spheres. Smooha (1999) has shown that the percentage of Arab citizens who identify themselves as both Palestinians and Israelis rose significantly between 1976 and 1995. According to Smooha, the politicization of the Arab minority in Israel since 1967 signifies a gradual integration into the Israeli public sphere, and hence, the demonstration of Palestinian identity in itself is part of an "Israelification process." Although criticizing the methodology of self-labeling used by Smooha, many scholars of the field have recognized that both Israeli and Palestinian spheres are highly relevant for understanding the identification, self-presentation, and political orientations of the Arab citizens of Israel. This recognition has brought scholars to identify and investigate the diverse strategies that enable the Arab-Palestinian minority in Israel to cope with the tension created by their sensitive location in the Israeli–Palestinian conflict. These strategies could be divided into two crude major theses: *separation* and *substitution*.

The separation thesis has different versions but it generally asserts that different dimensions of identification coexist in total separation, and each dimension gains prominence in different spheres. This separation is attained by means of psychological mechanisms such as compartmentalization and through the process of becoming politically indifferent (Peres and Yuval-Davis 1969). The separation thesis reverberates in later studies such as Rouhana's (1988), which argues for the distinction between emotional (Arab-Palestinian) and formal-instrumental (Israeli) elements of identity. Other versions of the separation thesis reject the distinction between a "shallow" civic component opposed to a deeply rooted but suppressed national component (Bishara 1999; Suleiman 2002). As 'Azmi Bishara argues, "in a long term social process the tool becomes a part of the person who uses it" (Bishara 1999: 176), and therefore Israeli identity is more than instrumental, even though it is perceived as contradicting Palestinian identity.

According to the substitution argument, Arabs in Israel tend to distance themselves from clear national or civic identifications and try to emphasize non-national identifications – communal, religious, clannish, or local (Bishara 1999; Ghanem 1998). This distancing is facilitated by their peripheral status vis-à-vis Jewish-Israeli society, as well as Palestinians living outside Israel. This double marginality enables the Arabs in Israel to define their identity without the need to commit themselves to either one of the two referent groups (Al-Haj 1993).

Soccer, I argue in this study, is an outstanding sphere for practicing both separation and substitution strategies. For this purpose, I have modified the separation thesis from the field of social psychology (which focuses on internal psychological mechanisms) into a combination of dramaturgic, macro-constructive and conflictual sociological approaches. Irving Goffman noted that individuals perform different roles depending upon their audiences and situations (Goffman 1959). A "role conflict" might emerge when there is a potential contradiction between the expectations stemming from different roles. A crucial precondition for a successful performance and impression management in such circumstances is the strict segregation of various spheres of life that maintains the separation of diverse audiences.

From this point of view, soccer is part of a wider strategy facilitating the spatial segregation of divergent identifications. The incident in Jordan resulted from an unexpected interruption of the separation strategy, within which soccer is used by fans, players, and managers as a means to gain acceptance by Israeli Jews. The contradictory expectations deriving from their being simultaneously citizens of Israel and members of the Palestinian people, have taught the Arabs in Israel, as a collective, to insert wedges between various spheres of life, and to assign different functions to each sphere. In this context, the soccer sphere is constructed to serve as an enclave of integration, in which the Palestinian citizens of Israel attempt to suspend their national identification as Palestinians; and in so doing, maintain inwardly and outwardly a circumscribed display – in time and in space – of civic partnership with the Jewish majority. In al-Wihdat, the different roles of the Kafr Kana residents as Palestinians and Israelis collided, since the audiences (Jewish Israeli players and Palestinian dwellers of a refugee camp) were not kept separate, and soccer's regular character as an "integrative enclave" could not be smoothly displayed.

The substitution strategy is also significant for understanding the importance of soccer for the Palestinians in Israel, since they do not fit the standardized model of national identity. One way to interpret the mushrooming of Arab soccer teams in Israel during the 1990s (see chapter 2) is to see them as a reflection of local patriotism, as a form of identification that does not endanger the Arabs' status as Israeli citizens. However, channeling local pride to the soccer field promises additional benefits. Despite trans-nationalist tendencies arising from the globalization of consumptive patterns, massive labor migration, and the decline of the nation-state's political power, national models of citizenship are still highly relevant (Koopmans and Stathan 1999); the meta-discourse of nationalism still governs people's minds and directs them towards certain foci of collective identification. Thus, when the option to adopt a certain national identity is seen as problematic, people may create alternative spheres that simulate several of the main attributes of a nationalist experience. Soccer provides many Arab men with a secure sphere of competitive masculinity, horizontal fraternity, and identification with flags and emblems; and at the same time, it avoids both Palestinian and Israeli national narratives (see chapter 6).

Due to the central place of soccer in the leisure culture of Arab men in Israel, and due to the increasing visibility of Arab soccer players in the Israeli public sphere, soccer is much more than another "interesting angle" for the investigation of Arab–Jewish relationships. The over-representation of Arab teams in the IFA is striking. While the Arabs in Israel make up only 16 percent of the population, in the 1997/8 season 42 percent of the senior clubs in the IFA represented Arab villages or cities, or Arab neighborhoods in the mixed cities. By the 2004/5, season the ratio of Arab teams was reduced to 36 percent, which is still more than double the relative share of the Arab population in Israel. In the 2003/4 season, Arab soccer was the focus of public attention as two Arab teams, from Sakhnin and Nazareth, played simultaneously in the Premier League (the highest division),[1] the former even winning the State Cup (see chapter 8).

Soccer as a political tool

The prominence, visibility, and success of Arab soccer teams and players mentioned above have both a political background and potential political implications. The sports arena has, on the one hand, a considerable symbolic power, and is therefore a sphere where political resources are readily available (Allison 1986). On the other hand, sports in itself is not stamped by any particular value system; it is a flexible tool for potential action in different directions (Hoberman 1997). These characteristics turn the sports arena into a "contested terrain" (Bourdieu 1988; Hartmann 2000), an arena in which struggles are waged over the potential meanings that can be attributed to it, and over the formulations of identities that are derived from these meanings. The concept of "contested terrain" reverberates with Gramsci's idea about culture as a political tool, which is used by the dominating groups in society but might be used just as well by subordinated groups to undermine the political status quo (Gramsci 1971). It follows that events which take place in the arena of sports have a role in struggles over the construction, shaping, and undermining of collective identifications.

Therefore, the construction of the integrative enclave is not a harmonious and coordinated process. Rather, the potential power of soccer games to produce symbols with a variety of different implications has made them a battleground of meanings: different social agents attempt to politicize or depoliticize soccer according to their interests. They try to articulate various meanings based on their ideology and their interests, and these meanings reflect different definitions of collective identities for the Arab-Palestinian minority in Israel.

Hence, soccer games in Israel are played on two different levels: the first level is on the field, where professional excellence is a requisite for winning. The second level is in the broader public sphere, in which power relations between various agents are expressed in the battle over collective consciousness. The main axis of this battle is the following subtle

---

[1] The Israeli soccer league is divided into six divisions (until 1999 only five). The top division was named in 1999 the Premier League, the second – the National League, and the third – the Countrywide League. For the sake of simplicity I use in this book the hierarchal number to refer to each division – second division, third division, and so on.

dialectic: an opportunity for integration into Jewish-Israeli society and acceptance by the Jewish majority versus a stage for promoting political protest and national pride. These aspirations are not totally contradictory and can even be complementary (Smooha 1999). Nevertheless, their simultaneous appearance entails an inherent tension on the level of subjective experience (Bishara 1999).

The tension between these two poles is related to the dual, elusive nature of ethnic minorities' empowerment in sports, especially in its *intensive inclusion* mode (Sorek 2003). In this mode, individuals and teams of the minority are intensively involved in the most popular sports of the majority, sometimes achieving notable over-representation in certain fields. On the one hand, this kind of ethnic empowerment always has its "subversive" aspect, which is identified with separatist tendencies or the aspiration to construct isolated social enclaves. On the other hand, when this empowerment is achieved within the framework of a state-oriented institution, it reaffirms the legitimacy of domination by the majority and represents integrative tendencies. These complicated relations are exemplified even in cases where sports empowers non-national ethnic minorities, such as the Pakistani minority in Britain (Werbner 1996), and the African-American minority in the United States (Hartmann 2000; Wiggins 1994). This dualism is especially visible, however, when the minority articulates its identity in nationalist terms and connotations (Boyle 1994; Finn 1991; Gallagher 1997).

In the case of Arab soccer in Israel, this duality is especially pronounced because of the intensity of the Israeli–Palestinian conflict, and because for the Palestinians, the establishment of the state of Israel meant a colossal tragedy of dispossession, exile, and colonization. At the same time, this state, with its exclusively Jewish symbols, is visibly present on the soccer field. The IFA, which constitutes the overall framework for soccer games, is a state organization, responsible for representing the state in international soccer. The second major prize in Israeli soccer is called the "State Cup," and the president of the state personally awards it. Important league games that are broadcast on television are preceded by the playing of the Israeli national anthem, *ha-Tikva*, and most of the teams – including Arab teams – belong to organizations historically identified with Zionist political parties. The stamp of the state is even evident upon the players' bodies through the symbols of the sports organizations, unmistakably Zionist in origin, printed on their uniforms. At the same time, as previously mentioned, this is the public sphere in which the visibility of Arab citizens is most pronounced.

Beyond arguing that there is a tension and that a battle over meaning is taking place, this study demonstrates that we can also identify a temporary winner in the battle, or at least temporary dominant meanings. As this book's sub-title – *The Integrative Enclave* – implies, I argue that the integrative orientation of soccer takes precedence in present-day Israeli soccer. This integrative orientation is constructed by several actors. Arab fans on the bleachers tend to cheer their teams in Hebrew and avoid national confrontation or political protest (see chapter 8); in the Hebrew media, soccer is represented mainly as a pioneer of coexistence between Arabs and Jews. This unexpected "alliance of meanings" stemming from the ad hoc shared interests of the Hebrew media and the Arab soccer fans is strong enough to overcome the more nationalist and highly politicized tones that can be found in the Arabic-language sports press (see chapter 5). The dominance of this integrative discourse is reflected as well by my findings that Arab men who go to soccer stadiums are more likely to vote for Zionist candidates and parties than those who do not attend soccer games. These same men are less likely to be proud of their Palestinian identity (see chapters 4, 6, and 8).

This exclusion of political protest and Arab-Palestinian national symbolism from the stadium is seemingly paradoxical. Since the removal of the Military Government in 1966, and especially since Land Day in 1976,[2] the Arab minority in Israel has been extensively politicized, and this politicization has been growingly articulated in Palestinian nationalist terms. The political calendar of the Arabs in Israel contains certain dates during which national history is commemorated, such as the *Nakba* (the destruction and expulsions of 1948), the Kafr Qasim massacre in 1956,[3] Land Day, and the bloody events of October 2000 when thirteen Arab demonstrators were killed by Israeli police. These days are marked by public and widespread rallies and demonstrations at which the Palestinian flag is raised and national songs are sung. Memorials to the martyrs – a pillar in the construction of many national identities – have been established to commemorate those who were killed in these events. Some Arab schools take their students on "heritage trips" to destroyed Palestinian villages. These trips emphasize the Palestinian

---

[2] On March 30, 1976 six Palestinians (five of them Israeli citizens) were killed by Israeli police during protests against governmental land expropriations. The day is considered a turning point in the development of national consciousness among the Arab-Palestinian minority in Israel.

[3] On October 29, 1956 a group of peasants from Kafr Qasim returned to the village from their fields, not aware that their village was under curfew. Forty-seven of them were shot dead by Israeli troops.

collective fate more than that of the actual villages that were razed. Further, since the signing of the Oslo accords in 1993, Palestinian national symbols are no longer illegal, and the Palestinian flag is commonly seen at political demonstrations held by the Arabs in Israel.

Against this backdrop, and in the light of the nationalist orientation of Arab-Palestinian sports in the pre-1948 period (see chapter 2), one might expect that the latent potential in soccer to provide a dramatic expression for the conflict between two mutually hostile social groups would turn the bleachers into an arena in which a vocal political protest would be manifested and the Arab-Palestinian minority's national identification would be strongly emphasized. This expectation becomes even stronger in the light of several well-known cases in which the success of national minorities in soccer turns the stadium into a central location for political protest and the expression of nationalist feelings. For example, the Athletic Bilbao team represents the Basque minority in Spain (MacClancy 1996); the Barcelona team represents Spain's Catalonian region; the Sporting Youth of Kabylia club in Algeria served as a rallying point for the Amazigh ethno-nationalist cultural movement (Silverstein 2002); and al-Wihdat – a Palestinian team in Jordan – gives its fans an opportunity to vocalize their identity as a national minority (Tuastad 1997).

Surprisingly enough, however, despite the significant place that Arab men in Israel give to sports in general and to soccer in particular, soccer is far from being a site for political resistance or explicit national identification.

One does not see Palestinian flags in the bleachers of Arab soccer teams; the songs, cheers, and swearing are largely taken from the verbal repertoire of Israeli soccer supporters as a whole, and mostly lack a national-based uniqueness. Outbreaks of violence are no more common at games between Arabs and Jews than at other games. In addition, the Arab soccer stars who play in Israel's leagues seek to downplay their national identity, instead emphasizing their professional identity. Even though the ethno-national cleavage constitutes the deepest chasm in Israeli society, and even though the Palestinian citizens have developed diverse forms of political national protest, these processes have only rarely and marginally diffused into the soccer bleachers, where the integrative discourse still prevails. This study strives to solve this paradox.

At the same time, it is noteworthy that this integrative discourse is not translated into a tangible change of the discriminatory character of the state. As a consequence, soccer might play a conservative political role that legitimizes the political, social, and economic inferiority of the Arabs in Israel. Seeing sports as a political sphere has been part of academic discourse since the emergence of neo-Marxist criticism of sports in the 1970s (Brohm 1978; Gruneau 1983; Hoch 1972; Vinnai 1973). These studies were followed by a plethora of Gramsci-inspired studies (Hargreaves 1986; McKay 1991; Sage 1998; Sugden and Bairner 1993), as well as a wave of feminist critique of sports in the 1980s and 1990s (Birrell and Cheryl 1994; Burstyn 1999; Hargreaves 1994; Lenskyj 1986; Messner and Sabo 1990; Theberge 1995). Still, the popular belief that sports is an autonomous area and that "one should not mix sports and politics" is very widespread in public discourse, even after years of academic criticism (Gruneau 1993).

The gap between academic discourse and public discourse on sports is not a coincidence; the attempt to mark a specific sphere as apolitical can be a successful tactic for achieving certain political goals (Allison 1986). This is precisely one of the secrets of sports' efficiency as a political weapon in social conflicts – it appears to be innocent, even somewhat childish, identified with "irrational" worlds, such as the worlds of leisure, play, and entertainment. The consistent presentation of Arab involvement in Israeli soccer as "apolitical" is a major component in the political function that soccer serves in Israel (see chapters 6 and 8).

"Modernity" as power

Another major attribute of sports that makes it powerful is its popular identification in many contexts with modernity. Functionalist writers view sports as a modern substitute for traditional foci of solidarity (Coles 1975; Curtis, Loy, and Karnilowicz 1986; Edwards 1973). The Weberian historian of sports, Allen Guttmann, considers sports to be an expression and reflection of the modern-industrial existence and a scientific world (Guttmann 1978). Norbert Elias and Eric Dunning see the evolution of modern sports as a major element in the "civilizing process" of British society, a process that is characterized by decreasing tolerance for sights of violence in the public sphere. As a result, a need emerged for a social sphere where regulated forms of violence were permitted (Elias and Dunning 1986).

In this book I am not interested in either validating or confronting these perspectives. Rather, I treat "modernity" first and foremost as a powerful discourse which plays a specific role in colonial contexts (Mitchell 2000), and sports as an important element in the production of this discourse. What is vital for understanding the political role of sports in the Israeli–Palestinian context is its representation as "modern," and the political assets that have been accumulated by this representation. The adoption of sports in general, and soccer in particular, has been a strategy of delineating the border between the modern and the traditional. This association between sports and modernity was used by the Palestinian elite in the pre-1948 period to promote a secular Palestinian national identity. The institutional development of modern Palestinian sports was tightly connected to what Habermas described as the "discourse produced by modernity about itself." Namely, sports, in the eyes of certain parts of the Palestinian elite under British rule, was a significant component in a "cultural model of modernity" (Delanty and O'Mahony 2002: 6), the basic normative, symbolic, and aesthetic structures underlying societies that consciously aspire to become "modern" (see chapter 2). After 1948, sports as a badge of "modernity" was used by the agencies of the state in order to present themselves as modernizing agents (see chapter 3). This successful representation still resonates in contemporary Israeli soccer (see chapter 8) and it has a significant contribution to the successful construction of the integrative enclave.

Methodology

This study is a sociological-anthropological-historical project which utilizes diverse research methods and presents the subject through a wide range of lenses, from microscopic scrutiny to a bird's-eye view. I have been guided by a holistic approach, which attempts to illuminate the phenomenon from as many angles as possible. The alternating movement – between the macro and the micro perspectives, between hard data and subjective perceptions, and between measurement and quantification and qualitative analysis and interpretation – focuses the view on the various angles of the subject under study. In this way, methodological choices do not overshadow the subtlety of the phenomena under investigation.

A major tool in this study was extensive ethnographic work in Palestinian towns in Israel, mainly in Sakhnin, but also in Nazareth, Kafr Kana, and others. This channel of research was the most challenging and the most problematic. As a 30-year-old Jewish-Israeli man who speaks Arabic, my presence in the field was far from being natural and unthreatening. With this profile I could easily have been sent by the Israeli General Security Service under the guise of an academic researcher.[4] I believe that in certain contexts I gained the trust of my informants and interviewees, since, as the book demonstrates, Arab

---

[4] On a similar problem see Rabinowitz 1997.

soccer fans have relatively frequent encounters with Jews. Still, even without being considered as a "secret agent," my Jewish-Israeli background was highly relevant to my interactions in the field. This fact has been an asset as much as it has been a burden, since it enabled me to learn extensively how Arab fans and players in Israel are strategically using soccer in their encounters with Jewish-Israelis like me.

The complexity and sensitivity of the ethnographic work emphasizes further the need for additional channels of investigation. Therefore, this book incorporates findings from historical archival research, textual analysis of the contemporary Arabic and Hebrew sports press, interviews with soccer fans and functionaries, as well as the statistical analysis of financial support for soccer clubs invested by local authorities (see appendix 2 for details on the database created for this purpose). The accumulated findings from these data sources are used to analyze both the discursive and institutional strategies employed in the soccer sphere.

In addition, I conducted two surveys which enabled me to add a correlative dimension to the study. Politicians, sports writers, local and religious leaders all try to harness soccer to their needs. Sometimes they consciously and intentionally attempt to shape collective identifications and to influence political behavior through the game. These attempts are motivated by the assumption that soccer has the potential to significantly influence the emotional bonds that individuals develop towards various social groups. These important assumptions can be tested by examining the statistical correlations between the degree of involvement in soccer on the one hand, and the sense of collective pride and voting patterns on the other hand. Two surveys investigated these correlations. One, conducted in Sakhnin in April 1999, encompassed 173 male interviewees between the ages of 16 and 40. The second survey involved 448 interviewees, a representative sample of the Arab male population in Israel between the ages of 18 and 50 (see appendix 1 for further details on sampling method and research design).

The structure of the book

The book begins with an historical introduction. In chapter 2, I examine the emergence of modern sports in Palestine and how it was viewed by certain segments of the Arab-Palestinian elite as a badge of modernity and as a necessary vehicle for forging a Palestinian national identity. The Arab-Palestinian sports infrastructure was leveled to rubble with the eradication of Palestinian urban centers in the war of 1948; chapter 3 examines the reappearance of Arab sports after the State of Israel was established. This time sports was used as a political tool in the hands of the government and other state-related institutions. Under the Military Government (1949–1966), sports in general and soccer in particular were part of an educational and propagandist program which aimed to distance the Arabs in Israel from any development of national consciousness and protest.

The recent prosperity of Arab soccer teams has been achieved by the generous financial support of soccer clubs provided by Arab municipalities. Therefore, chapter 4 examines financial documents containing information about support given to soccer clubs. This quantitative analysis is complemented by in-depth interviews with Arab mayors that illuminate the motivations behind this support.

Chapter 5 deals with the meanings attributed to soccer by the Arab press in Israel and the attempts of Arab sports writers to generate Palestinian and Arab national pride around Arab soccer teams and players. Interestingly enough, this assumed linkage between sports and national pride has no significant echoes among the fans, as chapter 6 demonstrates. That chapter deals with the complex relations between soccer fandom in various arenas (Jewish teams, Arab teams, the Israeli national team) on the one hand, and national identity and political behavior on the other hand. The chapter discusses the attempt of Arab fans to fashion the soccer arena as an apolitical arena and analyzes the potential for soccer fandom to serve as a "surrogate nationalism." In addition, the chapter discusses the ambivalent attitude of Arab fans towards the Israeli national team.

The mirror image of soccer as an integrative sphere is the isolationist reaction of the Islamic Movement. Chapter 7 deals with the Islamic Soccer League in Israel and points to the linkage between the ideology of the Islamic Movement and its need to establish a separate soccer league. In addition, the chapter explores the tensions and dilemmas created when soccer and political Islam meet. Chapter 8 illustrates the role of soccer in the formation of collective identities among the residents of Sakhnin, a town that is known in contemporary Israel as both a bastion of Palestinian national protest and Arab soccer excellence. The chapter points to the dialectic between the option of nurturing national pride around the local team and the aspiration of many of the supporters to preserve the soccer arena as an enclave of integration, thereby emphasizing the Israeli civic component of their identity. The final chapter evaluates – with a broad view – the role that soccer fulfills in Arab–Jewish relations in Israel, and speculates about future directions that may be taken as Arab prominence in Israeli soccer continues to grow.

2

Sports, modernity, and struggle in Palestine

On December 24, 1917, less than two months after the historical Balfour Declaration in which Britain declared its sympathy for the Zionist project in Palestine, the well-known Jerusalemite educator Khalil Sakakini wrote in his diary: "The Power! The power! This is the new education that we should disseminate ... the stronger will inherited the land" (Sakakini 1943: 117). Sakakini, who admired Friedrich Nietzsche and named him "the master of the philosophy of power in our era," had founded eight years earlier an elitist, nationalist, and secular school that was the first Arab school in Palestine to include sports in its curriculum. His sporting education stressed martial arts such as boxing and wrestling, a reflection of Sakakini's perception of sports as a tool that prepares the nation for war (Sakakini 1943: 52).

Sakakini was a pioneer who represented the tendency of his socio-demographic milieu to assign a specific political role for sports. From the first decade of the twentieth century on, sports was a significant element in the conscious attempts of a secularized intellectual elite to construct an Arab (and later, Palestinian) national identity and in their self-appointed mission of "modernizing" Palestinian society. Gradually, this modernizing mission became a tool in the anti-colonial struggle against Britain and Zionism, and in this context, sports was assigned the double mission of nurturing muscular power for beating the enemy and serving as a viable representation of genuine Palestinian modernity.

Sports and colonialism

The complex relationships between sports, colonialism, and modernity are crucial for understanding the sports dynamics in Palestine. British rulers used the sports they exported to the countries they conquered as a tool for

14

co-opting local elites and inculcating "British" as well as Christian values in the natives. All over the globe, from Ireland, through Africa, to India, sports games were assigned the role of "civilizing," "moralizing," and "moderniz-ing" people from "under-developed" cultures (Jacob 2005; Mahlmann 1988; Mandle 1979; Mangan 2001; Nauright 1997; Sugden and Bairner 1993). It is not a coincidence, therefore, that British games were considered by many non-Europeans as a cultural weapon used by the West to subordinate non-Western societies. In many cases, however, those same games were adopted by the local population and became, ironically enough, locales for the formulation of anti-colonialist nationalist sentiment. Such was the fate of cricket in India (Appadurai 1996), and that of soccer in Egypt (Di-Capua 2004; Wagg 1995), Yemen (Stevenson and Alaug 1997), and Zimbabwe (Stuart 1996). The globalization of the games enabled their reinterpretation as first and foremost viable representations of modernity rather than as symbols of foreign rule.

In the Middle East, competitive organized physical activities, including team ball-games, have been known for centuries, long before the Western colonial enterprise. Games such as polo (known in Arabic as *solojan*), hockey (*houksha*), versions of tennis (*tibtab*), and golf (*daho*), were played by Arabs in the Middle East at least since the Middle Ages as bureau-cratically organized activities (Alawi 1947; Al-Khuli 1995). Furthermore, the practice of maneuvering the ball and shooting it with the foot as a game was known to Arabs as to other civilizations (Khuli 1995). However, the codified and standardized versions of modern global sports as we know them today, and above all the game known as soccer in the USA, football in England, and *kurrat al-qadam* in the Arab world, were imported to Palestine at the beginning of the twentieth century, by immigrants from Europe (Tidhar 1961).

The identification of soccer with Europe in general and with Britain in particular, as well as the recognition of its political role, might explain why Ottoman authorities under the rule of Sultan Abdulhamid II (ruled 1876–1909) were very suspicious of it. Young men who played soccer in Istanbul before 1908 were pursued by the authorities (Okay 2002). There is no evidence that a similar policy was implemented in Palestine, and it is known that the first soccer club in Palestine was established as early as 1906 by Jewish immigrants in Jaffa (Kaufman 1998). Nevertheless, the first documented games played by the local Arab population are found only after the 1908 revolution in the Ottoman Empire (Tidhar 1961), which liberalized many spheres of life within it.

The process of soccer's institutionalization and formalization began after the British conquered the country in 1917. As has been stated, modern sports in general and soccer in particular have never been politically neutral in Palestine. Soccer arrived in Palestine loaded with both its colonialist function and the latent promise to "advance" its follower towards the mirage of modernity. Hence, contrary to Sakakini's aspiration that sports games would be pioneers of modern Arab nationalist consciousness, they were considered by the mandatory government as a mechanism that might promote interethnic cooperation between Jews and Arabs (Ben-Porat 2001c). As a part of this policy, and in 1921 (shortly after the first intercommunal riots in Palestine in 1920) the British "Temporary Government" in Palestine established a framework called Sports Clubs and invited Arabs and Jews to join them.

The Sports Clubs began to manage regular cup games in which both Arab and Jewish teams took part, and at least one team, that of the railway workers, included both Arab and Jewish players (Kaufman 1993). In fact, friendly soccer games between Jewish immigrants and Arabs had taken place even before World War One (Tidhar 1961: 17), but under British rule these encounters not only contradicted the general tendency of growing communal segregation, they were also politically motivated and initiated by the British authorities to pacify the anger of the Arab population who opposed the pro-Zionist British policy.

During the 1920s several Arab sports clubs were established in the large cities. This sporting activity was carried out mainly by working-class individuals and petits bourgeois while the upper classes remained uninvolved (Badran 1969: 311). In contrast to Sakanini's expectations, sports began its development in Palestine as a class-based, mainly masculine sphere, where Arabs, Jews, as well as British soldiers and functionaries interacted.

This state of affairs was relatively short-lived. Unlike the British perspective, Zionist leaders tended to view sports as an integral element in the project of nation-building and the "resurrection" of the Jewish people (Kaufman 1998). Therefore, British policy faced diverse Zionist attempts to establish competitions and sports projects for "Jews only." A significant example was the initiative of the Zionist sports association, Maccabi, to establish a formal soccer association affiliated with FIFA (the international soccer association). Maccabi was the first Zionist sports organization established in 1921 by the civic-liberal, non-socialist wing of the Zionist movement as an international umbrella framework for Jewish sports associations from different countries. Maccabi officials had considered the founding of such an association not only an integral part of the revival of the Jewish people in its homeland, but also as a means for weaving a network of international relations for the

Zionist project.[1] According to FIFA rules, however, only associations representing states could be accepted as members. Thus, Maccabi officials were compelled to invite not only the Zionist socialist political adversary, ha-Po'el, but also Arab teams to join the Palestinian Football Association (PFA). Therefore, in addition to the fourteen Zionist representatives that participated in the first meeting of the new soccer association directorate, one Arab delegate took part, a member of the Nusseibeh family, representing the Islamic Sports Club of Jerusalem. However, despite his involvement in this first session, Nusseibeh's name never again appeared in the directorate's protocols.

Nevertheless, during the first years of the PFA, Arab teams participated in the games of the association. A report submitted to FIFA in 1929 describes three soccer divisions in Palestine: ten teams in the first, twenty in the second (five of them Arab), and thirty-nine in the third (six of them Arab).[2] At this stage, the Palestinian Arabic press did not ascribe much importance to sports, and the sporadic reports on the subject were based on eyewitness accounts. On April 4, 1929, an exceptional report was published in the Arabic newspaper *Filasṭin* about a match held in Jaffa between the Islamic Sports Club and one of the Jewish teams of ha-Po'el. The generous coverage appeared thanks to a diligent spectator who recorded his impressions and sent them to the newspaper. He describes a large crowd and a high level of enthusiasm during the game, and he reports the Jewish team winning 5:1. He analyzes the reasons behind the Arab team's loss and calls for the introduction of professional training, "like the Jews and the Egyptians are doing." After two weeks, the return game took place, and ha-Po'el won again. This time, the newspaper blamed the loss on the hostile calls of the Jewish referee, who disqualified two goals scored by the Arab team.

Despite the PFA's formal claim that it represented all of the country's inhabitants, Zionist officials and players dominated it on all levels. With the exception of the 1932 championship, won by the team of the British police, all the other champions were Jewish teams. Furthermore, in official games of the Palestinian National Team the Zionist anthem *ha-Tikva* was played alongside God Save the King and the team itself was boycotted by the Arab-Palestinian players.

Not surprisingly, Arab willingness to serve as a figleaf for the association's neutrality did not last long. As early as 1930, the newspaper

---

[1] See: *The IFA Yearbook*, 1959, Archives of Sport and Physical Education, Wingate Institute, AD 1.21/31.

[2] Archives of Sport and Physical Education, Wingate Institute, AD 1.21/15.

Filasṭin expressed its resentment of this state of affairs. The editor, out of his awareness of the political role of sports, called for the establishment of a separate Arab sports association.[3] This idea was realized four years later in 1934 with the establishment of the General Palestinian Sports Association (GPSA). This association managed many sports competitions in addition to soccer. The immediate result of its founding was the departure of Arab soccer clubs from the PFA to join the Arab sports association.

Throughout the 1930s, parallel to these institutional developments, sports reports became more substantial and prevalent in the Palestinian press and they tended to conceive sports mainly as an educational mechanism. Accordingly, some newspapers dedicated significant space to reports about sports competitions in schools. The nationalistic and militaristic meanings of these events proved to be very explicit. Examples of this are the Arab flag that was displayed at these competitions and the fact that youth sports teams were named after historically renowned Muslim and Arab military commanders, such as Khalid Ibn al-Walid, Tariq bin al-Zayyad, and Ṣallaḥ al-Din al-Ayoubi. In May 1935, the association organized a major sports festival in Jaffa, in which, according to reports in *Filasṭin*, more than 5,000 Arab athletes competed in track and field, sword fighting, and horseback riding.[4]

Although the British authorities were initially interested in encouraging sporting activities among Arab-Palestinians, the affinity between the emerging sporting movement and the national movement was regarded with suspicion. With the eruption of the Great Revolt against the British mandatory government in Palestine (1936–1939) this suspicion became evident as some clubs were closed by the authorities out of concern that they would serve as a platform for political organization.[5] Practically, during the revolt the GPSA ceased functioning. By 1939, when the rebellion subsided, Arab soccer players remained without any institutional framework. The British authorities became even more suspicious about sports clubs and were selective in authorizing the opening of new clubs. For example, the police recommended rejecting the request to open the Sa'adi Sports Club in Jerusalem because some of the applicants were known to hold "extreme nationalist views" and the officer concluded that "the desire to form this club is motivated by forces other

---

[3] *Filasṭin*, July 2, 1930.   [4] *Filasṭin*, May 17, 1935.

[5] See, for example, correspondence from September–October 1937 between the district commissioner of Jerusalem and the district police officer of Ramallah about the decision to close the al-Bireh Youngmen Sports Club (Israel State Archive, "Bireh Youngmen Sports Club," M-843).

than the mere love of sport."[6] This state of affairs might explain the request of several Arab teams to rejoin the PFA (which was surely not considered as anti-British) in 1941. These teams finally split off once again from the association with the re-establishment of an Arab sports association in 1944.

1944–1947: the nationalization of sports

In May 1944, the National Sports Club of Jaffa initiated the re-establishment of an Arab sports association. Representatives from twenty-one clubs assembled in response to the invitation and decided "to establish an association to be called 'The General Palestinian Sports Association.' The directorate of this association should be exclusively Arab, without consideration of the citizenship of participatory teams."[7] Likewise, the National Sports Club of Jaffa decided to establish a preliminary committee for the drafting of a constitution. For this purpose, they enlisted the help of all the Arab clubs and urged them to send their proposals for the constitution. On July 22 of the same year, the inaugural meeting of the new organization was held in Jaffa. It was represented in the media as "The Arab Palestinian Sports Association."[8] At the meeting, the representatives of fourteen clubs from across the country were present. The involvement of various political parties in the sports clubs was noticeable (Badran 1969: 310). It is also worth mentioning that during the very same period, another Jaffan sports club (the Islamic Sports Club) initiated a plan to establish the Palestinian militia al-Najda, with the aim of preparing the Arabs in Palestine for a military conflict with the Zionists (Levenberg 1993: 126–154). The nationalist orientation of this association was reflected as well in the game calendar. The association did not play on November 2, the anniversary of the Balfour Declaration, a day which is remembered by Palestinians as the beginning of their downfall. A soccer game which was nevertheless played in Jaffa in 1945 was preceded by a moment of silence.[9]

The APSA had a number of committees, each assigned to a different sports branch. In addition to soccer, the association appointed committees for boxing, table tennis, volleyball, weightlifting, swimming, and

---

[6] Israel State Archive (ISA), "The Sa'adi Sports Club," M-843.   [7] *Filasṭin*, June 17, 1945.
[8] Unfortunately, the documents of this Association were lost in the 1948 war. Given this loss, the main source for its activity is the sports section of the newspaper *Filasṭin*.
[9] *Filasṭin*, November 2, 1945.

basketball.[10] The association was managed in accordance with six different regional sub-associations: Jerusalem, Jaffa, Haifa, Gaza, Nablus,
and the Galilee. In 1945, the sports section of *Filasṭin* estimated that the
number of active athletes exceeded 10,000. Eight months after its official
founding, the association included forty-five clubs, ranging from Acre in
the north to Bir-Saba' in the south. By 1947 the number had increased to
sixty-five clubs.[11]

The nationalist rhetoric in *Filasṭin*

The institutional prosperity of Palestinian sports was accompanied by
unprecedented coverage by the media. It is not a coincidence that the most
active newspaper reporting on sports events was the daily newspaper
Filasṭin. *Filasṭin* was one of the longest-running and most important Arab-
Palestinian newspapers under British rule. It was founded by the cousins 'Isa
and Yusef al-'Isa and published in Jaffa from 1911 to 1948. It became a daily
in 1929, and in 1946 its distribution was approximately 9,000 copies a day
(making it the second largest Arab newspaper). Its sales were based mainly
on the subscriptions of educated Christians, and it served as a platform for
writers who identified with the secular 'Istiqlal' party (Abu-Ghazaleh 1972;
Kabaha 1996).[12] While the founding of the newspaper was motivated
mainly by the desire to defend the interests of the Arab Orthodox (Rumi)
community, very soon, however, 'Isa al-'Isa found himself defending the
national Palestinian cause (Khalidi 1997). Although al-'Isa did not abandon
the Orthodox cause, *Filasṭin* tended to maintain a supra-religious
orientation in its writing (Abu-Ghazaleh 1972), frequently stressing the
unity of interests of Christians and Muslims in Palestine in the face
of colonialism. The newspaper was also the most prominent and consistent
opponent of the aspiration to see Palestine as part of a pan-Arab state and
instead was committed to the idea of a particularistic Palestinian identity.

Between 1944 and 1947, *Filasṭin* published almost daily a sports column
that was dedicated to spreading a nationalist ideology. The section was
entitled *Al-al'ab al-Riyaḍiyya* ("The Sports Games"), and its first editor
was Hassan Husni, a former sportsman and an Egyptian journalist living
in Palestine in the 1940s.[13] The very fact of the section's existence, as well as

---

[10] It is noteworthy that some of these frameworks, such as the table tennis association, were
active before the general association was founded.
[11] According to *Filasṭin*, the PSA decided as well to publish a bi-weekly periodical called
al-Jil. Unfortunately, none of *al-Jil*'s issues has survived.
[12] Istiqlal was a secular nationalist party that opposed the notable leadership in Palestine.
[13] Mustafa Kabha, personal communication.

its interpretative and pedagogic characteristics, teach us of a significant development in the Palestinian elite's attitude to sports in this period, especially when compared with the scattered reports of the 1920s and 1930s.

"Sports is an indicator of health, progress and social revival."[14] This statement, used as an argument to convince municipalities to financially support sports clubs, reflects the column's rhetoric, in which sports was presented as an integral part of modernization and "progress." In this sense the rhetoric was embedded in a prevalent discourse about body and modernity which had emerged in the region, especially in Egypt (Jacob 2005) and Iran (Schaeygh 2002), since the late nineteenth century. Following colonial penetration, this rhetoric incorporated as well explicit consideration of the relationship between national success and physical culture (Jacob 2005: 126–156). Therefore, sports' assumed power to cultivate modernity in Palestine has made it a necessary tool of both nation-building and anti-colonial struggle.

An important element in the above-mentioned discourse was presenting sports as a mechanism that strengthens the national body through strengthening the individual body. "Every person must look after his body, and adhere to the rules and obligations that the experts have agreed upon."[15] This pedagogic tone, preaching respect for the body, is a particularly noticeable characteristic of the sports section in those years. It recruited the help of doctors, approached on the initiative of the paper, whose quoted opinions were presented as a professional endorsement of the demands the section made of its readers. Well-informed instructions on how to take care of the body were often published, with a specific focus on certain organs: oral hygiene, health of the eye, and so on.

At the same time, despite the great importance of caring for the individual body, it was not usually proffered on its own. Most of the time, it was presented as a means to constructing national robustness:

One is forced to point out here that sports' most important virtue is that it is creating a generation of youths and adults with healthy bodies, free from sickness, who do not complain of feebleness and weakness. There can be no disagreement that such a generation is the standing army of the state, which it will call upon in its hour of need.[16]

There is a significantly distinctive feature of modern nationalism's construction of symbols which stems from the need to stress the "natural" foundation of the identity under discussion. George Mosse claimed that "the

---

[14] *Filasṭin*, November 1, 1945.   [15] *Filasṭin*, December 25, 1945.
[16] *Filasṭin*, February 7, 1946.

rediscovery of the human body" in Western Europe in the nineteenth century expressed a yearning for the original and the natural against what was perceived as the "artificiality of modern life" (Mosse 1985: 48). Renewed concern with the body was connected to the need of European nations coming into existence at exactly that time to emphasize their "naturalness." In this context, one can say that the Palestinian national movement, consolidating itself as a new entity in opposition to traditional, religious, and local identities which preceded it, also found itself in need of stressing "natural" and primary focal points of identification.

The *Filastin* sports section did not make do with a direct appeal to its readers, but tried as well to relay its importance through various agents of education, such as religious leaders or schoolteachers. In these cases, the rhetoric that tied caring for the individual body with the nation's needs was still preserved:

An Appeal to the Members of the Supreme Muslim Council

I am calling upon you as a soldier active on the sports field for many years ... I would ask you to direct the attention of the preachers in the mosques, and the speech-givers in the houses of God, so that through their speeches they may point the nation to sports, to urge them to care for their bodies, to ensure its cleanliness and activeness, to strengthen its limbs and to behave according to the rules of health, and its health will advance with us, it will become stronger in the workplace, in the struggle, and in increasing production.[17]

"The soldier active on the sports field" sees sports as an arena of conflict, or as a weapon in struggle, and thus the militaristic discourse can be found everywhere. Like a military leader, he tries to enlist all the powers and resources he can, including the preachers in the mosques, for the battle. The appeal to agents of traditional society was complemented by one to school principals who, in the opinion of the section's editor, were not doing enough to engage young people in sports:

In order to allow the youth to absorb knowledge, there is no choice but to strengthen his body and to look out for his health by means of the sports that we shall provide him – and not only in his "free time." And maybe no one knows that better than you ...

Gentlemen! Remember that you are living through a time that demands a special spirit in education, a modern education, right for our times. Remember that history demands of you that you create a new generation for Palestine, one that combines science and sports ... Remember that history urges you to raise an army of

---

[17] *Filastin*, June 1, 1946.

well-educated and healthy people, which will defend this country against the demon of colonialism.[18]

In addition to the focus on the human body, two other characteristics of modern sports which make it attractive for national movements are the discipline of the body and the ideal of maximizing physical output. These features explain both the instrumentalization of sports for national needs and the interpenetration of sports and the military sphere: "To sports, oh Arab youth – and leave the life of amusements and entertainment behind. Join the ranks of the young, and take your place in the front line of those serving your homeland, your nation, and humanity."[19]

It is noteworthy that in Arabic, the term used for sports is *riyada*, a word which was initially used to refer to the domestication and training of animals. When combined with *al-nafs*, the self, then the expression denotes a process of self-disciplining. Although *riyada* came to signify almost exclusively sports, the concept always retained a close connection to the tradition of self-disciplining (Jacob 2005: 134). Sports, according to *Filastin*, is certainly not an "amusement," but rather a service to the nation. It is not a sign of licentiousness, but rather one of accepting discipline. It is presented to the youth as an activity whose primary aim is not self-enrichment, but rather the general good. In October 1945, the sports section in *Filastin* posed a question to a number of leaders and public figures: "How would you like to see today's youth?" The answers that were quoted once more lead us to the connection between sports, modernity, nationalism, and physical health. Ahmad Hilmi Basha[20] said: "I would like the youngster to have a strong belief in God and strong nationalist feelings, to love sports a great deal, and to be expert in one of the sciences and one of the humanities, so that he will carry out his work well."[21] Rushdi al-Shawa, Mayor of Gaza said: "The youth is to the nation as the heart is to the body ... I see sports as the best means of equipping the nation with the youth it longs for."[22]

The youth, the heart of the national body, must be strong and healthy, with a national consciousness. The preparation of the people for the military confrontation just over the horizon is not merely physical; it must also be mental, and here, too, sports can contribute. To that end,

[18] *Filastin*, October 25, 1945.   [19] *Filastin*, September 26, 1945.
[20] A dominant leader in Palestinian politics in the 1940s, leaning towards the secularist Istiqlal party (Khalaf 1991: 74). In 1948 Basha became the Prime Minister of the provisional All Palestine government established in Gaza.
[21] Interview with Ahmad Hilmi Basha, *Filastin*, October 12, 1945.
[22] *Filastin*, October 17, 1945.

the sports column chose to emphasize the self-discipline and obedience of
the rules required by the game of soccer:

Soccer teaches us to obey the team's manager, and the referee teaches us to adhere
to law and justice. Soccer also teaches us how man must obey his conscience, and,
furthermore, how he must obey the commands and instructions of God. The crowd
also learns to obey the referee and the rules ... Obedience is one of the most
important qualities that the soldier in the battlefield must equip himself with.
The war will not be fought without obedience, and I request of everyone that
they obey whomever they are subordinate to, no matter whether you are players,
spectators or referees, and to heed to his every law, decision and limitation.[23]

European, Zionist, and Egyptian models

Palestinian sports by and large was oriented westwards. The European
powers are presented in *Filastin* as providing a paradigm of correct
sporting activity and as offering a model worthy of replicating, not
because sports is essentially European but because Arabs, who were
athletes in the past, abandoned it and are paying the price for that: "the
Orient has neglected sports for a long period. It was one of the main
reasons, if not the main reason, for its decline from its superiority."[24]

In addition, Palestinian sports had two main points of reference in its
regional environment. One point was Egypt, the local sporting power whose
institutions had been organized since the early twentieth century (Jacob
2005); also, since it was British-controlled there was greater access and
more ties compared to French-controlled Lebanon and Syria (since 1918),
and most of Palestine's international connections tended in that direction.
However, while Egypt was the elder sibling and provided a protective wing,
Jewish-Zionist sports was flourishing alongside that of the Palestinians, and
constituted a threat as well as a model for comparison. The existence of the
Jews' relatively impressive sporting infrastructure, as well as the international activity in the form of the Maccabiah Games[25] was a source of
envy. On December 13, 1944, a very brief piece was published in the sports
section under the headline, "Without Interpretation," which included the
following: "In Tel Aviv, Jaffa's neighbor, there are 48 children's

---

[23] *Filastin*, March 28, 1946.

[24] An article by Muhammad Taher Basha, a famous Egyptian athlete, published in *Filastin*'s
sports section on March 11, 1945.

[25] The Maccabiah Games, sometimes referred to as the "Jewish Olympics," gathered Jewish
athletes from all over the world in 1932 and 1935 in Tel Aviv. Inspired by these games, the
editor of the Palestinian newspaper *al-Difa'*, Ibrahim al-Shanti, suggested in the 1930s
establishing an Arab tournament to be called "'Antariah," following the name of a
mythological Arab hero, 'Antar, from the Jahiliya period (Kabaha 1996).

playgrounds, 15 school playing fields, three fields belonging to different teams, and one large international pitch." Only the following day did the paper point out the target of its statements – Jaffa city hall, which was not building sports fields. Zionists' hikes around the country were also seen as a sporting-patriotic activity, which had to be competed with: "We hear from lots of non-Arabs about their hikes in the country, and they know every path; the Arab youth must also hike."[26]

A recurrent motif in the press was the bewailing of the lack of funding for activities. The statements were directed at the nation's wealthy (who were accused of not investing in sports), against the mandatory government, and against the municipalities. Spectators who dodged entrance fees to sporting events also received a dressing-down. The complaints were also directed at school principals for the minimal attention they paid to sports in their curriculum, and also against the state-run radio station for its inadequate Arabic sports broadcasts (five minutes per week). That complaint may well have had an impact, because a short while after the protest was published, the radio station decided to increase the airtime to ten minutes. The statement that "this is how things are done in enlightened countries" frequently accompanied those claims. Thus, investment in sports was presented as a step towards modernization.

The tendency to compare oneself with British and Zionist sports went beyond the material aspect, and the European and Zionist use of symbols also constitutes a source of inspiration. The following quotation, taken from an article written in the early days of the sports section's existence, makes this clear:

When the French stand up to sing their national anthem, the "Marseillaise," or when the English rise and sing "God Save the King," or when the Jews sing their anthem, "ha-Tikva," I cannot but feel a great sorrow that we end our competitions and ceremonies in silence ... and so we ask of our authors and poets to do their utmost and act now for the sake of the homeland – they will be most favorably recorded in the history of our resurrection. Like other national anthems, the anthem ought to be a song of ten lines, it must incorporate love and sacrifice for Palestine, and it must disseminate a sporting spirit in the souls of our young.[27]

Women in sports

The nationalist rhetoric should be understood as well in the context of images of masculinity produced in a colonial context, in which the native's male body was described by the colonizer as weak and undisciplined (Jacob

[26] *Filasṭin*, March 10, 1945.   [27] *Filasṭin*, April 29, 1944.

2005: 122). To a certain extent, the argumentation of *Filasṭin* reflects an internalization of this image. Sports is considered as both an explanation for European physical superiority and a cure for Arab inferiority. The importance of sports for rehabilitating images of masculinity raises the question of what should be the place of women in sports. On this issue, therefore, the sports section showed inconsistency, where it would seem that opposing pressures exerted influence on the writing. On the one hand, women's participation in European sports, which constituted a model in many areas, became visible in the Olympic Games of the 1930s. On the other hand, the conspicuous presence of the female body in the public sphere, especially when it is related to the use of physical competitive force, might challenge the traditional division of gender roles.[28]

There is no better example of this tension than that in a couple of articles written by the same writer (who signed only as "Nir"), which were published two days apart. On September 20, 1945, an article was printed which, full of pathos, called on young Arab women to involve themselves in sporting activity, while emphasizing its national importance:

> Oh, educated young woman! Leave that which should not concern you to those men and women stricken with social diseases. Come gather at the broad sports field, come happy and cheerful to nature's bosom, until you can compete with the Western girls in their city and culture, and then you will be able to show everyone your pride in your achievements on the broad and open sports field.

After only two days, his attitudes changed from one extreme to the other. The need to emulate Western girls was toned down, and the appeal to go out into nature's bosom was replaced by the demand to stay at home:

> **Housework = Sports!**
> Mankind has learned from experience that a woman who does housework is of fine health, with plenty of strength and energy. And are you aware, dear reader, of the reason for this? When a woman is looking after her child, when she caresses him in order to put him to sleep, she is continually active from dawn till dusk – and that is undoubtedly a sporting activity. And when she prepares food she is doing sports, which strengthens the muscles in her arms – and when she cleans the floor of her house she is doing her daily sports. Afterwards, she needs to rest, and in this regard she is like every sportsman who plays soccer, basketball, or any other sports at all ... Furthermore, women feel satisfaction when they succeed in completing the required housework. Oh, Arab sisters, get to your housework. And do not let it exasperate you, but fulfill your duties – that will make the men respect you, and you will thus achieve two important aims: carrying out your daily work, and

---

[28] Similar to the alarm created in American physical education circles by the participation of French women in the track and field international competitions in the early 1920s.

strengthening your bodies. Onward, young woman – beseech of the pen to write you a glorious page in the history of our new revival.

This drastic change (probably a result of pressure applied on the writer) reveals the logical and moral imbroglio that the sports section was entangled in with regard to women's status in sports. He praised and commended sporting activity because of its importance to bodily health, its contribution to national unity, and owing to the need to imitate European countries. The exclusion of women from sports was liable to contradict each one of those three justifications. The solution that the writer found was to expand the meaning of the word "sports" in order to include traditional female activities that did not threaten the existing gender order.

The struggle over international recognition

During the first year of the APSA's existence, it founded a countrywide soccer league, managed on a regional basis. The champion of each of the six regions advanced to the Palestine championship. As a lesson learned from the Zionist dominance of the PFA and as an expression of the escalating hostility between the two collectives, the APSA's laws explicitly prohibited the participation of Jewish players.[29] Soccer gained the recognition of the Arab leadership, and national and local leaders honored the players with their presence at important sporting events. The final game of the first Palestinian soccer championships took place at al-Baṣa stadium in Jaffa on June 3, 1945, under the patronage of Ahmad Hilmi Basha. All of the Arab mayors of Palestine and the honored citizens of numerous Arab villages were invited to the competition between the Islamic Sports Club of Jaffa and the Orthodox Union of Jerusalem. According to *Filasṭin*, as many as 10,000 spectators witnessed the Jaffa club win the game 2:0, receiving a silver plaque that had been donated by the Arab National Bank.

It is noteworthy that in mid 1945 Ahmad Hilmi launched a campaign to promote himself to a dominant position in Arab political life, in opposition to the Husseini family, by using the financial tools he controlled (Khalaf 1991: 98). Thus, the support of the Arab National Bank (which he chaired), as well as the generous coverage of the event by *Filasṭin*, are significant.[30] They suggest that the parts of Palestinian society that were interested in the

---

[29] *Filasṭin*, September 13, 1947.
[30] Also significant is that money for the Arab National Bank was collected in soccer games during the same period (*Filasṭin*, April 17, 1945).

promotion of sports in the 1940s were relatively secularized elites who opposed traditional familial authority. In addition, the use of soccer by Hilmi Basha and his supporters to mobilize popular support indicates the popularity of the game among Palestinians during this period.

Two minutes of silence in memory of the victims in Syria and Lebanon[31] preceded the game, during which both the players and the observing crowd stood to attention. In fact, the solidarity with Syria and Lebanon was not limited to ceremonies. The APSA organized boxing, weightlifting, and wrestling competitions, in which all profits were donated to the war victims. At the end of June 1945, the central committee of the APSA decided to send financial support to the war victims in Syria and Lebanon via the Syrian Sports Association. Likewise, it implored the Palestinian sports clubs to aid in gathering donations.

Despite the humanitarian motivations and the ethno-national solidarity that surely stood behind the united efforts of the APSA to help their Arab neighbors in need, these efforts did not lack pragmatic considerations. During those years, the APSA worked to create ties with other Middle Eastern countries, and Arab-Palestinian athletes participated in competitions in Jordan, Syria, Lebanon, Egypt, and Iran.[32] However, this activity sparked off opposition. The Zionist PFA, the official representative of Palestine on FIFA, vetoed competitions between national teams and the APSA teams. In December 1944 the APSA attempted to register in FIFA as the official Palestinian association, but failed since Palestine was already represented by the PFA. Therefore, the management of the APSA attempted to enlist the help of the national associations in Egypt, Lebanon, and Syria in their struggle for international recognition. On March 15, 1945, the following excerpt appeared in the sports section of the Palestinian newspaper *Filasṭin*:

A sports delegation led by the APSA is expected to travel to Egypt in order to plan games between Egypt and Palestine at the beginning of next month. We are asking the delegation to discuss the issue of the Palestinian Football Association, which is not Arab, and is recognized internationally and representing us against our will. Likewise, we are asking Egypt to intercede on our behalf and insist on the elimination of the PFA. This association [the PFA] does not represent anyone but itself and its community, and not the Arab-Palestinian people. If this is impossible at this

---

[31] On May 29–30, 1945 the French army, in a harsh reaction to anti-French demonstrations in Syria and Lebanon, shelled and bombed Damascus from the air, resulting in the loss of some 400 lives.
[32] *Filasṭin*, February 16, 1945.

time, then we demand two-thirds of its seats, and the last third will remain with it according to the governmental laws of the country.

This association was founded in 1922 [sic; 1928] and represented Palestine internationally while the game among the Arabs was still in its formative stage. Twelve members manage this association. None of them are Arab, it is located in Tel Aviv, and until this day it still represents Palestine. It will be a great injustice if this association continues to represent Arab Palestine internationally when our games and our association are already organized and among our youth there are stronger, better and more professional athletes than them. The Arab teams cannot visit Palestine and play with us if this illegal association refuses to let them. Egypt is also forced to comply with this if it wishes to keep the international order and laws that are followed in other countries. As long as this irregular and exceptional situation does not come to an end, efforts must be invested in Egypt in order to establish an Oriental Sports Association that will begin operation immediately.

The frustration of Arab athletes, as reflected in the newspaper, led them to seek additional solutions. For instance, the option of merging Palestinian soccer with the Syrian Association was raised (for this purpose the Central Committee of the APSA reverted to the one-time use of Palestine's forgotten nickname from the time of Faisal's revolt in Syria, "Southern Syria"),[33] but this proposal was dropped for reasons that are unclear. In contrast, however, the Weightlifters Association became, in practice, a subsidiary of the Egyptian Association.

In 1946, with support from the Lebanese and Egyptian associations, the Arab Association made an official appeal to FIFA to be accepted as a separate association (or, according to a different version, to found an independent association in mandatory Palestine). In November 1946, as a result of this request – and worried that it would lose its international legitimacy – the Zionist PFA was spurred into inviting the Arab teams to join its ranks. The APSA, in reaction, formulated a letter of refusal, which all the Arab teams were asked to send to the PFA.

Meanwhile, the Arab Association's request to join FIFA was rejected, leading to the convening of a joint conference of the region's Arab associations. The Arab associations expressed their protest and demanded that FIFA reconsider the issue. Accordingly, in the summer of 1947, FIFA's executive committee proposed that the next conference form a neutral association in Palestine, headed by people not belonging to either of the two "races" (so stated in the Association's protocol).[34] By

---

[33] *Filasṭin*, March 27, 1945.
[34] Protocol of the directorate of the Football Association, Archives of Sport and Physical Education, Wingate Institute, AD 121/1.

the time the conference took place, the country was deeply mired in war, so no meaningful decisions were made.

Requiem

On November 28, 1947, one day before the United Nations' historic vote on the partition of Palestine, the following excerpt appeared in the sports column of *Filasṭin*:

Our aim is to make Palestine Arab forever, and that's what every Arab in this country and in the sister countries, is hoping for. Then, we want a strong and respected state, abundant with grace and importance. None of these will happen unless all of us become strong and healthy, competent of bearing the burden, and confident in our vigor and power as a nation that has to survive. Then, we should be ready to serve our country and best choose the path that will lead us to this level. If we wish our country to reach this aim, we must look for the best facilities to realize it.

Sports claims to be the best tool for achieving this goal. A wicked condition of a country stems, in most cases, from the presence of an occupying state that opposes the country's independence. Naturally, the interests of the occupying state contradict those of the occupied people or of the resistant people.

The occupying country invest a great effort toward the corruption of the occupied people, their deflection from thinking about their country's interests and causing them to think instead about their personal interests and satisfying "bread and amusements." If someone is still resistant, the conqueror reacts harshly and punishes him by various means.

Thus, the reformers have no escape from finding a way to publicize their ideas among the people and to spread their doctrines and opinions with no fear of resistance or oppression.

By way of sports they can reach the target, as occurred in Sweden, Czechoslovakia and Hungary, and like we want to occur in Palestine. In the next issues we will discuss what was happening in each of these countries, and then we will talk about Palestine.

The sports editor's long-term plans were never implemented. The intercommunal war that erupted two days later ended sports writing and gradually ended all sports activities as well. The end of the war left Arab-Palestinian society with a divided homeland and 700,000 refugees. The Arab-Palestinians who remained under Israeli control have lost the elites of the large cities (Morris 1987) who were the generative and initiative power propelling Palestinian sports during the 1940s. When the dust of the war settled, no independent Arab sports infrastructure survived. Instead, the institutional vacuum was filled by a new power that used sports as a political tool for completely different purposes.

3

The emergence of the integrative enclave

Although the majority of the Palestinians who lived in the territory which became Israel were uprooted in the war and their return was prevented to ensure a Jewish majority, 156,000 Arab-Palestinians remained in Israel, became Israeli citizens, but lived under the strict Military Government until 1966. The emergence of Arab soccer as an "integrative enclave" has roots in these first two decades of the state's existence. During those years soccer was used by both the state apparatus and by the Palestinian minority for different purposes, and in order to fulfill different needs, but the combined effect of these forces was shaping Arab soccer as a sphere of limited integration.

As Yoav Peled and Gershon Shafir argue, Israeli political culture has been characterized by a continuous tension between three partly contradictory political goals and commitments: the colonial project of settling the country with a specific group of people, the ethno-national project of building a Jewish nation-state, and the liberal project of establishing a democracy. The tension between the first two commitments and the third commitment was partly solved by ensuring that most of the non-Jewish population remained beyond the state boundaries. The existence of the remaining Arabs, however, forced the political leadership to find creative solutions to reconcile between the divergent commitments. Therefore, as Shira Robinson (2005) has demonstrated, from the very first years of the state's existence, its apparatus implemented extensive and diverse practices towards the Arab-Palestinian minority to ensure a limited form of inclusion, one that simultaneously emphasized their liberal inclusion in the project of state-building, excluded them from the project of nation-building, and made them the victims of the colonial project. The fact that they belonged to the Arab side of the Arab–Israeli wars made them a suspicious "fifth column" in the eyes the authorities and further emphasized the exclusionary tendencies alongside careful attempts to contain, control, and discipline them.

During the first decade of the state's existence, these contradictory goals were reflected in incoherent and inconsistent policies towards the Arab minority (Bauml 2001; Robinson 2005). The late 1950s and the early 1960s, however, witnessed two interrelated processes which significantly shaped this policy and made it somewhat more coherent. On the one hand, those years were characterized by growing unrest among the Palestinian citizens, which was accompanied by significant attempts to become politically and nationally organized; on the other hand, among the Israeli authorities there was a growing awareness of the permanence of the situation, namely, that the Palestinian citizens were not going to leave the country and there was therefore a need to establish a long-term and comprehensive policy towards them (Bauml 2001). From this period the practices of partial and limited integration were not merely a product of cross-pressures but were of a partly pre-planned and organized policy.

It is not a coincidence that those same years were the crucial period when Israeli authorities were involved in monitoring the development of Arab sports clubs and sporting activities. The promotion of the athletic realm was considered an especially useful tool for constructing a partial citizenship, as well as disciplining and surveying a minority with potential separatist aspirations and identification with the enemy. On the one hand, it mobilized people's bodies to a practice which conveys a universalistic promise and which cannot be identified as Jewish (and therefore exclusive), and on the other hand, it was frequently sponsored and organized by the state (Ben-Porat 2003) and therefore was identified with it and legitimized it.

The Military Government, the Histadrut, and Mapai

Before illustrating the political importance of sports after 1948, it is necessary to explain the system which governed the Arab minority in Israel in those years. The Military Government was formally established in 1949, although it functioned virtually since the first Arab localities were occupied by Jewish forces in 1948. It was imposed on three areas which included the vast majority of the remaining Palestinian population: the Galilee in the north of the country, the "Little Triangle," a strip of land adjunct to the north-eastern armistice line with Transjordan, and the Naqab/Negev desert, in the south. The Military Government was practically the only state organization that was responsible for the Arab population, replacing many of the functions fulfilled by governmental ministries vis-à-vis the rest of the population. Instead, the Military Government coordinated its activities with the Adviser to the Prime Minister for Arab Affairs (APMAA). The Military Government imposed severe restrictions on movement, breadwinning, and political organization (Jiryis 1969; Lustick 1980). In addition, many of the Palestinians who remained in Israel were prevented from returning to the homes they left during the war and their property was expropriated, while their new status as Israeli citizens did not protect them from this policy.

Another important organization which was involved in this system was the Histadrut (The General Federation of Hebrew Laborers in the Land of Israel), the Israeli trade union congress, founded in 1920. Its initial goals were to provide a federation for all Jewish workers in the British Mandate of Palestine, promote land settlement, workers' rights against management, and Jewish employment despite the lower wages paid to Arabs. It became one of the most powerful institutions in the State of Israel, the largest employer in the state, and an important tool in the nation-building project. In 1959 the Histadrut decided to accept Arabs as almost equal members (except for voting rights which was finally granted in 1966), and changed its name accordingly by omitting the word "Hebrew."

Following this decision, an Arab Department was formed in the Histadrut. Most of the functionaries in this department were members of the ruling party, Mapai, which was interested in gaining Arab votes in parliamentary elections, and minimizing votes for the non-Zionist Communist Party. Most scholars agree that there was an almost complete overlap, coordination, or even a symbiosis, between the interests and the activity of the government, the Military Government, the Histadrut, and Mapai (Bauml 2001; Lustick 1980; Rosenhek 1995). Therefore, Histadrut activities were aimed as well at assisting the government in preventing the emergence of an independent Arab leadership and promoting the interests of Mapai. To advance these goals the Histadrut organized the Arab workers into trade unions, established HMOs in Arab localities, and attempted to encourage "Israelization" through educational and cultural programs, including sports.

A study of the development of Arab sports in those years reveals two main elements in this policy: dependency-creation and co-optation of the young elite. These efficient mechanisms of control were mentioned, among others, by Ian Lustick (1980) as he tried to explain why, despite the clearly uncomfortable situation of the Arabs in Israel, there were no significant outbreaks of political agitation until 1976. One must not underestimate the importance of these two strategies in the realms of employment, licensing, and other day-to-day areas. But sports has certain unique characteristics of its own: the potential to present sports as an apolitical sphere actually can assist the rulers in using it as a political tool (Allison 1986). Therefore, the power exerted by sports is sometimes invisible, and therefore more effective, since "every power which manages to impose meanings and to impose them as legitimate by concealing the power relations which are the basis of its force, adds its own specifically symbolic force to those power relations" (Bourdieu and Passeron 1977: 4).

Accordingly, the exact same practices that parts of the Palestinian elite tried to employ in the name of their national struggle against the Zionists and the British later served the Israeli state, through the Histadrut, in establishing its rule over a population whose loyalty was seen as fragile and situational.

Sports, partial citizenship, and control

Almost nothing remained from the pre-1948 Arab sports infrastructure in Palestine. Soccer teams ceased to exist, as did the independent Arab sports press. The major Palestinian sports stadium, in the al-Baṣa neighborhood in Jaffa, was confiscated and in 1960 it became the home stadium of the Histadrut's flagship soccer team, ha-Po'el Tel Aviv.[1] There were, however, two rare exceptional categories. First, sports clubs that represented Christian religious institutions, such as Terra Santa in Jaffa, and the Orthodox Club in Haifa, survived the war, signifying the relative caution of the Zionist forces in their treatment of important churches (Morris 2004: 418). To the second category, which is more relevant to the topic of this chapter, belong sports clubs established by the Histadrut-affiliated organization ha-Brit in Nazareth and Haifa. Ha-Brit (The Alliance of the Workers of the Land of Israel) was an Arab trade union founded by the Histadrut in the pre-state period, and in effect, it formed the organizational infrastructure for what was to become the Arab Department of the Histadrut later.

While before the founding of the state sports clubs affiliated with the Histadrut were extremely marginal on the Palestinian sports map, after 1948, and especially since the late 1950s, the Histadrut became the leading and dominant power in redeveloping Arab sports in Israel. As early as the mid 1950s the Histadrut began offering courses to train Arab sports coaches. Ha-Po'el (in Hebrew – "The Worker," the Histadrut sports

---

[1] In 1968 the stadium was destroyed and rebuilt and is known today as the Bloomfield stadium, the home field of ha-Po'el Tel Aviv.

organization) was already involved in the efforts to develop Arab sports, and two soccer teams affiliated with it, from Lydda and Jaljulia, began playing in the Israeli Football Association in 1955.

A significant change took place in 1959, as a part of the general crystallization of the above-mentioned semi-integrative policy of the state. From this point on, the matter was no longer one of local solutions offered to specific villages or towns, but, rather, a wide-reaching, uniform policy of the Histadrut, fully guided by the APMAA and the Military Government. In the early 1960s, dozens of ha-Po'el sports clubs were opened in Arab villages. By 1964, ha-Po'el teams from Nazareth, Ramleh, Acre, Shafa 'Amr, Kafr Kana, Beit Ṣafafa, Majd al-Kurum, Ṭira, Kafr Qasim, Kafr Qara', Qalanswa, Jaljulia, Ṭaibeh, Kafr Yasif, Jisr al-Zarqa, Tarshiha, Sulm, 'Eilabun, and Me'ilya, joined the IFA.

The opening of these clubs was strongly encouraged by the government. A letter sent on March 24, 1962, from the office of the APMAA to the Ministry of Education explicitly stated that: "We have political interest in nurturing sporting activities among the Arab and Druze[2] populations. We are interested that this activity will be carried out by the *Histadrut*, which has already expressed its readiness to take care of that through *ha-Po'el* and the municipalities."[3] A significant indication of the political function of these clubs is that although this letter expressed interest in promoting Druze sports clubs, in 1964 there was still not a single ha-Po'el soccer team in the Druze villages (which were considered to be already loyal to the state).

The Histadrut also helped in establishing sports grounds by using money from the Islamic Waqf funds, released by the APMAA. In addition, in the early 1960s the Histadrut held training workshops for sports coaches which the Ministry of Education and Culture helped finance. Every year, at the end of the soccer season, the Histadrut organized a special game between a top Arab club and an "All-Star" Arab team, with players taken from other teams. The APMAA and the head of the Arab Department of the Histadrut were regular guests of honor at the games.

The association of the Arab ha-Po'el teams with the ruling Mapai party and the Histadrut gave them an establishment stamp, and even though they did not give rise to popular opposition, they did pose a

---

[2] The Druze religion is a break-off of Shi'ite Islam, but today they are not considered by most Orthodox Muslims as Muslim. They are spread mostly in Lebanon, Israel, and Syria. In Israel, the Druze are one-tenth of the Arab population. They have been allies of the Israeli authorities since 1948 and Druze men are required to serve in the Israeli security forces. Only a small minority among the Druze in Israel define themselves as Palestinians (Amara and Schnell 2004).

[3] ISA, 23/845, "Arab Sports Clubs."

challenge to political elements with a national consciousness. Accordingly, the early 1960s saw the formation of independent teams with Arab names, such as al-Ahali and Abnaa al-Balad. An examination of the joint action taken by the Histadrut and the government reveals a clear policy, the basis of which was the creation of dependency on the part of Arab citizens on the sporting infrastructure provided by the state. Sporting activity that took place within the accepted frameworks was warmly supported, but independent Arab sports organizations were prevented from taking root.

In some places the Histadrut activists were able to silently shut down these clubs (Bauml 2001: 259) but they were not always successful. For example, at the beginning of the 1960s, an independent Arab league was set up in the Triangle area. This league included teams from Ṭira, Qalanswa, Kafr Qasim, and Ṭaibeh. Activists of al-Arḍ (literally, The Land – a political group with an Arab nationalist agenda which emerged in 1959 and was banned by the Israeli authorities in 1964), were involved in running these independent sports clubs. Facing obstacles in setting up a nationwide political organization, some of al-Arḍ's dominant activists, including Ṣaleh Baransi and Husni 'Iraqi, tried in 1963 to use sports clubs as a symbolic and organizational tool.[4] These attempts attracted the Security Service's attention, and it followed the clubs' activities closely. In April 1964 the Military Government intervened, canceled an independent sports competition, arrested the leading organizers, apparently out of concern that they were dealing with organizing a nationalist opposition (Lustick 1980).[5] It appears that this intervention was not the first or the only one of its kind, and it followed the dismantling of a sports club in 'Arabeh (in the Galilee), which the Military Government considered to be the basis for a Syrian spy network.[6]

Yisrael Bar-Yehuda, the transportation minister from the Zionist leftist Mapam party, intervened and asked for explanations. Rehav'am Amir, the APMAA, answered in a letter, quoting the sarcastic accounts of the local officer who made the decision to ban the competition:

The club in Kafr Qara' was established in August 1963 as a club for sports and culture. The Military Government consistently followed its "sporting" activity, which was distinguished by the relative absence of sports and the abundance of "culture." Ṣaleh Baransi and Husni 'Iraqi, known for their extreme nationalism and

[4] Interview with Sabri Jiryis, December 11, 1999.
[5] See *ha-'Olam ha-Zeh*, no. 1390, April 29, 1964, and no. 1407, July 26, 1964.
[6] A letter from Rehav'am Amir, the APMAA to General Nisiyahu, May 7, 1964 (ISA, 23/845, "Arab Sports Clubs").

their activity in al-Arḍ were their patrons and mentors. Calls for unifying the Arab nation, songs of praise for Naṣir, and hopes for returning of the status of the Arabs to what it was before the state was established, constitute this obsolete culture.[7]

Ṣabri Jiryis, a leading activist in al-Arḍ, wrote about this subject in his book, *The Arabs in Israel*:

al-Arḍ has therefore been "accused" in an excessively heavy-handed way, of help-ing to open independent sports clubs in certain Arab villages. On one occasion, the Military Governor of the Central Region declared a village in the Triangle a closed area, in order to prevent a soccer match between teams from Galilee and the Triangle. The establishment of sports clubs among the Arabs of Israel is regarded as an unforgivable sin by the Military Government and its associates. Indeed, what need is there to form independent sports clubs? It was long ago decided that the Arab department of Histadrut, the General Federation of Jewish Labor, which is under absolute control of the Mapai Party, is alone allowed to establish clubs in the Arab villages, which clubs alone are allowed to form soccer teams, and that these circles alone are empowered to decide how soccer shall be played, and with whom.
(Jiryis 1969: 138–139)

The attempts by nationalist activists to use soccer as an organizational and symbolic platform again prove the political potential of soccer. However, considering the power imbalance between the state and al-Arḍ activists, the potential of soccer as a producer of national consciousness could not be realized. The reaction of the Military Government clarified the structural boundaries within which the Arabs in Israel were permitted to form their collective identification and to be organized for political protest.

Brotherhood of peoples

Between 1948 and 1968 the Histadrut and the APMAA published a daily in Arabic, *al-Yawm*, which was considered a major propagandist instrument of the government. Ironically, *al-Yawm* was located in the offices of *Filasṭin* in Jaffa, used its equipment and presented itself as its successor (Caspi and Kabaha 2001); in a very limited sense, it was. Starting in 1960, *al-Yawm* began publishing a sports section, edited by Na'im Zilkha, an Iraqi-born Jew. Similar to *Filasṭin*'s sports section, that of *al-Yawm* was also characterized by a tendency to present sports as an educational tool; this time, however, the focus was completely different. *Al-Yawm*'s sports section stressed the positive role of sports as a symbol of the brotherhood of peoples.

---

[7] Ibid.

Starting in July 1964, the sports section was published as a weekly two-page section (out of the newspaper's six pages). In the first extended section the editorial column stated:

I am confident that we will succeed, with the help of the brother athletes and the spirit of sports, to serve the sporting movement in the Arab sector, extend its boundaries and promote friendship and brotherhood between the Jewish and Arab athletes in this homeland. By this we will promote the celestial mission that we took on our shoulders to support this homeland with faith and loyalty for the sake of all its sons.[8]

The sports realm as seen by *al-Yawm*'s editors is a rare opportunity for imagining the not-necessarily-Jewish Israeli nation, a concept which contradicted the political reality in other spheres of the Jewish state.[9]

Al-Yawm's sports section struggled against the potential of soccer to become a site of political protest. Even Ṣallaḥ al-Din al-Ayoubi, a symbol of Muslim military prowess, was recruited once in order to deliver a pacifist message through sports. In an op-ed written by Elias Katila, he praised the spirit of knighthood which "frequently governs sports," and mentioned that even Ṣallaḥ al-Din gave his enemy, Richard the Lionheart, his own sword and horse after the latter lost his. Then the author added: "and in our days, nations are not measured by their military ability and their war skills, but by the level of consciousness of their sons, their morals and treatment of human principles."[10]

The *al-Yawm* sports section was only one arm of the sports propaganda system. Na'im Zilkha went to Arab villages to lecture on the importance of sporting activity, which sometimes was not looked upon kindly by the villages' local elder leadership. In May 1963, the Israeli Broadcast Authority began airing a weekly Arabic sports program on the radio, and within a year this had risen to three programs a week. Zilkha had a permanent slot on these programs. It is likely that the decision to broadcast Arab-Israeli sports was a response to the interest in Egyptian soccer, which was broadcast by Egyptian radio and was followed by Arabs in Israel.[11]

---

[8] *Al-Yawm*, July 7, 1964.

[9] Four decades after this editorial was published I met Na'im Zilkha in his apartment in Ramat Gan, where he insisted that he truly believed in this message and thought that sports had an important role to play in improving the relations between Jews and Arabs (interview with Na'im Zilkha, January 21, 2000).

[10] The Qadi Elias Tawfiq Katila, *al-Yawm*, October 13, 1964.

[11] Some of my interviewees from the Triangle, who were teenagers in the early 1960s, mentioned that their first experience as a soccer audience was through radio broadcasts from Egypt (interviews with Jawdat 'Odeh, October 8, 1999; Nawaf Muṣalha, February 23, 2000).

One of the most visible expressions of the institutional attempts to use sports for establishing political legitimacy was the special place dedicated to athletics in the celebrations of Independence Day in the Arab localities. These celebrations were visible "spectacles of sovereignty" (Robinson 2005: 183–260) in which the state apparatus attempted to demonstrate its power in the Arab localities and mobilize the citizens' bodies to the state-building project. As early as 1953, 5,000 people reportedly watched games and athletic demonstrations performed by schoolchildren from Nazareth and the surrounding villages. The event was attended by the military governor of the Galilee as well as other military government soldiers (Robinson 2005: 248). However, from 1959 onward, the sporting festivals on Independence Day seem to be more systematically organized. From this year, the government organized local sports competitions for Arab schools on Israeli Independence Day. At these festivals, which were highlighted in *al-Yawm*, speeches stressed that this was the way for Arabs in Israel to express their joy at the state's celebrations.[12]

Special attention was given by the Histadrut to nurture its Arab flagship team, ha-Po'el Shabbab al-Naṣira (The Youngsters of Nazareth), a team that joined the IFA in 1960. The team's budget was generously supported by the Arab Department of the Histadrut, especially after the independent Arab sports clubs were shut down in spring 1964. In 1963 the annual budget of the team was 600 Israeli Liras (IL).[13] In 1964, however, the team received 3,500 IL from the Arab Department of the Histadrut.[14] In addition, the Nazareth municipality received a loan from the Construction Fund of the Histadrut in order to build a stadium for the team.[15]

Ibrahim Shabaṭ, who was appointed as the Histadrut cultural and sports coordinator in Nazareth, explained in *al-Yawm* that the team's management has two roles: "1. To disseminate the spirit of sports among the team's members and among the Arab youth in general. 2. To strengthen the friendship and brotherhood between the two peoples in the country, the Jewish and the Arab, through encounters between sports teams."

This message was projected as well through flyers which were distributed during the Games of Shabbab al-Naṣira, which stated, for example:

The management invests the best of its efforts to strengthen the mutual understanding and friendship between the two brother peoples … let's welcome our guests, *ha-Po'el Ṭabariya* [a Jewish team] with sporting spirit and dignity, according to our regular habit of hospitality. Long live *ha-Po'el* Nazareth. Long live the sublime sporting spirits. Long live the brotherhood between the two peoples, the Arab and the Jewish.[16]

The efforts of the Histadrut to make an Arab team a symbol of coexistence contradicted the political reality which ruled beyond the stadium, and the contradiction was frequently expressed in absurdist incidents. For example, as an Arab club which played under the control of the Military Government, the team was still required to submit an application for a travel permit from the district governor before every away game.[17] In addition, tense games between Shabbab al-Naṣira and Jewish teams brought the Jewish–Arab conflict into the soccer sphere. On March 16, 1964, the Hebrew newspaper *ha-Boker* reported that the team had been involved in a violent incident between the fans and players of both ha-Po'el Shabbab al-Naṣira and ha-Po'el Migdal ha-'Emek, which represented the neighboring Jewish town. The incident reverberated far beyond the soccer field. Following the event, the joint Arab–Jewish Communist Party called for a general strike in protest of violence against "the Arab sector," and indeed, the following morning, hundreds of workers from Nazareth did not appear for work in nearby Migdal ha-'Emek. The paper noted that "the events of last Saturday are none other than a spontaneous outbreak that demonstrates, in an extreme fashion, the ongoing shaky relationship between the populations of Nazareth and Migdal ha-'Emek." Radio Cairo even interrupted its broadcasts to report on "an armed ambush carried out on an Arab sports team from Nazareth by a Jewish sports club."

Two months later, in May 1964, the city of Nazareth celebrated the promotion of its team from the third to the second division. More than 6,000 spectators from Nazareth and the surrounding area came to watch the promotion game against Beitar Kiryat Shmona – a game that Nazareth won 8:0. When the game ended, thousands of fans stormed the field and carried the players on their shoulders through the streets of Nazareth, accompanied by encouraging cheers from the city's inhabitants.[18] *Al-Yawm* celebrated the victory with much enthusiasm and declared a special discount for advertisements which congratulated the team for their achievement. For over fifteen years, Shabbab al-Naṣira was the dominant Arab team, and as such was a source of pride for many Arabs.

---

[16] Ibid.   [17] *Ha-'Olam ha-Zeh*, no. 1419, November 18, 1964. p. 16.
[18] *Al-Yawm*, May 25, 1964.

Arab men's desire for sports

Up to this point, I have described sports as part of a political plan employed by the state. This plan by itself, however, could not have been sufficient to make sports an institution with integrative orientations. These orientations were shaped as well by bottom-up pressures, stemming from the peculiar conditions of the Arab Palestinian minority after the 1948 war, and especially among Arab men.

The Arab rural population in Israel underwent far-reaching changes in their social structure in the decades following the state's founding. According to Ian Lustick, from 1948 to 1963, 55 percent of Arab-owned land in Israel was confiscated by the state (Lustick 1980). This massive land confiscation, on the one hand, and the increasing dependence on the Jewish economy, on the other, both led to accelerated processes of proletarianization in Arab society, especially from the late 1950s on (Zureik 1979: 130–133), years which were the formative period of Arab sports in Israel. Between 1959 and 1968 the percentage of Arab employees who worked in agriculture shrank from 45 to 31 (Bauml 2001: 129). These processes had a number of consequences with a bearing on physical culture and leisure habits.

First, wage labor creates a clear distinction between work and leisure time; indeed, "leisure" is a result of counting work hours in industrialized society (Walvin 1978). Therefore, urbanization and proletarianization tend to bring about an increase in sporting activity. The sharp change from a mainly agricultural society to one that supported itself from wage labor also had an anomic effect on the social tapestry of the Arab village, which became detached from traditional village life and the relatively stable regularity of the agricultural year. The local attempts at forming sports clubs constituted an effort at reorganizing society around alternative fulcra that were more suitable to the changed conditions.

According to memories of both Arab soccer players and Histadrut activists, some of the elders in the Arab villages regarded sporting activity with suspicion mixed with disparagement. At best, they regarded the sight of barely-dressed young men purposelessly running around after a ball a waste of time, and at worst, as a licentious, "un-masculine" activity.[19] This generational gap should be viewed in the context of the conception of modernity within the factions of Palestinian society that

---

[19] Interview with Suleiman Ghantus from Sakhnin, September 26, 1999; interview with Nawaf Muṣalha, February 23, 2000; interview with Naʾim Zilkha, January 21, 2000; interview with Victor Shaharabani, March 2, 2000.

remained in Israel, and the role that soccer played in shaping this image of modernity. As 'Azmi Bishara describes it:

To the Palestinians, as a people, Israeli modernism severed the historic continuum of the Palestinian process of modernisation. This process had begun well before 1948. With the foundation of the state of Israel in 1948, Palestinian society lost its political, cultural and economic elite. More importantly, Palestinian society lost the Palestinian city, having been reduced to a village society, separate from but dependent for its subsistence upon a Jewish city that refuses to allow integration. Moreover, with the loss of agriculture as a basis for subsistence, village society became neither rural nor urban. The only avenue to modernisation that remained open to the Palestinians, therefore, was that laid out by the Jewish state and the only alternatives available to Palestinians were marginalisation, imitation or, in the best of circumstances, pressing for some rights.   (Bishara 1998a: 171)

Consistent with Bishara's argument, I suggest that soccer, which was described in the Arab nationalist rhetoric of the 1940s as a viable representation of modernity (see chapter 2), was reloaded with similar meanings. However, while before 1948 the "modernist" aura of sports was used to promote a modern Palestinian national identity, after 1948 the same aura was used by the state apparatus to portray the state itself as an agent of modernity. "Modernity," with all its positive connotation of progress and optimism, was identified with the state that supplied the sporting facilities. This development was in part a result of the opposition expressed to the game by some of the traditional leaders. The young Arabs who were looking for material support for their sporting activity found a receptive audience in the Arab department of the Histadrut.[20] Ian Lustick pointed to the attempt of the Histadrut to cultivate ties with the younger generation, grooming them to replace the older notables as new leaders. "To these younger men, the government, and in particular the Histadrut, have presented themselves as sympathetic to the frustration of the new 'modern' generation as it confronts the traditional social and political forces" (Lustick 1980: 211–213).

Being appointed to the position of sports coordinator under the auspices of the Histadrut was one of many possible opportunities that the Histadrut could offer young Arabs who were prepared to serve its interests in Arab localities (Lustick 1980: 211–213). Na'im Zilkha, for example, was involved in persuading Nawaf Musalha, a soccer player and the "star" of the independent team in Kafr Qara' to join the Histadrut (as part of the struggle against the independent teams in the

---

[20] In the Histadrut's archives, one can find a large number of letters from the inhabitants of Arab villages requesting help so that their village could also set up a sports club.

Triangle in 1964).[21] Muṣalha joined ha-Poʻel and was completely co-opted. He was later hired for a position in the Histadrut without the required education (Bauml 2001: 137), and began a long career in the Histadrut and Mapai. In 1999 he became Deputy Foreign Minister in Barak's government.

Finally, while both Palestinian women and men suffered from the coercive practices of the Military Government, they experienced them differently. For the Palestinian men in Israel, the repeated Arab defeats in war and subordination to the Israeli Military Government constituted a significant threat to their masculinity. In addition, Arab men lost large parts of their lands, while land was an important element in the peasant masculine image before 1948 (Katz 1996). Furthermore, by preventing political organization and neutralizing public protest, the military regime restricted the activity of Arab men in the public sphere and reduced masculine roles to providing their families with livelihoods (Hawari 2004). Feminist studies posit that modern sports has emerged in Western countries as an answer to the "masculinity crisis" created by the rapid social and economic changes in the early twentieth century (Messner and Sabo 1990). Sports emerged as an exclusive masculine sphere which is marked by an idealization of qualities associated with the extreme potential of the male body (Messner 1988). Similarly, for Arab men in Israel, sports became an important sphere for the rehabilitation of the undermined image of masculinity, where they could be part of a competitive muscular activity, which does not involve the risk of confronting the authorities. And indeed, in the 1960s it was very hard to find evidence for organized sports among Arab women.[22]

Soccer had a limited potential to simulate military battles and therefore the possible combative image of this sport was a subject of concern for the authorities. A discussion held in the office of the APMAA in April 1962 concluded that: "It is recommended to encourage basketball, volleyball, track and field, and table tennis. It is recommended not to encourage wrestling, boxing, weightlifting and soccer."[23] From the governmental point of view, the "dangerous sports" included combative and warlike sports – exactly those sports which were the most desired for oppressed

[21] Naʻim Zilkha, interview.
[22] A letter of protest against this state of affairs, written by Widad Ishak, an Arab woman, was published in al-Yawm on August 11, 1964.
[23] Conclusion of discussion on sports activities in the Arab sector, in a letter sent from the APMAA to the Histadrut and the Ministry of Education, April 16, 1962. A similar recommendation appears in the conclusion of a discussion at the ha-Poʻel center, from November 26, 1963 (ISA, 23/845, "Arab Sports Clubs").

men who needed them to compensate for their political subordination. This policy, if it was ever seriously implemented, completely failed. In the long term, it is exactly in the "dangerous sports" where Arab men became extremely over-represented, or even gained complete dominance.[24]

Soccer, especially, was too popular to defeat and therefore the policy was modified. Instead of opposing it, soccer was encouraged if it was played in a framework which is easy to supervise, namely, the Histadrut-sponsored clubs of ha-Po'el. Even in other "dangerous" sports the Arab athletes were integrated into the establishment frameworks. As early as 1959, an Arab weightlifter, 'Ali Khudruj from Acre, was the first Arab athlete to win an Israeli national championship. In subsequent years, 'Ali and his brothers 'Adnan and Muhsin, dominated Israeli weightlifting. In 1963, Ramzi 'Asali, an Arab Christian from Haifa who volunteered for military service, represented Israel in international boxing.[25]

It was not only the government which was forced to admit the popularity of soccer and to adapt its policy accordingly. The Arabic newspaper, al-Ittihad, the mouthpiece of the Communist Party and the only legal avenue for political protest for the Arabs in Israel, had virtually ignored the Arab teams of the Histadrut until 1964. From early 1965, however, this approach drastically changed. From January 1965, al-Ittihad published a sports column which gave special attention to the Arab teams in the Israeli leagues (and especially to ha-Po'el Shabbab al-Nasira, the leading Arab team), frequently complaining about the racist treatment they received from Jewish audiences, the referees, and some unidentified elements in the establishment. It is plausible that the editors of al-Ittihad understood well the political gains which Mapai was trying to achieve through these teams and therefore initially chose to ignore them. It is likely, as well, that these teams became so popular that it was much safer to identify with them and provide alternative interpretations to that provided by al-Yawm.

The post-Military Government period

The Military Government officially ended in December 1966, but its legacy refused to vanish. This legacy included: seeing the Arab citizens as a security problem, strict surveillance, restriction of their personal and

---

[24] In the field of boxing, Arabs have gained domination, both in terms of achievement and on the institutional level. The office of the Israeli Boxing Association, for example, is located in the Arab village of Kafr Yasif. Ironically, this is a sphere where it is more common to hear athletes from the Jewish minority complaining about discrimination.

[25] *Ha-'Olam ha-Zeh*, no. 1344, June 5, 1963.

collective independence, and the inculcation of mutual fear between Arabs and Jews (Bauml 2001: 195–196).

In the realm of sports, as well, the governmental policy followed the same logic which prevailed under the Military Government. Shmuel Toledano was the APMAA between 1965 and 1977. In an interview I conducted with him he explained the outlook that guided the government regarding Arab sports clubs during this period:

Regarding sports, we asked ourselves whether it would be good for the Arabs of Israel to have sports, and we came to the conclusion that it would be. Why would it be good? We knew that it was impossible to set up a youth movement for them with nationalist outlooks like ours . . . so we thought that sports was definitely the right answer to [free] time. After all, they had a lot of time.

But we preferred for it to be within the framework of existing clubs – Maccabi, ha-Po'el, and so on – and not separate sports clubs. This was the policy for years. The policy was no Arab banks and no Arab factories, nothing. Regarding sports, we had an interest, definitely, that the Arab youth would have something to do, that they would be busy with sports and not with other things. So we took matters into our own hands and supported and encouraged – again, as far as it was possible, within existing frameworks – Maccabi and ha-Po'el . . .

As soon as a youngster is unemployed, has nothing to do, he hasn't got anything to do with his nationalist aspirations in the way that a Jewish youth does – Gadna,[26] the army – he hasn't got all that, so obviously the concern about nationalist tendencies is bigger. Not that that is for sure – someone can be unemployed for a long time, someone might have nothing to do, but he won't go in that direction anyway. But starting to take drugs and so on, from a broad national perspective, we saw that as a negative thing. They didn't have any power, or money, or a leadership that would organize for them independent teams. So most of the teams came into the existing frameworks. The Histadrut, and us, we supported that. And when you've got a body that is giving you financial help, and soccer shirts, and helping with the field, one can assume that they'll come to it. They've got no problem of belonging here. It's not like the party issue. We wanted them to join the existing parties and not to set up independent parties. For years that was the policy, and in the end it failed. The Arabs have got a problem – why should an Arab join the Labor Party, Meretz, or Likud? But with sports, there's no problem to be in ha-Po'el Ṭaibeh or Maccabi Ṭamra. It doesn't hurt their pride or nationalist feelings.[27]

Toledano clarifies that the spirit of the Military Government continued even after its formal removal. The State of Israel opposed the establishment of independent Arab sports clubs, out of awareness of the mobilizing potential in the hands of whoever is running the soccer team.

---

[26] Pre-recruitment military education for Jewish-Israeli high school students.
[27] Interview with Shmuel Toledano, April 3, 2000.

And indeed, in 1966 the authorities shut down the independent club in Ṭaibeh and two years later the General Security Service recommended shutting down the club in Ṭira, the last nationalist club in the Triangle (Bauml 2001: 261).

However, as a counterbalance, the state continued to support whoever wanted to be incorporated within the state-supervised system. According to Toledano, this support achieved two aims: it eliminated the dangerous vacuum of free time, which could threaten stability by way of crime or Arab national identity; and it blocked a potential alternative – the emergence of independent sports clubs that could develop into a base of political or organizational power. The sports clubs that the state provided could be attractive for young Arabs because of sports' apolitical image (as opposed to political parties).

Facing the difficulties of establishing "nationalist" teams, players and fans who resented ha-Poʿel teams for their affiliation with the Histadrut found an ironic substitute. Following the end of the Military Government, more political parties beyond the ruling party, Mapai, were able to access Arab localities and recruit voters. Accordingly, other sports associations could more easily open sports clubs in the Arab towns and villages. The main rival of ha-Poʿel, the Maccabi association, was concerned that ha-Poʿel's activities within the Arab population were giving it a political advantage in the various sporting institutions.[28] Also, the ha-Poʿel teams could not answer the needs of all of the young athletes; there was just not enough room in their ranks. In addition, facing the "danger" of the nationalist teams, the Maccabi teams were seen by the Histadrut as a support for the government's policy of suppressing the first, and therefore the Histadrut even encouraged their establishment – against its sectorial interests, but in accordance with the government's goals.[29]

Maccabi tried to penetrate Arab localities even before the end of the Military Government. In a few isolated cases, mainly in places with the relevant local or personal connections, some Arab teams joined the Maccabi association even in the mid 1950s (in Furaydis and Meʾilya), but then it faced the imbalanced competition with ha-Poʿel.[30] With the end of the Military Government, however, many Maccabi-affiliated sports clubs were set up countrywide; and even more ironically,

---

[28] In the Israeli Football Association, as well as in other sports, representation was determined by the number of active athletes (Reshef and Paltiel 1989).

[29] Interview with Victor Shaharabani, March 2, 2000.

[30] In Meʾilya, for example, the Maccabi team switched to ha-Poʿel in 1964. *Al-Yawm*, April 27, 1964.

some Arab teams joint the small Beitar sports association, which belonged to the Revisionist Zionists, the militant right-wing movement established by Ze'ev Jabotinsky.

In many Arab villages, the division between the Maccabi and ha-Po'el soccer teams overlapped with the villages' familial alliances, political coalitions, and class-based dividing lines. The competitive and achievement-oriented character of soccer matches allowed the different groups in these villages to display dramatic representations of the conflicts between them. A repetitive pattern that can be seen, for instance, in the villages of Sakhnin, Kafr Kana, Umm al-Faḥm, and Judeideh, was division along class lines.

It is historically difficult to determine the extent to which the financially stronger families moved closer to the Zionist establishment and the extent to which that proximity contributed to an improvement in their financial situation. Yet, it is clear that many of the Arab villages developed a positive correlation between financial standing and the breadth and depth of contact with government and Histadrut officials. Accordingly, the ha-Po'el teams were very often identified with the rich families, while Maccabi became "the people's team."[31] On the political plane, ha-Po'el's establishment image meant that Maccabi attracted social groups whose political tendencies were more nationalist. It is noteworthy that the countrywide survey I conducted showed that the political gaps between the fans of Arab Maccabi teams and fans of Arab ha-Po'el teams were still valid in the year 2000 (see table 3.h in appendix 3). Despite the importance of the rivalry between ha-Po'el and Maccabi, however, Arab soccer remained nevertheless within the state's rules of the game. Attempts to form an independent and separate Arab framework ceased after 1968, and reappeared only after about two decades, with the formation of the Islamic League (see chapter 7).

In 1971, following a request from the Arab Department of the Histadrut, the Israel Lands Authority began to allocate pieces of land to the ha-Po'el clubs in the Arab villages and towns with the express purpose of building sports fields.[32] Against the background of the long-term governmental policy to reduce Arab control of the land, the decision

---

[31] This is in paradoxical opposition to the declared ideologies of the parties behind the sports clubs – ha-Po'el was founded as the sporting organization of the Workers' Party, and Maccabi was set up by the civic-liberal, non-socialist minority of the Zionist movement.

[32] See correspondence from November 1971 between Ya'acov Cohen from the Histadrut and Re'uven Aloni from the Israel Land Authority on this issue (ISA, 23/845, "Arab Sports Clubs"). Victor Shaharabani, head of the Histadrut's sports department between 1962 and 1987, argued in an interview I conducted with him that the decision taken by the Israel Lands Authority was a strategic one.

to allocate land purely for sporting purposes further supports the argument that the Israeli power-holders saw sports as a political tool for ruling over the Arab minority.

Players crossing the borders

Until the late 1970s Jewish and Arab teams were almost completely ethnically (Jewish or Arab) homogeneous. Rare exception can be found in Haifa, where Bulus Bulus starred on a Jewish team, ha-Po'el Haifa, in the late 1950s, and Ḥasan Bastuni[33] started to play for Maccabi Haifa in 1963. A Jewish player, Ze'ev Zeltser, played during the same period on ha-Po'el Kafr Qasim. The most famous exception was 'Ali 'Othman from Beit Ṣafafa (an Arab neighborhood in west Jerusalem) who joined ha-Po'el Jerusalem's senior team in 1967, when he was only fifteen years old. According to the memories of old soccer fans, 'Othman quickly gained a reputation for being a stubborn and determined defence player, a "real man" who would stand up to anyone. Out of a sense of identification with 'Othman, many Arab fans came to watch him play in games throughout the country. For more than a decade 'Othman was seen by many fans as a symbol of the Arab as fighter and resister, so different from the collective Arab self-image shaped by the wars of 1948, 1956, and 1967, and by their subjection to the humiliating Military Government. Identification with 'Othman contained the possibility of reinforcing masculine, national self-respect, without having to risk the potential sanctions involved as a result of identifying with other heroes, such as the Fatah movement, which was beginning to gain momentum at exactly the same time.

In the 1976 Montreal Olympics an Arab soccer player who played on the Jewish ha-Po'el Tel Aviv team, Rif'at Ṭurk, represented Israel on the international stage for the first time. This appearance heralded a new period of growing integration of Arab players on Jewish teams and vice versa. This process is related to an historic turning point in the social meaning and function of Israeli soccer. Especially since the early 1980s, instead of ranging between entertainment and politics, soccer increasingly began to be seen as a type of commodity (Ben-Porat 1998). The rules of the market gained an ever-increasing influence over the dynamics that channeled soccer players between clubs. Jewish clubs with a

---

[33] Hassan Bastuni was the nephew of Rustum Bastuni, who was a Member of Parliament on behalf of the Zionist Mapam party. Bastuni is famous for rejecting even the existence of an "Arab Nation" and calling for recognition of an Israeli identity which would unite both Jews and Arabs (Lustick 1980: 116–117).

distinctive ethnic characteristic that, until then, had been successful (the Bulgarian Maccabi Jaffa, the Yemenite Shimshon Tel Aviv, and so on), began to wane, and big money became the language of soccer.

The rules of the market determined that a club's success depended mainly on the extent of its financial support, and indeed, since 1983 no team outside one the three main cities (Tel Aviv, Jerusalem, and Haifa) has been crowned champion. According to one significant criterion, a correlation between the size of a club's hometown and the division it played in began to appear. The absence of any large Arab towns in Israel (Nazareth, the largest Arab town in Israel, had a population of 65,000 in 1999, making it the twentieth largest city in the country) immediately ruled out the possibility of continued Arab representation in the top division. Young talents in Jewish or Arab localities of a small size are quickly scouted by the senior clubs, and move to play for them, where their economic future and social prestige look far more secure.

This dynamic prevented for a long time the coalescence of a successful Arab team supported by a traditional core of fans, as was the case with the large teams in Israel. In the lower divisions, the two-way flow of players between Jewish and Arab clubs increased, as well. In the early 1980s, the generation of Arab players from the beginning of the 1960s reached positions of leadership in the elected munucipalities, which accordingly began to be more generous in their support of soccer teams (see chapter 4). Jewish players were bought as reinforcements by nearly every Arab team that aspired to promotion, a further factor that reduced the possibility of crystallizing national pride around these clubs.

Instead of the formation of an Arab flagship team, the position of Arab players improved on an individual basis. The most symbolically significant phenomenon was the prominent presence of Arab players in the Israeli national team. By representing the State of Israel, Rif'at Ţurk (thirty-four international performances between 1976 and 1986) and Zahi Armeli (played twenty-eight times between 1982 and 1986) symbolized the tension and contradictions inherent in being an Arab citizen in the Jewish state. It is true that Arab athletes previously had represented Israel at the international level, but this had been in marginal sports, such as boxing and weightlifting, which do not receive the same level of public attention as soccer. The presence of Ţurk and Armeli on the national team presented Jewish and Arab soccer fans alike with fundamental questions as to what they had in common, as well as what separated them. Ultimately, Ţurk's and Armeli's representing the State of Israel raised few objections from the Arab population. Further, the dismissal of Shlomo Kirat, a Jewish defender on the national team, following racist comments he made about Ṭurk and Armeli, clarified that the Israeli national soccer team played an inclusive role with regard to the state's Arab citizens. Ṭurk and Armeli, as well as other Arab stars who played in the top teams in Israel's Premier League, were role models for many young Arabs, who saw in soccer a path for upward mobility and a way to escape the marginality of being Arab citizens in the Jewish state.

The 1990s and the 2000s: accelerated development

The 1990s saw a marked rise in the number of Arab teams playing in the Israeli leagues (figure 3.1). In the 1996/7 season ha-Po'el Ṭaibeh was the first Arab team to play in Israel's senior league. Ṭaibeh's promotion inspired a wave of hope among many Arab soccer fans that there might be a permanent Arab presence in the top division, but, to their disappointment, Ṭaibeh was demoted after only one season, partly because of the lack of a suitable home field (Ben-Porat 2001a). In 2003, Arab presence in the top league was renewed with the success of Ittiḥad Abnaa Sakhnin (freely translated – Sons of Sakhnin United) and al-Aakha al-Naṣira (The Brotherhood of Nazareth) in climbing to the Premier League, and in 2004 Arab soccer gained unprecedented local and international media attention when the team from Sakhnin won the Israeli State Cup (see chapter 8).

The stories of Ṭaibeh, Sakhnin, and Nazareth, however, are only the tip of the iceberg of a widespread phenomenon – that of more and more Arab teams reaching the middle divisions. In the 1976/7 season, only eight Arab teams played in the top four divisions. In 1992, twenty-one Arab teams played in those divisions, and within seven years that number almost doubled to forty teams.

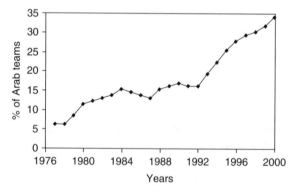

Figure 3.1: *Percentages of Arab teams in adult IFA divisions, 1977–2000 (excluding the lowest division)*

Table 3.1: *Ticket sales for the second division in the 1997/8 season**

Team**	Population in 1996 (1,000s)	Ticket sales in 1997/8***	Number of tickets per 1,000 pop.
Kafr Kana (A)	13.0	5,651	434
Taibeh (A)	25.3	7,245	287
Sakhnin**** (A)	19.4	2,925	151
Nes Tziona (J)	22.3	2,759	124
Kiryat Gat (J)	46.1	4,493	97
Yavne (J)	28.9	2,298	90

*Not including season-ticket holders. Only localities represented by one team are included, where that team is the senior one.
**A = Arab town; J = Jewish town.
***Data from the Israeli Football Association.
****Given a punishment of eight away games, five of which were closed to supporters.

The Arab teams' achievements are even more striking when one takes into account the strong correlation between the size of the team's home-town and its representation in the higher divisions. Because Arabs in Israel are spread out in smaller localities than those that Jews live in, the starting point from which they must climb to the senior divisions is lower. To bring this point home, the median number of residents of localities that were represented in the second division in the 1997/8 season was about 50,000,[34] and in the third division about 29,000.[35] In contrast, the Arab teams represented much smaller localities. In the 1997/8 season, three Arab teams played in the second division, representing localities whose residents numbered between 15,000 and 25,000; in the third division ten Arab localities were represented, the median number of residents of which was about 13,000.

Also, interest in Arab teams rose in the 1990s in comparison with Jewish teams, which is demonstrated by the large number of tickets sold by Arab teams relative to Jewish ones. Table 3.1 presents the number of tickets sold by different clubs in the second division for the 1997/8 season, relative to the locality's population. The Arab teams are

---

[34] The calculation only includes a locality when the team representing it is the locality's top team (for instance, teams based in Tel Aviv are not counted for the second division, because the city is represented in the Premier League).
[35] As above.

Table 3.2: *Percentage of Arab men aged 18 to 50 who participated in various modes of soccer consumption*

Activity	%
Watching a live broadcast of a game of the Israeli national team	77
Watching a live broadcast of a game in the Israeli Premier League	77
Reading the sports section in the newspaper	76
Listening to a soccer radio broadcast in Arabic	53
Watching the weekly TV sports program of the Israeli Broadcast Authority in Arabic	42
Attendance at local soccer games	39
Listening to a soccer radio broadcast in Hebrew	35
Watching the television summary program of Israeli Premier League	33
Attendance at a Premier League game	19

compared with Jewish teams that represent towns of similar sizes. The numbers in the table reflect not only the popularity of soccer among Arabs, but also the fact that Arab teams attract Arab fans on an ethno-national basis, beyond the local level.

The higher interest of the Arab public in soccer is reflected as well in television ratings. Among the twenty most-watched non-regular television programs by Arabs in Israel in 2001, fifteen were broadcasts of soccer games. Among the Jewish public, only four of twenty programs were broadcasts of soccer games.[36] The countrywide survey I conducted in 2000 demonstrated a similar pattern. Table 3.2 illustrates that by presenting the percentage of Arab men aged 18–50 who took part in various modes of soccer consumption.

As the table demonstrates, the interest in the general Israeli soccer sphere (Israeli Premier League, Israeli national team) is higher than the interest in the local sphere. Furthermore, 21 percent of interviewees said that they watched every single game out of ten games played by the Israeli national team in 1998/9 in the preliminary stage of the European Championship, and 43 percent watched at least half of these games. Only 22 percent did not watch any of these games.

The interest in the Israeli Premier League and the Israeli national team is most likely related to the noticeable presence of Arab players in these frameworks. During the 1990s more and more Arab players earned positions on Israel's senior teams – and on the national team. After a

---

[36] Noam Segev, www.ynet.co.il, November 21, 2001.

decade in which there were no Arab players on the national team (six years of which saw the Intifada in the West Bank and Gaza Strip, which may or may not be connected), two were recruited in 1998: Najwan Ghrayeb and Walid Bdeir. Ghrayeb and Bdeir became cultural heroes; Arab journalists closely followed their successes; the players starred in commercial companies' advertising campaigns; and babies are even named after them.

'Abbas Sawan from Sakhnin who joined the national team in 2004 became an Israeli hero on March 26, 2005, after his stunning last-minute goal earned Israel a 1:1 draw with Ireland in a World Cup qualifier game. Four days later Walid Bdeir replicated the exact same achievement in a game against France when he equalized the score in the eighty-third minute. Thanks to these goals, Israel found itself momentarily with a chance to qualify for the World Cup for the first time in thirty-five years. In the following days, politicians, broadcasters, and commentators in the Hebrew media competed against each other in glorifying the contribution of soccer to the integration of the Arab minority in Israel. Although some voices in the Arabic language media were more restrained (see chapter 5), joy and pride were the popular feelings among the Arab public. The sky above Sakhnin, for example, was lit up with fireworks after Sawan's goal against Ireland.

Arab soccer stars gain extra attention from both the Hebrew and Arab media, and they do their best to avoid "rocking the boat" with any politically controversial statement. They are professionals who are subjected to the disciplinary forces of the market, which dictate political neutrality. Their aspiration to play in the Israeli national team might be motivated as well by their desire for international exposure which might be followed by international careers. These factors sometimes create gaps between their personal and familial history, and the way they present themselves in the media. Bdeir's grandfather was murdered by Israeli troops in the Kafr Qasim massacre in 1956. Sawan's familial biography also epitomizes the price paid by the Palestinian side of the conflict. His family's village of origin, Muraṣaṣ, was occupied in May 1948 and its inhabitants, including Sawan's grandparents, became "internal refugees" in Israel.[37] The State of Israel has never taken responsibility for the massacre in Kafr Qasim, and the perpetrators' punishments were

---

[37] The internal refugees in Israel are Palestinians who were uprooted from their villages in the course of the 1948 war, but found refuge within the borders of the state and became its citizens. They have continuously voiced their demand to return to their villages, only to be met by the refusal of all Israeli governments. See Cohen 2003.

minimal (Rosenthal 2000). Similarly, Israel has refused to resettle the "internal refugees" in their towns and villages. However, neither Sawan nor Bdeir have ever tried directly to use their stardom as leverage to demand that the state take responsibility for the atrocities committed against their grandparents. The soccer environment in Israel has never been an appropriate incubator for national protest.

Following Sawan and Bdeir's goals, an Arab Member of Parliament, Ahmad Ṭibi, told the media that they should adopt the slogan – "No Arabs – No Goals." This was a play on a shivering slogan that emerged at the beginning of the second Palestinian uprising (2000–2004) and the wave of terrorist attacks against Israeli civilians which accompanied it. The slogan, which appeared as wall graffiti, bumper stickers, and on internet forums, stated simply: "No Arabs – No Terrorism," hinting that expelling all Arabs is necessary to prevent terrorism. A public survey from April–May 2003 showed that 33 percent of the Jewish public in Israel supports the expulsion of the Arab citizens of Israel (Arian 2003). The Arab citizens, for their part, consider pro-transfer attitudes of Jews as a tangible threat. The uprooting of 700,000 Palestinians in the 1948 war is an important element in their collective memory and therefore their presence on their land is never taken for granted.

These concerns took on an ironic twist in a game between Sakhnin and Beitar Yerushalaim (Jerusalem) on April 4, 2005, several days after the victorious goals of Sawan and Bdeir. Although the Hebrew media was quite sympathetic to the two soccer heroes, in the game between Beitar Jerusalem and Sakhnin, the crowd of Beitar fans booed Sawan and raised a sign: "You do not represent us, 'Abbas Sawan." The fans from Sakhnin, on the other hand, hung a large sign in front of Beitar's fans in Hebrew: "There are Arabs – There is World Cup." In other words, the goals of Sawan and Bdeir, hoped Arab soccer fans, might serve as an antidote to their exclusion, an insurance policy against their expulsion.

The flexible significance of soccer

Palestinian sports has come a long way since the days when Jewish athletes were boycotted by the Arab-Palestinian sports association, up to that spring evening in 2004 when the president of the Jewish state handed the cup to the captain of the Arab team from Sakhnin. In its formative years, Palestinian nationalists used sports as a nation-building tool, but under Israeli rule after 1948, sports in general – and soccer in particular – became a tool for limited and selective integration, downplaying the national identity of the Arabs in Israel.

Neo-Marxist approaches in the sociology of sports have maintained that this is the role that sports must necessarily play, in that its optimistic ideology creates an illusion of a lack of structural restraints and thus serves the status quo (Brohm 1989 [1975]). Critics of this approach justly argued that the inhibition of national consciousness or political protest is not necessarily the only role that soccer can play. Even in the particular case of the Palestinian people, there is some evidence to the contrary. As I showed in chapter 2, when the Palestinians were a majority, in the Mandatory period, soccer was used to promote anti-colonial nationalist consciousness. Five decades later, under the autonomous rule of the Palestinian National Authority, the Palestinian national soccer team arouses an extravagant popular enthusiasm in the West Bank and Gaza Strip. Its international games attract people from all strata and regions. After winning third place in the Pan-Arab games in June 1999, the Palestinian national soccer team was welcomed in Gaza by thousands of cheering fans waving Palestinian flags. By contrast, when the same team visited the Palestinian towns inside Israel, Sakhnin and Nazareth, three months later, its two games did not attract more than a few hundred spectators – far fewer than an ordinary league game in those towns.

The Palestinians under Jordanian rule provide another example of soccer as a forum for Palestinian nationalism. Indeed, the Jordanian policy towards sports was derived from the aspiration to promote cultural unity after the drastic demographic transformation following the 1948 war (Khalifeh 1986). However, the Palestinians in Jordan express anti-establishment collective national pride in the soccer sphere, through their flagship team, al-Wihdat (Tuastad 1997). In the Israeli–Palestinian case, a number of factors separated soccer from the minority's nationalism and political protest. Primarily it has been the huge gap in the power held by the state, on the one hand, and a society that lost its elites in 1948, on the other, and the ability of state agents to create the triangular association of sports, modernity, and the state.

When Palestinian society was torn apart in 1948, soccer was not rooted in the popular culture of the peripheral towns and villages that remained under Israeli rule. The collective memory of the Arab-Palestinians in Israel does not contain any recollections of pre-1948 Palestinian sports, mainly because the urban population that organized it was exiled from the country. The construction of an organizational infrastructure during the 1950s and 1960s with the help of governmental and semi-governmental bodies, and the prevention of any independent organizations, created a cognitive association between the game and the political status quo. The Arabs in Israel identify soccer with "Israeliness"; this Israeliness in turn would seem to contradict Palestinian nationalism (Bishara 1999). Soccer in Israel, then, is seen as an opportunity for integration, while expressions of Palestinian nationalism within the sporting arena are taken as a threat to that opportunity.

From an historical and socio-economic perspective on the order of events, Arab success in soccer came too late for it to serve as a locale for national protest. Just as soccer's sporting infrastructure in the Arab towns and villages was starting to bear fruit at the beginning of the 1980s, the rules of the game changed. The laws of the market damaged the ability of ethnically or nationally identified teams, or teams representing small localities, to achieve notable success. The achievements of Arab teams since the mid 1990s happened in spite of these developments and the short visits of Arab teams in the Premier League provide the exception that proves the rule.

Still, the success and prominence of Arab teams is very impressive. The major agents behind this success are the Arab municipalities which provide disproportional financial support for soccer clubs. The next chapter is dedicated, therefore, to analyzing and interpreting this support and the role it has played in shaping the integrative orientation of soccer.

4

Soccer and municipal "labor quiet"

On a summery May evening in 1999, it seemed for a moment that the city of Nazareth had shunted aside the bitter conflict between Muslims and Christians that had embittered the life of its residents for two years. At the epicenter of the quarrel was a disputed area adjacent to the Church of the Annunciation, where the municipality wanted to prepare a square for the anticipated thousands making the pilgrimage in the year 2000, and upon which the Islamic Movement demanded to build a mosque because of its proximity to the grave of Muslim holy man Shihab al-Din. For a long time, this conflict nearly paralyzed the municipality's activities, leaving deep fissures in the city's social tissue. But on that evening, thousands of people flowed into the streets to welcome the heroes of the Maccabi al-Aakha al-Naṣira soccer team who were returning from Ramat Gan after winning a last-second victory that secured its place in the second division. A long caravan of buses had brought about 3,000 supporters to the game. The returning fans had alighted from the buses at the southern entrance to the city, and began to march – singing, dancing, and drumming. The mayor of Nazareth, Ramez Jeraisy, usually a well-dressed, necktied gentleman, had himself traveled to Ramat Gan and had delivered a pep talk to the players at half-time; now he was carried on the shoulders of the singing fans. Songs of praise for the team were interwoven with rhythmic chants: "Wihda Waṭaniyya: Islamiyya-Masihiyya" (National Unity: Muslim–Christian).

Not always was al-Aakha al-Naṣira the city's standard-bearer. From the 1960s through to the mid 1970s, it was ha-Po'el Shabbab al-Naṣira, many of whose players and supporters were Christian. Shabbab al-Naṣira did not only represent Nazareth: in those years it was the premier Arab team in the country (see chapter 3). The demographic retreat

of Christians before Muslims in the city (Emmet 1995: 72–74) was reflected also in changes in the sports hegemony. Al-Aakha, whose fans came
mainly from the Muslim "Eastern Neighborhood," and whose soccer
stands were totally devoid of Christians, slowly climbed the ladder of
divisions, while its Christian rival continued to descend.

For years the Nazareth municipality had been under the control of the
Communist Party. Although the party was based on Christian–Muslim
partnership, growing dissatisfaction with the lack of services and the
apparent neglect of Muslims and their neighborhood played a role in
the emergence of the local branch of the Islamic Movement as a political
actor since the late 1980s (Emmet 1995: 254–283). In 1994, the Muslim-
born, secular and communist poet Tawfiq Ziyad, charismatic mayor of
Nazareth since 1975, was killed in a road accident. Ziyad's personality
was an important factor in maintaining Muslim–Christian unity and
preventing the eruption of inter-communal conflict. His deputy, Ramez
Jeraisy, who replaced him as mayor, did not enjoy the prestige of his
predecessor, and members of the Islamic Movement exploited his
Christian identity in order to undermine the legitimacy of his leadership.
One of the ways in which Jeraisy sought to buy the hearts of the residents
was through generous financial support for al-Aakha, the pride and joy
of the residents of the Eastern Neighborhood. The municipality created
an irregular position – Director of the Department of Soccer (in addition
to the Director of Sports) – who, upon assuming this position, in effect,
invested his time and energy in the advancement of al-Aakha al-Naṣira.
According to Ahmad Hilu, who was appointed Director in 1997, the
municipality funded approximately two-thirds of the team's budget.[1]

This support produced the anticipated results. In 1997/8 the team,
fortified by many players acquired from outside Nazareth, climbed
from the third division to the second division. The disc of songs released
on the occasion of the latter ascent extols the unity within Nazareth –
with its minarets and its churches – and preaches Muslim–Christian
amity. In the 1998/9 season, in which the interreligious tension almost
reached physical violence, the team managed to successfully finish in
eighth place, thus ensuring its place in the second division for the next
year;[2] and four years later it climbed, for the first time in its history, to the
Premier League, where it played for a single season.

---

[1] Interview with Ahmed Hilu, May 10, 1999.
[2] At the end of that year, the second division was split into two: the upper part (places 1–8)
joined those descending from the top division and was called the "National League" (second
division). The lower group was attached to those coming up from the third division and was
called the "Countrywide League" (third division).

We return to the parade of the celebrating fans. The procession reached Nazareth's main street, Paulus VI, and advanced towards the soccer field. In the meantime, Mayor Jeraisy had left the procession to prepare for the victory celebration that had been planned for later in the evening at a local banquet hall. On the way to the soccer field, the fans had to pass near the area of contention. As they approached the area of the Basilica of Annunciation, the calls for unity died out, being replaced with a different cry: "With spirit, with blood, we will redeem you Shihab al-Din!" Jeraisy's place atop the shoulders of the fans was taken by Salman Abu Ahmad, the Islamic Movement's representative in the Nazareth municipality, and a former member of the al-Aakha al-Naṣira management.

The relationship between the soccer teams and local politics could not be more faithfully illustrated than by the two local politicians, astride the twisting human chain of happy soccer fans, conducting the chorus that was singing political slogans. Attempts by local politicians in the Arab municipalities to channel the tremendous energy latent in soccer towards different goals is one of the main factors in the disproportionate representation of Arab localities in Israeli soccer leagues. This phenomenon raises the question: why does soccer rate such an important place in the local politics of the Arab population in Israel?

The over-support for sports clubs by Arab municipalities

Although the budgets of the teams is considered "Top Secret" and so hidden from the external investigator, conversations with managers, journalists, and others close to the teams point to the importance of municipalities, which provide the lion's share of the budget of most teams (at a conservative estimate, between 70 and 80 percent of the budgets for most of the teams in the second, third, and fourth divisions). The rest of the budget is covered by fans' personal contributions and by commercial sponsorship (in the middle divisions, but not in the lower ones). Therefore the financial base of the Arab soccer boom in Israel is determined by the municipalities; the measure of their support for the teams determines chances for advancement to a higher division. The data points to a significant gap between the support given by Arab municipalities and that given by Jewish municipalities.[3] In 1998, Arab municipalities spent

---

[3] Support for the sports organizations comprises only part of the investment in sports, but this is the investment for which relatively accurate figures are available. There is also investment in sports infrastructure, which depends in large part upon the ability of the municipality to collect funds from external sources, such as the National Lottery or the Toto Facilities Fund, about which I was unable to acquire information.

Table 4.1: *Support of Arab and Jewish municipalities for various sports (thousandths of all regular municipal budgets for 1998)*

	Arab municipalities	Jewish municipalities
Soccer	8.06	3.34
Basketball	1.30	2.20
Volleyball	0.38	0.17
Track and field (for schools)	0.28	0.07
Boxing	0.08	0.03
Handball	0	0.18
Swimming and water polo	0	0.07
Tennis	0	0.04

on average 1.07 percent of their regular budget on support of sports clubs. Jewish municipalities of an equivalent size spent an average of 0.64 percent of their budget for the same goal. The average support for soccer clubs in Arab municipalities reached 0.83 percent of the budget, whereas among Jewish municipalities of an equivalent size, average support for soccer clubs reached 0.29 percent (see appendix 5 for details about the database built for these calculations).

Soccer is the major sport among the Arab minority in Israel. Approximately 79 percent of the funds budgeted for sports clubs in 1998 was earmarked for soccer teams (as against 53 percent for clubs in Jewish localities). The most significant investment disparities, aside from soccer, are in volleyball (which receives especially generous support in the Druze villages of the Galilee, Christian villages, and mixed villages) and also school track and field and boxing (see table 4.1).

Possible explanations

The data raise two questions. First, how does one explain the overly generous support of the Arab municipalities for sports clubs? Second, how does one explain the partiality for soccer among Arab municipalities?

In my conversations with them, Arab sports writers and soccer fans usually explained this over-investment by arguing that in the Arab localities there are no other options for leisure time – no cinema, no clubs, no libraries. Although this shortage might partially explain the gap, I doubt that it can be considered as the best account. True, the Arab municipalities have suffered years of discrimination with regard to public support for public facilities. They have, however, the autonomy to choose the manner in which the leisure culture of the inhabitants will develop. Their investment in the local sports organizations is not necessarily less expensive than nurturing many other potential recreational and cultural institutions. The decision to supply funds for soccer clubs and not for a drama club or religious activity, for instance, derives from the way in which the municipal leadership perceives the leisure needs of the residents, or from the manner in which they are interested in influencing their leisure patterns.

An alternative explanation may lie in the difference between the status of local government in Arab towns and villages in contradistinction to its status in Jewish localities. In the Arab communities, more than in the Jewish ones, the municipalities are the locus of political, social, and economic struggles. A primary reason for this is that the Arab citizens have limited access to the political centers of power on the state level, which turned the municipality into a default sphere of direct political influence (Ghanem 1995; Rosenfeld and Al-Haj 1990). The relative importance of the local arena is expressed in the relatively high percentage of voters in local elections compared with voter turnout during elections for the Knesset (Paz 1990). Another reason for the relative importance of the Arab municipalities is the weak economic infrastructure in the Arab towns and villages, which turns the municipality – in most Arab localities – into the largest employer (Ghanem and Ozacky-Lazar 1999).

The mayors of the Arab municipalities are represented on the Committee of Mayors of Arab Municipalities and on the Follow-Up Committee,[4] and many see these bodies as a springboard to national leadership among Arabs in Israel (Rosenfeld and Al-Haj 1990). They are also over-represented in the Center for Local Government, in which they comprised one-third of the membership in 1999, thus carrying considerable weight in this important political body (Ghanem and Ozacky-Lazar 1999). Municipal elections are, in some localities, the ultimate tests of strength for local clans and social and political forces (Ghanem and Ozacky-Lazar 1999); and occasionally the contests are highly fractious.

The local soccer team has an important function in the framework of these struggles. Aware of the mobilizing power of soccer teams,

---

[4] A committee established in 1982 by Arab mayors, parliament members, and representatives of extra-parliamentary Arab organizations, in order to coordinate the collective action of the Arab minority in Israel. The FUC is involved in organizing nationwide strikes and demonstrations, especially on Land Day and the commemoration of the events of October 2000. The decisions of the FUC are widely followed by the Palestinian public in Israel. Unofficially, it is even recognized by the Israeli authorities as a leadership body, for coordinating and negotiating strikes and rallies.

local politicians tend to believe that achieving control over a team is an important political goal. Many Arab mayors elected during the 1980s and 1990s were previously directors or members of a team administration,[5] and they learned to convert the prestige and the status which they acquired in these positions into political assets. An intense struggle over control of the local soccer team is a frequent feature in many towns. An instructive example – though extreme in its severity – occurred in Taibeh in 1990. The lack of agreement between the two major clans of the city – Haj Yihya and Musarwa – over the composition of the administration resulted in two separate teams arriving for a Saturday game, each claiming to play for ha-Po'el Taibeh. The game was canceled until ha-Po'el Taibeh's internal squabbles were settled.

Although the political importance of soccer in Arab towns is highly relevant for any discussion of Arab soccer in Israel, as an explanation for the gap in municipal support for soccer clubs, it provides only a partial understanding, since it is somewhat tautological: it is still not clear why struggles over local rule are conducted through the soccer team.

A third possible explanation relates to the desire of minorities for cultural assimilation into the majority society. The prominence of national and ethnic minority involvement in certain sports is attributed to aspirations for cultural assimilation (Bazzano 1994; Nelson 1998; Soto and Travert 1997; Wilcox 1994). In the case of Arabs in Israel, the prospects for cultural integration into the general Israeli public sphere are limited. The majority of the Jewish public, as well as the mainstream Hebrew media, do not view Arabic culture as an integral part of general Israeli culture. Furthermore, in the dominant Israeli discourse Arab and Jewish cultures have been constructed as mutually exclusive (Shohat 1989). When Arab culture does receive public attention, it is presented as exotic, with emphasis on its folkloristic dimensions. On the other hand, Jewish tradition and most of the Hebraic culture that has developed in Israel are not the culture of the Arab citizens, and they cannot identify with it. Yet, in the soccer arena, the players, functionaries, and fans share a universal language, according to which earlier cultural backgrounds grant no *a priori* advantage to either side, thus facilitating the development of imagined egalitarian interaction. The success of an Arab sports club may be perceived by the municipality as an opportunity to rescue the Arab town from social marginality (deriving from political inferiority) through cultural integration into an arena which does not threaten the Arab pride of the residents.

[5] For example, Jalal Abu-Tu'ama from Baqa al-Gharbiya.

Yet another explanation may come from Norbert Elias's theory of the "civilizing process" (Elias 1978), which was further developed together with his student, Eric Dunning (Elias and Dunning 1986). According to Elias and Dunning, the main function of sports in society is to provide a "safety valve," a social enclave in which moderate and regulated forms of violence are permissible. The primary goal of leisure hours is "to arouse pleasurable forms of excitement" and competitive sports enters a category of what Elias and Dunning named "mimetic activities": activities which create excitement by means of building up tension that mimic risk in real life.

According to this logic, in the stands young Arabs can exhibit aggression in a controlled manner, releasing frustrations in a way that does not undermine the status of existing bodies of authority. The mayors who are concerned with their political survival cultivate the local team that, every week, supplies the youth with an arena that creates excitement and limits expressions of aggression to well-defined periods of time and within clearly demarcated spaces. This viewpoint enables one to explain as well the popularity of soccer compared to basketball in the Arab community; the structure of soccer enables – actually demands – the demonstration of higher levels of aggression. In basketball, there is less meaning to the question "how forcefully was the ball thrown?" In soccer, on the other hand, the force of the kick is significant: "a rocket," "a missile," or "a bomb" are battle images which soccer permits and sports journalists frequently use; but such descriptive terms would sound absurd in the context of a basketball game.

Another angle of observation, which may have some explanatory value, is gender, i.e. the difference in patterns of inter-gender relationships between Arab and Jewish societies. According to a study conducted by the sociologist Hannah Herzog, of 246 women elected to municipal councils in the November 1998 elections in Israel (14 percent of those elected in 1998 were women), only three were Arabs. Namely, much more than in Jewish towns, Arab local politics are controlled almost exclusively by men. Therefore, these politics are more subject to male internal and external pressures, and municipal resources tend more to meet male needs. The soccer bleachers in Israel are a male-dominated sphere among Jews and an almost exclusive male sphere in Arab localities (see chapter 8), and therefore massive support for soccer clubs reflects the marginalization of women.

In addition to the previously discussed explanations, there are measurable demographic and economic differences which may also explain the exceptional investments in sports made by the Arab municipalities in comparison to their Jewish counterparts. Arabs in Israel have lower levels of education than Jews (Semyonov and Yuchtman-Yaar 1992), and earn less (Plaut and Plaut 2002). Studies of sports consumption consistently demonstrate that both people's level of education and their level of income correlate positively with the rate of involvement in sports, both as participants and as spectators (Bourdieu 1984; White and Wilson 1999; Wilson 2002). At the same time, those having limited education and income tend to be more involved in specific sports, both because of material reasons (some branches of sports require less expenditure) and as a consequence of cultural factors. That is to say, certain sports have become signifiers of a "popular" class, while other sports are elitist and closed off to whomever lacks the right "cultural keys" (Bourdieu 1984).

We see, then, that the exceptional investment of Arab municipalities in sports clubs in general stands in contradiction to expectations anticipated in the aforementioned studies, whereas the relatively high investment in soccer can be explained by the gaps in education and income between Jews and Arabs. If the class approach is applicable to our case, Israeli soccer, as a popular game, is a marker of class culture cutting across ethnic borders; but because more Arabs swell the ranks of the lower classes, soccer has a more central status in the Arab public.

The gaps in the economic status of Arab and Jewish towns can explain the choice of certain kinds of sports. The greater the expenditure necessary for a particular sports the more likely it is that it will be found in wealthier localities. While it is difficult to improvise facilities and equipment for sports like swimming or tennis, soccer has become the most popular sports in the world in no small part because of the rudimentary facilities required. It can be played just about anywhere, and there is no need for special equipment, not even for a commercially manufactured ball (Frankenberg 1957). Soccer played in a formal framework does require a much greater investment, but the public demand for such investment exists in those places where people experienced the game themselves as players in informal frameworks. Mason (1995) explains the magic of soccer by emphasizing that many people can watch the game that they themselves play, and this allows them to imagine themselves as players on the field. Therefore, in those sports-supporting municipalities, we may assume that the economic standing of the residents will predict which branch of sports the council will support. Thus, support for soccer can be considered inversely proportional to the level of the population's income.

Yet another significant difference between Jews and Arabs in Israel is to be found in the age structure. In 1995, 40 percent of the population of the Arab localities were 17 years old or younger, as compared with

33 percent in the Jewish localities. Fully 62 percent of the Arab localities were 24 years old or younger, compared with 44 percent in Jewish localities.[6] Since the average age of "in-the-stands" soccer fans is relatively low, investment in the local team provides entertainment for an overwhelmingly young population. It may be assumed that municipalities with older populations will promote more varied forms of leisure activity than those with relatively young populations.

It is worthwhile to mention one factor that does not explain the disproportionate level of investment in sports by the Arab municipalities, but does sharpen the questions asked since it may explain this relationship in an opposite direction. I refer here to disparity in the level of inequality. The Arab localities tend to be more homogeneous class-wise. In 1997, the average of the Gini index for income levels in medium-size Arab towns (5,000–35,000 persons) was 0.325, compared to 0.389 in Jewish towns of equivalent size. Since the variance is small in both cases, this is a significant gap ($t = 12.16$). It may be assumed that as the social and economic gaps in a town grow larger, so too will the municipality's investment in the representative sports grow as a means to increase local solidarity. Therefore, according to this logic, the disparities in sports funding between the Jewish and Arab municipalities do exist – despite the relative equality in the Arab localities.

Not all the above explanations can be tested quantitatively. But at least those explanations based on demographic and economic gaps can be checked by the correlations between the above-mentioned variables and the investment in sports. In order to examine the independent weight of these variables in explaining disparities in investment in sports and soccer, I have placed them in linear regression equation. The independent variables in the regression equation are: education (measured by the ratio of high-school diplomas held by the locality's adults); the average wage in the locality; the Gini inequality index for the average wage; the ratio of residents younger than 17, and the ethno-national identity of the locality ($0 = $Jew, $1 = $Arab). The significance of including the last variable in the equation is as follows. If, despite the removal of the economic and demographic variables, the ethno-national variable still explains the variance in investment, then some weight may be given to at least some of the unquantified explanations which were not included in the equation, or to a combination of them. Should it be found that the ethno-national variable does not explain the variance in club support, then the probability that these assumptions carry weight in explaining the variance decreases.

---

[6] According to data of the Israeli Central Bureau of Statistics census for 1995.

The table in appendix 5 presents the results of two linear regressions in which the dependent variables are (a) the ratio between support for sports clubs and the total budget of every municipality; and (b) the ratio between support for soccer clubs and general support for sports clubs (calculated for 111 municipalities that support sports clubs). The results demonstrate that after removal of the demographic variables that were checked, the nationality variable still has explanatory value, though minor, for the differences in sports investment. The "nationality variable" is a black box containing all the differences between Arabs and Jews which were not examined in the regression. They are difficult to quantify: political inferiority of a national minority, patterns of gender relations, the status of the local government in the social life of the town or village, and the need for maintaining "safety valves" for managing the level of excitement generated among the population and the release of aggression. Similarly, 83.8 percent of the variables are still not explained by the demographic variables.

The table further indicates that the income gaps between Jewish and Arab localities do not explain the disparities in sports investment, whereas the correlation between education and sports investment is clearly negative. This is to say that it is not financial factors which motivate the mayors to invest their meager resources in the support of sports organizations, but other factors. This finding contradicts expectations raised by studies on the relation between education and involvement in sports. At first glance, it would have seemed that sports is a path of mobility which bypasses education (Bourdieu 1978; Semyonov 1986; Stuart 1996), i.e. because of their inferiority in education, Arabs are more inclined than Jews to expect that investment in sports will facilitate socioeconomic mobility. The empirical data, however, do not support the "mobility argument" in the case of public investment in Arab sports. The main investment of Arab municipalities in sports is not in the local human infrastructure, but in the acquisition of reinforcement players and in short-term investments. Empirical proof may be found in the relatively small number of Arab teams in the youth leagues. In 1998, 42 percent of all adult clubs were Arab, compared with only 28 percent of the youth clubs and only 3 percent of the children's teams. Some of the municipalities also support school teams. In Arab localities, support for these teams is higher than in Jewish localities, but in both sectors, the amounts are negligible compared with the overall level of support for the soccer teams.

Despite these facts, the theory of mobility aspiration is not without basis if, instead of discussing economic mobility, we discuss "prestige mobility." It appears that the local pride emerging from the success of the Sakhnin team and the prestige gains of Sakhnin within the Israeli public sphere (see chapter 8) are not out of the ordinary. It is reasonable to assume that similar results have been obtained by successful soccer teams in Jewish peripheral towns such as Bet She'an and Kiryat Gat, basketball teams in the Druze village of Yarka and the Jewish town of Migdal ha-'Emek, and volleyball teams in the Jewish town of Hatzor and the Muslim–Druze–Christian town of 'Usfiya. If we assume that low educational attainment levels are correlated with social marginality and low town prestige, then such an explanation matches the regression equation: a low educational level explains why there is such widespread support for sports clubs; but still, since the marginality of the Arabs is also linked to their identity as "the other" in the state of the Jews, the identity of Arabs also explains some of the noted variances in investment levels.

It is worthwhile to mention that the level of inequality within a town makes a modest positive contribution to predicting the level of support for the sports organizations. This finding suggests the possibility that local sports clubs have a vital political function – though not necessarily derived from conscious choices – to blunt social tensions in the town. As we shall see later, this conjecture is reinforced by statements given by mayors when asked to explain their motives for supporting the sports organizations.

As opposed to the overall investment in sports – which still leaves us with the "black box" of differences between Arab and Jewish towns – the results do not support the possibility that the political inferiority of the Arabs as a national minority causes them to show particular interest in soccer. The exceptional support for soccer by the Arab municipalities is mediated clearly by the economic gaps between the Jewish and Arab localities, as expressed in the average wage. This is to say that while the high investment in sports in general is related to the social marginality of the Arabs in Israel and the ability of sports to promote the town's prestige, the popularity of soccer is related to its organizational simplicity and low cost. With the exception of the USA – where soccer is played primarily by members of the middle class because of unique socio-historical reasons (Markovits and Hellerman 2001) – all over the world soccer is traditionally the game of the masses and underprivileged; although in recent decades there has been an increase in the number of the well-to-do who regularly attend games of the leading teams.

It should be clear that maintaining a professional or semi-professional team is not inexpensive. It appears that the game's popularity derives from its technical simplicity and the low expenses for every child who wants to play in the alleyways or on a rocky field. The extensive acquaintance of diverse social groups with the game leads them to favor a soccer team and to pressure the municipality to support soccer instead of other sports. Even if another sports should enjoy temporary success and popularity, its chances for continued public financial support are slim if it has to compete for funding with a successful soccer team. For example, the YMCA Nazareth basketball team gradually climbed into higher league divisions and in the mid 1990s was on the verge of ascending to the Premier League. But this occurred at the same time as the star al-Aakha al-Naṣira soccer team was in the ascent; and thus, financial support for the basketball team shrank to the point where, in 1999, the same year that al-Aakha al-Naṣira climbed to the second division, YMCA Nazareth was disbanded.

What do the mayors say?

During November–December 1999, I conducted sixteen in-depth interviews with Arab mayors, eleven from the Galilee, five from the Triangle, and one vice-mayor from the Naqab/Negev. The interviews took place in a tent erected by the Arab mayors in front of the prime minister's office in Jerusalem, to protest against the government's responsibility for their financial crisis. The interviews could not supply rational explanations for the investment in the sports organizations; the explanation I always received was the lack of other options for leisure activity, an account whose limitations I explained earlier. The goal of the interviews was mainly to understand how the mayors connect their support for sports organizations with their professed political aims, and to elucidate the motivations or fears which drive them to do so. Except for two cases, all the mayors I asked to interview agreed. One may assume that the time and place of the interviews increased their tendency to paint their towns' situation in gloomy colors, and it may well be that this influenced the way they viewed – in retrospect – their investment in sports in this context. It is also reasonable to assume that the interviewees did not mention non-altruistic motives – such as the creation of additional jobs in order to increase political clout – when they related to their town's affairs (they were mentioned in informal conversations, however, in oblique accusations of other mayors).

The first part of this chapter took a positivistic approach and isolated variables from an external viewpoint. The following section is devoted to understanding the *Weltanschauung* of the people behind the numbers. The discourse of the mayors shows that the investment in sports is derived from two kinds of motivations: first, apprehension of the repressed energy of the youth which is liable to explode if they have too much free time; and second, nurturing of local pride. These two motivating factors are not independent of each other.

Black time and repressed energy

Every sports club you open guarantees the closing of some café, to the point where the youth gather with the beers and all the negative phenomena which we see in general in this era. So you have somewhere to go. Why is everything so quiet on Saturday? Because they are all at the soccer fields. There is no other activity.   (A mayor from the Galilee)

It also solves a lot of problems for me. There is no crime. Better that people talk about sports and not make a *balagan* [Hebrew colloquial word for "mess"] in my community. Let that occupy their time. If someone has no job – it is better that he should engage in sports. For a youth who puts his energy into sports, there is little chance that he will turn to crime.   (A mayor from the Triangle)

Although there is not enough evidence to support this assumption, both social theory and popular belief assume that sports might reduce social exclusion and urban crime, and this belief motivates municipal authorities to invest in sports (Long and Sanderson 2001). This popular belief is well reflected in the mayors' rationalizations for their financial support for sports clubs. However, the words they choose to describe their motivations reveal more than that. The similarity between Elias and Dunning's functionalistic perception of sports and the discourse that the mayors employ in justifying the support for sports in their communities is impressive. One discerns that Elias – strongly influenced by Freud – and his student/partner Dunning appear to share a collectivist psychodynamic view of the masses. The image of repressed energy on the verge of eruption, seeking release, appears repeatedly in the words of all the local politicians with whom I spoke – the fear of the blind power of the masses and of the directions it may take are, according to the politicians, a prime motivation for pouring money into sports in general and soccer in particular.

Another recurring motif is the concept of time. It seems that nothing worries the mayors more than the existence of an empty time bubble in the schedule of the young people, one that is liable to be filled immediately with crime, primarily using and dealing drugs. The following excerpt from an interview with a mayor from the southern Triangle illustrates the attitude towards empty time and repressed energy (all emphases are mine – T.S.):

There are no other activities in the Arab sector with which the children and youngsters can use to fill *their empty time*. All they have is sports. Therefore we have to invest.

[Q. What will happen if there is free time? What do you fear?]

My fear is of ... you know that in the Arab sector, many young men use drugs, theft, problems. We have people *with nothing to do* so they start problems, fights, theft at night. They engage in drugs because *they have nothing to do*. Also because they don't even have work. There is unemployment today. They are all in the street. If a girl walks, they begin to bother her. They have an effect, these fellows who *have nothing to do*.

[Q: What is there in sports that helps fight drugs and crime?]

Sports gives them something to do, they can *release their energy*. Then *they have no energy left* for drugs or to do bad things. All they have to do is [invest their energy] in the health club or in soccer or in basketball, and so we overcome all their bad qualities. *If the energy remains inside and you don't know how to empty it out* – then they start to go wild. They go wild with blows, with theft, with noise, with illegal driving, and this has an effect upon the population, on the village, on the residents. If he has a place like a health club, like a gym, like a swimming pool, then he *releases all this energy* into something positive.

Another mayor from the Triangle:

Usually youth seeks employment and something to do *with leisure time*. If it is after school or after working hours. So where are there places in the Arab village? Either in the café or in the main square where all the young people and the youth gather and from there begins this matter of crime and drugs and mixing of young people from good families with young people from families in distress, and thus is created the matter of drug commerce.

[Q. How do you prevent this with sports?]

First of all, sports, in my opinion is *preventative treatment*. First of all, the young man has somewhere to go when he has a sports club or he has a sports hall, or he has a soccer field, a basketball court, a swimming pool, and then certainly he will prefer to spend his *free time* in these places and will not go spend time with negative people, with juvenile delinquents.

The value of soccer is not found so much in what soccer has to offer; its value is derived more from its ability to fill a vacuum that may be filled with other things. The perception of a cultural institution as a "preventative treatment" indicates that the mayors consider soccer as a default option and not as a genuine desire. A Galilee mayor well known for his munificent support for the soccer team explains:

I say that it's good that I have a way to gather the community, otherwise where would it be? *This is the release of our youth*. We have no community center and we have no swimming pool – my support is for educational cultural activity.

I am afraid that this community, if it does not find a place to *fill its leisure time*, it will slide to forbidden things, to crime. I have no other way; *there is no vacuum in life.*

The vice-mayor of an Arab municipality from the south, who invests relatively little in soccer, declares that he would like to invest more but he is unable to do so, and therefore all the feared evils befall him.

First of all, sports allows the youth to *let loose*. You know *that when the youth does not let loose, then he seeks release in other things* – he can deal with drugs, he can commit crimes – he can indulge in all the negative things . . .
    [Q. How does sports prevent this?]
It can make things much easier. For example, why in the south, in the Negev in general, lately you hear a lot about crime – youth has nothing to do, in general he has no – the youth *has no employment* – first of all unemployment, the first thing is unemployment. There is no sports activity.

The surveillance practice is summed up not only in "directing energy" and channeling it in the direction of the soccer stands. There is also a perception of active involvement in order to rein in the violence even within the arena:

I personally believe that this develops immunity against deviation in the direction of drugs and violence and all sorts . . . I personally am also involved in soccer, and I lay down a clear formula – if there is violence, no support. There is quiet, there is support. The measure of the quiet is the measure of the support. I decided this and it works – until today it works. And the fact is that when a soccer game is over you see no quarrel and no altercations and no stones and nothing – business as usual.   (A Galilee mayor)

The question of the ability to rule and to discipline the youth is especially critical in a society in which the patriarchal authority structure has been weakened. Patriarchal authority was not limited to the confines of the family – it was conferred also upon the teacher in school; obedience to him derived from the obedience to the adult male figure at home. In the past, the teacher was granted exaggerated authority, and hitting pupils was acceptable educational practice. In the words of the mayors one detects problems of authority: the youth are perceived as throwing off restraints, and modern society is per- ceived as having failed in its mission of disciplining them. Thus, sports is perceived as an instrument of discipline within the framework of modern society:

Sports is discipline – because you behave according to *rules* in the sports. It is based upon physical development, mental development, and motor skills. Children aged

4, 5, and 6 when you start with them, and then they grow. *A certain level of discipline and level of rules.* We do not live in anarchy. Our problem here is that democracy has become anarchy. Democracy has rules. You must also learn *to enter the rules* and to understand and to live *by the rules* and to live with democracy. Sports means education to being a good citizen in the future *with all the discipline.*

Sports is one of the occupations that can instill *discipline* into people. No getting around it, today, with all that goes on in the school and democracy – and the lack of violence against … the teacher enters and cannot speak – *he has no control* over children, because this is anarchy, this is total anarchy. But sports, in my opinion, is the key to healthy society. Healthy mind in a healthy body, and that's all there is to it.

The threat of free time is connected not only to drugs and crime. Some of the mayors also fear political extremism that may undermine the internal stability of their town or village and damage its image in the eyes of the government and in the eyes of the Jewish public. In September 1999, a few months before the mayors' strike, the involvement of youths from two Galilee villages in Hamas-instigated terrorist attacks in Haifa and Tiberius was uncovered. When asked for the motives behind his massive funding of sports activity in his village, the mayor of one of these villages tied his support to the sports' ability to restrain extremism:

This is physical education; this is cultural education; this is education of love, that one should relate seriously to the other. It is also the recognition between village and village and also between Arabs and Jews. This is a very important area; supreme priority must be given to sports.

[Q. What education do you give through sports?]

A kind of education – first thing, that *they should not be extremists.* This is the first thing, that there should be no extremists at all. To distance them.

[Q. Extremists in what sense?]

That they should be *good citizens*, both to the village and to the state in general. I see that sports can deliver such results … If you find a solution for this generation from the beginning – if you do not provide him with *a framework to pass his time* he is liable to fall into hands – or he will go and become negative – or he will reach hands … and they brainwash him.

For the above-quoted mayor, investment in sports is an instrument in the struggle for the souls of the youth against political forces capable of under-mining the village's standing. Sports, from his point of view, is a tool for the advancement of dual integration: personal integration of the individual into the village and collective integration of the village into the state. As has been documented through the excerpts of interviews with the other mayors quoted, there is repeated reference to the fear of free time that may allow repressed energy to erupt and cause chaos and lead to loss of control over the foci of authority so dear to the hearts of the mayors.

Local identity

Another recurring motif is the effort to strengthen the ties of youth to the local community and to develop local pride. One can distinguish between three types of motivation for inculcating local pride: (1) strengthening of the tie to the community and the sense of partnership between the residents as a supervisory tool derived from the struggle against the "black time," those periods of youth's free time when the authority has no control over them; (2) strengthening of the local pride as an attempt to calm internal tensions between different groups in the village; and (3) strengthening of local pride as an end in itself.

The sequence of ideas expressed by a mayor from the Triangle in the following paragraph illustrates these motivations:

If he engages in sports – *and all his energy* – especially ages thirteen, fourteen, during adolescence with all their energy … you come and direct him – for what is adolescence – *this is the age of lack of discipline – of disobedience* – of desire to show – all the psychology of adolescence. You come to this boy – *all of his energy* – he goes and invests in sports – invests to be IN with his buddies, IN in soccer, IN in basketball. Not to be IN in drugs, not to be IN in acid parties. Thereby he feels *belonging to a team* ["team" said in English], *to a group, belonging to an age group, belonging to a village group. He belongs to the village; he belongs to those of his own age.* He has memories, even when he will be more mature, in the future at age forty, fifty years old – even should he travel to wherever he travels he will always say *I am a son of this village* – because he *belongs* to these people and will be prepared to give to these people and to sacrifice, to give, even to donate. This is the category of *belonging* – this contributes to his *belonging* also in the future, when he will be an adult.

The sense of "belonging" that the interviewee tries to create derives from the need for discipline. Sports is seen as a socialization implement that connects the individual to the community and strengthens his commitment to its norms and values. At the end of the above quote, it seems that the speaker considered strengthening of belonging to be a value in itself – the thought about a child's attitude to his village at the age of 50 attests to a perception that local pride is important even beyond its contribution to dealing with current problems.

Sports is also a means for relieving internal tensions. The Nazareth example of the place of a soccer team in Muslim–Christian relations is not an isolated case. Another Galilee village with mixed population underwent a period of inter-communal conflict. The mayor says:

You need things that make the community involved, as one says. So what is common to them all – it is soccer. *Soccer can unite them all. And that's the fact – unites them all.*

[Q. Does it really unite?]

Yes, in my opinion it unites. The team called Maccabi [name of the village], in our case, then Maccabi [name of the village] belongs to all, it is no one's private property. It is a symbol that *unites – all unite* after the team – if only we had many things which *unite.*

[Q. There are not many things which unite?]

There are, but the more things there are which unite, there will be quiet in the village, "*labor quiet,*" we need such *labor quiet.* We had a case in the village where they tried to describe it as Muslim–Christian. Thank God this is behind us. At the time there was the quarrel, the municipal council could not function. Because you have no *labor quiet.* You cannot plan a project and begin work. Every thought and every moment is sunk in squabbles, in fights, in all kinds of ...

"The things which unite" are means of achieving "labor quiet." The instrumental attitude is not only towards the soccer team receiving support, but also to the local identity which is crystallizing through it.

The discourse which describes strengthening of local pride as a goal in itself is quite rare. Not incidentally, this discourse combines local pride with national pride. The mayor of a town with a successful soccer team says:

I believe – I want to educate youth and a public who have a spine – proud of itself, *proud of its national identity.* Not fanatic, but let him say what he has. That he should respect himself and thus others will also respect him. This is our team, of the north, of the Arabs, of Galilee, and it warms the heart. I want the national pride – that *all should know that Arab feet are not inferior to Jewish feet.* Every person has potential, every one. Why not make it prominent, why not be proud?

Ashworth (1970) maintains that modern competitive sports creates in the individual a feeling that his team's ability is measured in equal and "natural" terms, without the initial advantages that the "artificial" social hierarchy gives. The gaps in political power and economic resources are suspended, as it were, and for a moment the collective can examine its "true" worth as compared with another collective. Against this background one can understand the binding of the national pride – by reduction – to a body. After emphasizing the importance of a "spine" comes the implied assertion that if "everyone knew that Arab feet are not inferior to Jewish feet" then there would be recognition of the Arab's "real" worth, without "artificial" differences created by the political power ratios.

Another Galilee mayor, who provides massive support to sports organizations, says:

In my opinion, a national team has to be based on national, local players, even built by local coaches. This is the product of which one can be proud.

[Q. Why don't you apply that? You finance the team [the local team has many players from the outside.]]

I have to build an infrastructure – this is the alternative. And this is an alternative which will yield fruit only in a year or two. So let's say that in the recovery program for the sports we will really make sure that in the near future we will not need to acquire outside players. In all the branches. And everything will have to be locally produced – in quotation marks, "national."

... This will continue until the children grow up and thus the world of sports is run and we entered the same dilemma. But, should the day come when I see that 90 percent of the players on the field are acquisitions – I would rather drop down a division and not continue in the same direction.

Not without reason did the interviewee choose to draw a parallel between national identity and local identity. The Palestinian national identity of Arabs in Israel is liable to threaten Jewish citizens, and therefore the mayor feels a need to frame the national aspect in quotation marks, while being interviewed by a Jew. This is a concrete example of the assertion that in certain cases the aim of emphasizing the local identity is to dilute the potential of Palestinian national identity to threaten the Jewish public (see chapter 8). This is not a particularly difficult undertaking, considering the proximity and similarity of the emotional load of these two identities. This is because the Palestinian-Arab national identity is often mediated by local identities (Tamari 1999) and because both cases involve territorial identities that take for granted a "natural" connection between the individual and her or his homeland. The ability to reinforce the local identity through a representative sports team depends upon the ability to present the players as expressing the "true essence" of the place. The aspiration to climb to the senior divisions, however, forces the acquisition of outside players. The overt contradiction between the need for nurturing collective local pride through local players, and the massive presence of "reinforcement" players is resolved by portraying the situation as only temporary.

The conservative role of soccer

The municipalities are the main financial patrons of the Arab soccer teams, and therefore they are the primary agents that create the field and maintain it. Through the statistical analysis I tried to explain the disparity in sports investment between Arab and Jewish municipalities. It is worth noticing that the regression equations provided only partial explanations. The graph in appendix 5 shows that only 16.2 percent of the variance in degree of support for sports organizations, and only 37.6 percent of the variance in support for soccer as compared with support for sports in general, are explained by the variables examined. This measure dictates caution in deducing far-reaching conclusions, but the trend of the influence of the variables checked supplies a certain indication as to the validity of a number of conjectures.

First of all, the excessive investment by the Arab municipalities in soccer in particular, as compared with other sports, is related to the economic gaps between Jews and Arabs more than to other variables investigated. Opposingly, the excessive investment of Arab municipalities in local sports organizations in general is related mainly to education gaps between Jewish and Arab localities. I do not interpret these findings as evidence that sports is seen by Arab local leaders as a possible path to individual mobility – this explanation is refuted by the "inverted pyramid" of investment in the teams. The common denominator of low education and Arab identity in Israel – the two factors which predict support for sports organizations – is social marginality, which might be crucial in the aspiration to gain public recognition or acceptance through a successful soccer team.

Furthermore, the regression equation shows that the excessive support granted to sports by Arab municipalities is weakly correlated with additional factors which distinguish between Jewish and Arab authorities and which are difficult to quantify. Possible explanations include the aspiration to cultural assimilation of the Arabs as a minority in the state, the support of Arab municipalities in the construction of an exclusively male arena for a sector where masculinity is threatened, the relative importance of the local government in Arab localities and viewing soccer as a tool for acquiring internal political resources, and the perception of soccer as a "safety valve" for the release of young people's aggression. In open interviews, mayors rationalized their support for soccer clubs primarily by the need to redirect the repressed energy of youth in directions that do not impair the stability of society, and to prevent the formation of "black holes" in time. Sports is seen by some of the mayors also as an instrument for instilling discipline which can cope with crises which befall the traditional foci of authority facing modernity. Many of them attribute to sports the ability to strengthen the bond between the individual and the community, and to nurture identity and local pride.

Those Arab mayors who spend considerable sums in nurturing the local soccer team in an effort to strengthen the ties between individuals and the local community have strong grounds for their decision. A statistical correlation between local pride and presence at the soccer stadium is found in Sakhnin (chapter 8), as well as in the countrywide survey. Yet, the countrywide survey makes clear that such a correlation exists only when examining the most loyal fans (11 percent of the interviewees who attended more than ten games). In other words, the faithful fans of the local teams tend to choose local identity as a source of pride with greater frequency than their colleagues, those who are occasional spectators and those who never attend games.

One could easily discern the striking similarities between the perception of sports by Arab mayors in the late 1990s and the way it was seen by the government and the Histadrut in the 1960s (see chapter 2). In both cases, sports is seen mainly as a disciplinary mechanism, a patch which might fill dangerous voids at times, and an attraction which might divert the youth from crime, drugs, and undesirable political deviance. These similarities raise the question: what are the relations between the role soccer plays in these two spheres, the municipal and the state?

It seems that while on the experiential subjective level soccer serves as a collective pain relief, on the macro-sociological level it is a stabilizing tool in a society in which many of the foci of traditional authority have been undermined and relations with the state are marked by alienation. Even the modest contribution of a degree of internal inequality in the town for explaining the difference in support of sports clubs suggests that in their support of the soccer clubs the mayors individually view sports as a means of guaranteeing stability in their town or village; and indirectly, of prolonging their rule. The support given to local soccer clubs by Arab municipalities, however, has ramifications that deviate from the usual municipality–resident relations; it is also relevant to the social location of both the mayors and the soccer fans with regard to the state. Nowhere is this phenomenon as evident as in the relation between attendance in the local soccer stadium and the tendency to vote for Zionist parties in the parliamentary elections.

During the first decades after the state was founded, its governments chose to encourage voting for Zionist parties (preferably for the ruling party, Mapai); and this meant that a vote for an independent Arab party was considered regressive and undesirable by the authorities. Today, there is less establishment pressure on the Arab citizen to vote for Zionist parties; ruling parties are more concerned for themselves and are less interested in whether or not the vote remains within "the Zionist camp." Similarly, since 1992 there has been a steady decline in the percentage of Arab votes for Jewish-Zionist parties (51 percent in 1992,

33 percent in 1996, 30 percent in 1999, and 27 percent in 2003). In addition to the voting patterns, Arab involvement in elections for the prime minister and the Knesset is significant. Participation in elections is perceived as attesting to the integration of Arab citizens into the Israeli political system (Neuberger 1996); and consequently, feelings of bitterness and frustration at the state are translated into relatively low voting percentages, as occurred in the 2001 elections for prime minister.

The countrywide survey from 2000 revealed that attendance at soccer games is associated with certain behavior in parliamentary elections. Figure 4.1 compares the vote distribution among those who attend soccer games with those of other interviewees. The comparison clearly shows that stadium spectators, both in local games and in the Premier League have a greater tendency to vote in Knesset elections and to vote for Zionist parties than do the other interviewees. However, while several

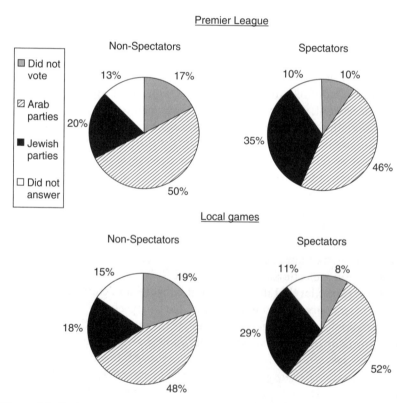

Figure 4.1: *Voting patterns among young Arab men in Israel: a comparison between interviewees who attended and those who did not attend soccer games*

variables are controlled (age, level of religiosity, level of newspaper reading [as an indicator of social involvement] and level of proficiency in Hebrew [as an indicator of ties with Jews]), the predictive power of attendance at Premier League games became statistically insignificant, while the predictive power of attendance at local games remained higher than that of Premier League games, and was statistically significant (table 3.e in appendix 3).

These findings suggest that the correlation between attendance at the stadium and political voting behavior is not merely derivative of background variables. With all due caution in deriving causal conclusions from such correlative research as this, these findings suggest as well the possibility of a "91st minute effect" – i.e. soccer fulfills a role in preserving the legitimacy of the state among the Arab-Palestinian community, and it is not merely a reflection of this legitimacy. According to this interpretation, by their generous cultivation of soccer teams, the mayors control an arena that grants legitimacy to the existing socio-political order and to the ideology which makes possible its existence. In light of these findings, the similarities between historical governmental understanding of sports and its contemporary use by Arab municipal leaders are far from being coincidental, and can well be explained by the political role these leaders are playing. Antonio Gramsci (1971) argued that political power is the combined result of force and consent, and that consent is a result of political and ideological leadership referred to by Gramsci as hegemony. Semi-autonomous institutions of the civil society are playing crucial role in the consistent maintenance of this hegemony by making certain ideas, especially those legitimizing the political status-quo, self-evident and part of a "common sense." Gramsci's theory of hegemony has been adopted by sociologists of sports to analyze the role that sports plays in class relations (Hargreaves 1986) and in ethno-religious conflict (Sugden and Bairner 1993). The case of Arab soccer in Israel is an interesting illustration of the relevance of Gramsci-inspired arguments to the relationship between a nation-state and a national minority.

Although the level of involvement of the state and the army in organizing the sports clubs in the first years of the state negates much of their qualification as "semi-autonomous," since the 1970s both Arab soccer clubs and the municipalities which finance them have emerged as part of the civil society of the Arab citizens of Israel. Through financing these clubs, through the glorification and celebration of their success in the Israeli sphere, and relying on the needs of Arab men for some of the crucial features of the soccer sphere, Jewish-Zionist hegemony has been legitimized. Municipal support for sports may fulfill an important role by

safeguarding the political status quo and preserving the restrained attitude of Arab citizens of Israel towards their state.

By its very definition, hegemony is never a complete domination and it
is always contested. In the context of Arab soccer in Israel, the main
agents which have been producing the counter-hegemonic meanings
since the mid 1990s are the Arabic newspapers, whose role will be
analyzed in the next chapter.

5

"These points are Arab": nationalist rhetoric in the sports press

Previous chapters have emphasized the integrative aspects of soccer and the historical role it played in inhibiting national protest among the Arab-Palestinian minority in Israel. Soccer's conservative role has been challenged by the new Arabic press that has been developed in Israel since the mid 1980s. Analyzing Arab soccer in Israel as a "contested terrain" is meaningful mainly because of the vocal and concrete opposition of Arab sports journalists to the hegemonic meanings produced both in the stadiums and in the Hebrew media.

This active and extensive nationalist tone in the Arabic press is relatively new. The effect of the 1948 war on the Arab-Palestinian media was similar to its implications for the Palestinian independent sports infrastructure. Namely, the media elite – most of the publishers, editors, and journalists – were exiled and Palestinian newspapers ceased to exist (Caspi and Kabaha 2001). Under Israeli rule, these newspapers were replaced by official mouthpieces of the Histadrut and the Zionist parties. The only newspaper that survived the war was *al-Ittiḥad*, the mouthpiece of the Communist Party, which had expressed an oppositional line but was subjected to strict censorship. Since the mid 1980s however, the Arabic press in Israel has experienced relative prosperity in the number and diversity of newspapers and has undergone a significant shift in political tone. This shift is described by Caspi and Kabaha (2001) as a "transformation from a [status quo oriented] mobilized press, to a nationally conscious press, self mobilized for the struggle of the Palestinian minority in Israeli society."

In the late 1990s Arabic-language newspapers with countrywide distribution in Israel included one daily paper: *al-Ittiḥad*, the paper of the Communist Party; a semi-weekly privately owned paper, *al-Ṣinnara*; and a number of weeklies: the privately owned *Kul al-'Arab*, *Ṣawt al-Ḥaq wal-Ḥurriyya* (mouthpiece of the Islamic Movement – northern faction), *al-Mithaq*

81

(mouthpiece of the Islamic Movement – southern faction), *Panorama* (privately owned), and *Faṣl al-Maqal* (mouthpiece of the National Democratic Assembly).[1] In addition, dozens of local weeklies were published.

All these papers featured a sports section. In the leading four (*al-Ṣinnara, Kul al-'Arab, al-Ittiḥad,* and *Ṣawt al-Haq wal-Hurriyya*), the sports section appeared as a separate section, composed of 10 to 16 pages (in *al-Ittiḥad,* a daily paper, the sports section appeared only on Sundays). The findings presented in this chapter are based upon the sports sections of four secular newspapers representing a variety of political outlooks: *al-Ṣinnara, Kul al-'Arab, al-Ittiḥad,* and *Faṣl al-Maqal*; the Islamic sports press will be examined in chapter 7, which is devoted to the Islamic League.

Throughout the world, the sports section is the most creative and emotive part of the newspaper, rich in imagery and metaphors and employing colorful language. This linguistic wealth, as well as the symbolic power, which various social agents attribute to sports, turns the sports section into a fascinating site for examining the discursive strategies employed by various social actors interested in advancing different codes of identity. The way in which the news is presented and the accompanying commentary reflect the tensions and contradictions in the existential condition of the Arab-Palestinians in Israel. The sportswriters belong to a relatively educated class, and most have a firm national consciousness. One might say, in a rough generalization, that the Arab sports press consciously and intentionally attempts to champion Arab and Palestinian national pride in its soccer commentaries. Despite their differences in tone and style, there is more similarity between the secular newspapers than divergence in this regard. The rhetorical bricks by which national pride is constructed may be described as follows: (1) an explicit call for solidarity between the Arab teams; (2) emphasis upon the Arab identity of players and teams; (3) use of botanical and agricultural images in describing Arab athletes; and (4) the use of martial metaphors, with specific references to the Arab–Israeli conflict.

Arab solidarity

Maher 'Awawde, editor of the *Kul al-'Arab* sports section, has a regular column called "Cocktail" in which he frequently calls for Arab solidarity:

It warms my heart when I see two Arab teams on the high peak of the table – ha-Po'el Majd al-Kurum and Maccabi Ṭamra on the Everest summit. The meeting

---

[1] The National Democratic Assembly was established in 1996 by 'Azmi Bishara. The party emphasizes an Arab nationalist line, and calls for collective national rights for the Arab citizens of Israel.

between these two reflects the Arab light in the fourth division . . . This is the peak of the good for us. The meeting between ha-Po'el Majd al-Kurum and Maccabi Tamra is a meeting between brothers . . . From this journalistic platform I call upon the crowds of both teams to take clean air into their hearts, regardless of the results. First of all and after all we bear the same number (Mahmud Darwish still lives among us).[2]

The text promotes an Arab-Palestinian pride both by its substantive argument and through its usage of a concrete Palestinian national icon for greater emphasis. First, the high ranking of the two Arab teams (in first and second place) constitutes proof of an "Arab quality" – tested in the objective conditions of the soccer game – and hence is endowed with a quasi-scientific seal. Secondly, the hint that 'Awawde is sending to his readers is clear even to those who have only a basic and superficial familiarity with Palestinian poetry. He refers to the famous poem of the Palestinian poet Mahmud Darwish, *Raqam Hawiyya* (Identity Card Number). In this famous poem, written under the Military Government, Darwish symbolizes the proud standing of the Arab citizen in the face of the Israeli state's attempt to undermine his identity. By recalling this poem in this context, 'Awawde attempts to take the Arab reader beyond the immediate context of the game and to make the question about the winner's identity in the sportive encounter irrelevant.

Beyond that, the call for Arab fraternity on the soccer field has its background in the reality of the Israeli soccer leagues. In Israeli soccer, the intermediate and lower divisions are organized by geographical region. As a result, from the fourth division downward, Arab teams form a majority in some of the sub-divisions, and hence inter-Arab encounters are very common. In the lowest division, where the Arab teams constitute the majority (54 percent in 1998), inter-Arab competitions form 38 percent of the games. Even in the first three divisions (which are not divided into geographical sub-divisions) there are several Arab teams, so inter-Arab games frequently take place.

Statistically, inter-Arab competitions tend to be tense and tumultuous compared to other games. I have checked the protocols of the disciplinary court of the IFA in the period between September 1997 and March 1998 and found that in this period thirteen games were interrupted before regulation time due to "unsporting" behavior; of these, nine were inter-Arab competitions, three were Arab–Jewish games, and one was an inter-Jewish encounter. These inter-Arab expressions of hostility heightened

[2] Maher 'Awawde, *Kul al-'Arab*, February 25, 2000.

the sense of urgency among the sports journalists to encourage the players and fans to demonstrate Arab solidarity.

The nurturing of national pride around successful "brother" teams is easier than dealing with the mediocre achievements of the Arab teams. During the 1998–2000 seasons the sports section in *Faṣl al-Maqal* mainly covered second division games, since there were no Arab teams in the Premier League. The newspaper tended to solve the problem of the dull achievements of Arab teams during these seasons by referring to an imagined internal ranking among the Arab teams themselves, emphasizing the relative position of each Arab team compared to the others. The main headline of the sports section frequently refers to the Arab team that is ranked highest, even if it is ranked eighth place in the general table.

For example, the headline "The second division is Kanawiyya" means that among Arab teams in the second division, Kafr Kana is ranked in first place. The creation of this internal table constitutes an imagined autonomous space in which an independent Arab league is acting outside the auspices of the Jewish majority. In times when athletic achievements are scanty, this discursive strategy may be an option for those who seek to nurture Arab national pride.

Sometimes the Arab newspapers even call for mutual assistance among brother teams. At the beginning of the 1998/9 season, the Arab team of ha-Po'el Ṭaibeh was beaten by Nes Tziona (a Jewish team) 1:5. A week later, Sakhnin (an Arab team) beat Nes Tziona with the same score. The main title in the sports section of *Kul al-'Arab* associated the two games: "Support Your Brother, Either as an Oppressor or as the Oppressed!" Then it reminded the reader about the Ṭaibeh defeat and added: "Sakhnin thought and responded – for your eyes Ṭaibeh!"[3]

Another example of this emphasis of solidarity can be found in *Faṣl al-Maqal*. Following the "Arab Derby" in the second division between Sakhnin and Nazareth (Sakhnin won 3:0), the editor, Walid Ayub, summarized the game by writing: "Indeed, these points are Arab – Sakhninian, Nazarethian, Shafa-'Amrian, and Taibawian – even if the victory was Sakhninian." Namely, the points stayed at home and Sakhnin's victory is a victory for all Arabs.

Sakhnin gained particular sympathy from Arab sports journalists even before it reached the Premier League, partly as a result of the exceptional unification between the two old local teams in the city, ha-Po'el and Maccabi (see chapter 8). The magic word "unification" awakens dreams about Pan-Arab unification and concrete ambitions for unifying the

---

[3] *Kul al-'Arab*, October 16, 1998.

efforts of the Arab minority in Israel at the state level. Another attempt at unification (which has ultimately failed) in Kafr Kana, excites Walid 'Ayub from *Faṣl al-Maqal*:

From this stage I call upon all sports zealots to put their hands together with Faysal and Yusif [the first names of the Maccabi and ha-Po'el Kafr Kana managers] so that they will give us a Kanawian Arab team that will glorify Kafr Kana. We say it concerning Kafr Kana, and we all hope that the brothers will hear our voice and comply with our call. May they be a model that will be adopted in other Arab places, such as Nazareth, Ṭaibeh, Umm al-Faḥm, Shafa 'Amr . . . and more.[4]

A year later, when unification was almost realized with the support of Waṣil Tah, the mayor of the Kafr Kana, Maher 'Awawde (*Kul al-'Arab*) wrote:

And in order to open a new page everyone has to cover the past and its pains. The mayor should be an ideal model for everyone, in spite of the future losses, and will be a breakthrough to Kanawian unity first and Arab second, as the one who paved the way to the noble unity (I hope the Arab members of parliament and Arab parties will learn this).

'Awawde, whose Pan-Arabic ideas are frequently echoed in his writing, wishes to "cover the past," when the Arabs were divided and quarreled. He hopes that the unification in Kafr Kana will be like a stone thrown into the water that creates expanding circles of unity by a ripple effect, from the local unity in Kafr Kana to Arab unity, and from the sports sphere to the political domain.

The Arabness of Arab teams: Jewish players as alien weeds

In Nahaf [an Arab village], ha-Po'el Nahaf fought until the last minute for the ticket to the third division. Its last game was against Maccabi Ma'alot [a Jewish team], a weak team marking time at the bottom of the division table, who needed points as though they were oxygen. Those in the know and the spectators saw that the three Jewish reinforcement players, Abuṭbul, Erez, and Perets, did not make their usual effort, and the rumor [circulating] in Nahaf was that they had sold the game to Ma'alot in order to save it from dropping at the expense of an Arab team, ha-Po'el Kabul or ha-Po'el Sakhnin . . .

What we want to say is that in light of their meager budgets, these teams [which employ reinforcements from the outside] should rethink their calculations; such reinforcement brings no benefit. As a rule, it is the local players who play with joy and with loyalty to the team's interests and advancement. They are motivated by

---

[4] Walid 'Ayub, *Faṣl al-Maqal*, June 4, 1998.

their belonging to their village and to their people and to their team which are proud of the success; the outside player sees the Arab team as no more than a station along the way, which he can leave or betray if he lacks money. He is certainly not loyal to the team, and does not feel part of it.

Almost any Arab team playing in the fifth division or higher (Israeli soccer is currently organized into six divisions) includes Jewish players. The high frequency of this phenomenon perturbs many Arab sports journalists, who repeatedly call on the clubs' managers to field their team with local players. *Fasl al-Maqal* even called upon the Arab teams to include only Arab players, claiming that their failures stem from their giving up on their Arabness, and arguing vigorously that their successes were based mainly on fielding Arab players and coaches:

There are many reasons for Taibeh's location at the table's bottom and many reasons for its decline from the highest division. One of them (although not the most important) is the abundance of foreign strengthening players that has caused the loss of its Arabness and its particular character that distinguished it among the Arab audience that accompanied the team.[5]

'Awawde's column in *Kul al-'Arab* also takes a very firm position concerning the Jewish players:

Our Arab teams and their boards are always participating in the marathon race after the outside players, and the money is flowing [to the outside players] in times of unemployment and deficit in the municipalities ... Personally, I feel senses of failure and embitterment when I enter our Arabic stadiums and the Hebrew language is increasingly heard and when I look upon the players, searching – maybe I will find our children. However, we are a minority – like in the parliament.

The dominance of the Hebrew language in the audience's cheers and slogans and in the instructions given to the players annoys 'Awawde. He sees the soccer sphere as an opportunity for the strengthening of Arab national pride through supporting teams with a clear national identity. However, his frustration is twofold. First, contrary to his previous expectations and hopes, the soccer sphere reproduces on the field and in the stadium the power relations between Arabs and Jews that prevails outside them; and fans and coaches balk at the chance provided by soccer to eliminate this power imbalance. Secondly, it is a "self goal," the Arabs themselves perpetuate their inferiority by preferring to invest money in Jewish players.

---

[5] Walid 'Ayub, *Fasl al-Maqal*, June 4–5, 1998.

Another example of protest appears in *al-Ittiḥad*:

The (sense of) belonging began to disappear from the souls of the village's children because they feel the discrimination and the favoritism of their team's management in favor of strangers. Therefore they began to walk in the footsteps of material things, ignored their activity, and left soccer ... From where do they [the managements] have the wherewithal to bring Moshe, Johnny, and Alon? How can they succeed in this and still cover the debts of the past? Are they able to forgo the reinforcement players and base themselves on the local youth team?

The protest against the employment of "Moshe, Johnny, and Alon" confirms that the call to build upon "local youth" means to build upon Arab youth. The quote from *al-Ittiḥad* echoes *Kul al-'Arab*'s – the problem with reinforcement players is not only that resources are wasted on them: they are also a blow to the teams' Arab identity.

The style of protest against the reinforcement players is instructive not only about the desire to crystallize an Arab national identity, but also about the nature of this identity in the eyes of the writers. The rhetoric employed by 'Awawde in discussion on the Jewish reinforcement players reveals much about the primordial dimension of national identity, as he sees it. The metaphors and images are frequently taken from the world of the family or from agriculture and nature. The following segment illustrates his perception of the nation as an expanded family:

It infuriates me ... !
It infuriates me – the great amount of money which is thrown out, with no plan, for some anonymous reinforcement, while our children are burnt on the coals [i.e. waiting in vain] of the Arab managements ...
It infuriates me – to see Arab monies being transferred to the Jewish banks despite our meager resources and our poor situation. It infuriates me, the lack of our managements' appreciation and the marriage to others, and the true and real father's disregard for our children because he is the son of the clear Ḍad.[6]

The problem with the preference for the Jewish reinforcement players lies not only in the strengthening of "the Jewish banks" at the expense of the Arab municipalities. Bringing in Jewish players constitutes *a violation of imagined kinship rules* that affects society's borders. The writer attributes to the Arab authorities the function of being a "true" and "real" parent to the local players, and therefore, by preferring the Jewish player, they are not fulfilling the obligation expected of a parent to his/her children. Furthermore, the context in which the "son of Ḍad" is mentioned implies

---

[6] The writer refers to the letter Ḍad, a letter which is unique to Arabic and is difficult for non-Arabs to enunciate. Therefore, the letter is considered as a symbol of the Arabic language.

that the ability to pronounce the letter is an inborn ability, which passes from the true father to the correct son, serving as an unassailable proof of the strength of the son's moral demand upon his father.

The use of botanical and agricultural metaphors is common to many nationalist discourses. These make possible the creation of a link between national identity and territory and to present this connection as part of the world's natural order (Malkki 1992). Among Palestinians inside and outside of Israel, the use of agricultural metaphors plucks especially sensitive strings. If we were to distill the Palestinian national narrative into a single sentence, we would say that the lands of the Palestinian *fallah* (peasant) were stolen by Zionists. In the Jewish state that arose, the proud Arab *fallah* became a hired worker with no possessions, subject to the authority of his Jewish employer. Throughout the state's existence, the major points of friction between it and its Arab citizens have focused on those places and times when the state has sought to appropriate Arab lands. Therefore, it is not by chance that all interactions between Arabs and Jews in the state, including the area of sports, are liable to raise the land issue to the surface:

My soul is wounded when I enter the (soccer) fields and sense the lack of Arab belonging, to the point where my tongue stops cheering and suffers temporary paralysis. The questions begin to trouble me: What has happened to us? Are we not able, through our will, to protect *our stolen lands?* Why are our fields filled with strangers, why do we not *sow in the proper seasons*, and what is it that we lack to the point that we sense inferiority?

I awoke after the game and the conclusion is unavoidable, and if only the others would wake up early to the reality, and begin *to fertilize the local soil*. It is difficult for my feeling to accept the hurrahs for Moshe and Yitzhak, and others.[7]

Infiltration of the soccer field by Jewish players is compared to the theft of lands. The failure to cultivate local players is compared to agricultural carelessness and neglect of the land. Because the local earth is not properly fertilized, it is overrun with unwanted weeds from alien fields, weeds with Jewish names: Moshe, Yitzhak, and others. There is no point in asking whether 'Awawde is enlisting the nationalist idea in order to promote soccer, or whether he exploits soccer in order to advance a nationalist agenda: for him and others, the Arabs should play soccer, and soccer should be Arabic.

The converse side of the protest against the reinforcement players is the praise for those who increasingly put Arab players on the field. Here,

[7] Maher 'Awawde, *Kul al-'Arab*, August 6, 1999.

too, the agricultural metaphors come into play: "Bravo Ittiḥad Abnaa Sakhnin – nine *Sakhninian blossoms* in the lineup – the land can be plowed only by its calves."[8] The Sakhnin players, sometimes blossoms and sometimes calves, belong to the soil. This is the natural and self-understood bond, not like the artificial tie of the reinforcement players. Again, the use of botanical and agricultural metaphors in descriptions of the soccer game emphasizes the "naturalness" of the Arab identity.

Following land, the major focus of friction between the Arab-Palestinian citizens and the State of Israel revolves around *construction*. The restrictive area plans for Arab localities which the government approves result in many houses being built without license. The government's attempts to demolish illegal buildings generates almost cyclical confrontations with the inhabitants of these houses who have become – unwillingly – flag bearers of the Arab minority's struggle. This friction is not lacking from the sports sections, and in addition to the agricultural and botanical metaphors, we frequently find the building motif, especially in 'Awawde's columns. In summarizing the first half year of the Arab teams in the second division for 1999–2000, 'Awawde analyzes the surprising success of Sakhnin. He lists a number of reasons, and the first is:

The land of Sakhnin is built with Sakhninian concrete – represented by Samer Mi'ari, Shadi Zbeidat, Bassam al-Hamuli, Niḍal Shala'ata, 'Abbas Sawan [home players of Sakhnin] who played together for a long time and who are able – with only a fleeting glance – to know the location of the (other) player and his movement. In Kafr Kana they read the area plans for the physical boundaries which restrict their construction, and they reached a firm decision that the Kanaite unity is preferable to the reinforcement lines which affect the local Kanaite construction like the bomb on Hiroshima and Nagasaki.

This time the local players are compared to strong concrete walls, while the reinforcement players are compared to a powerful weapon (atomic bomb) fired to destroy the building. The insistence upon local Sakhnin concrete is responsible for the team's success. The Kafr Kana management also receives compliments on its decision to base itself on local players. In the game between Nazareth and the Jewish team ha-Po'el Bet She'an, the Nazareth team frittered away the advantage it held almost till the end, allowing Bet She'an to force a tie. 'Awawde writes that Nazareth "gave the Bet She'an team *the cement for building the tie settlement.*" Namely, the Bet She'an players are the settlers, but the Arab team itself supplies the cement for construction. There is more than a hint at the fact

---

[8] Ibid.

that many of the construction workers who built the settlements on the West Bank and in the Gaza Strip were Arab-Palestinians.

The Arab–Israeli conflict in the Arab sports press

The comparison of the soccer field to a battlefield is a common rhetorical tool used by sports journalists everywhere. However, although the Arab sports press in Israel reports on many Arab–Arab games, the warlike images appear only when they describe a game between Arab and Jewish teams. Very often the journalists interweave the descriptions of the game in concrete historical contexts relating to the Arab–Israeli conflict. For example, before an important game between Sakhnin and ha-Po'el Be'er Sheva' (a Jewish team representing this southern Israeli city), 'Awawde wrote:

> The Sakhninian commando unit and its weapon (and I hope it is modern) are going out to Be'er Sheva'. The line they have to cross is the Negev's Bar-Lev line. The Egyptians succeeded and Ittihad Abnaa Sakhnin likes tradition. Tomorrow is the moment of truth. Will it be a fake or a cruise towards the target?[9]

In Arabic, the theme "a fake or a cruise" contains a rhyme, *al-tazyif aw al-tajzif*. The cruise hints at the crossing of the Suez Canal by Egyptian soldiers during the first hours of the 1973 war. In a few hours the fortification line that had been built by the Israeli army, named after the IDF Chief of Staff Haim Bar-Lev, collapsed. 'Awawde's mention of the Suez crossing and Bar-Lev line are not lapses. They genuinely represent the column's consistent attempts to nurture Arab national pride around the Arab soccer teams through cognitive associations with Palestinian and Arab national myths. An Arab–Jewish competition taking place in the south of the country is associated with the Egyptian–Israeli battles of the 1973 war, and Sakhnin's players are requested to keep the tradition going and defeat the Jews (ignoring temporarily the presence of several Jewish players on the Sakhnin team).

The Lebanese–Israeli frontier is also used to assist in cultivating national pride. In March 2000, it was already quite clear that the Israeli army were soon going to withdraw from Lebanon. At the beginning of that month, al-Aakha al-Naṣira, the team from Nazareth, hosted ha-Po'el Be'er Sheva'. Nazareth led the game 2:1, but in the ninetieth minute a Be'er Sheva' player scored a goal with his hand. The Jewish referee, Arik Haymovich, at first confirmed the goal, and faced a shower of fruit and bottles thrown by the infuriated audience. After a minute the

---

[9] Maher 'Awawde, *Kul al-'Arab*, April 23, 1999.

line referee reported to the main referee that, from his angle, he saw clearly that the goal was scored by hand, which caused Haymovich to cancel the goal. 'Awawde links the events of this game to the fights between the IDF and the Shi'ite Lebanese guerrilla militia, Hizballah. The material thrown at the referee is likened to the Katyusha missiles Hizballah launched over the Israeli border city, Kiryat Shmona:

Arik Haymovich remembered Kiryat Shmona and its missiles and asked for a real peace process. The borders of the Nazareth team refused the agreement that he wrote and took back their legal rights, which are recognized by the [Israeli Football] Association and by the refereeing rules. Nazareth fans have drawn the map of rights.

Further, 'Awawde said of Be'er Sheva' players and the team's manager, Eli Gino: "Gino thought that he is the Maginot line in the Association, and ha-Po'el Be'er Sheva' players wanted to rob the legitimate and real rights."[10] In this text, Nazareth fans are compared to Hizballah warriors and Be'er Sheva' players are the state's representatives who surrender only after being hit by missiles.

The warlike metaphors are also used to describe the players' characteristics. For example, an article from *al-Ittiḥad* states: "Sakhnin can be proud of several Arab players who became stars. The team continues this tradition today and offers the Arab audience the human tank, Wisam 'Iṣmi, and the fida'i, the son of Arab, Abed Rabah." Used in this context, the fida'i (literally, the one who sacrifices himself) is an image taken from the modern Palestinian national mythology. The image of the fida'i – adorned with a kafiah, holding a Kalashnikov gun, and ready to sacrifice himself in the battle – has symbolized the Palestinian armed struggle since the mid 1960s until the first Intifada (Kimmerling and Migdal 1993). The choice of warlike symbols to describe the Arab players is especially deliberate because of the noticeable presence of Jewish players on the Arab teams. These players are presented as mere appendages to the real fighting power, the Arab players.

Hesitant integration

The conspicuous presence of Arab players on leading Jewish teams opens a door for an integrative interpretation. Such an interpretation does indeed exist, although in a tentative and hesitant manner. In all the newspapers, Arabs playing for Jewish teams in the top divisions were

---

[10] Maher 'Awawde, *Kul al-'Arab*, April 14, 2000.

termed "our ambassadors." Ambassadors, of course, are sent only to other nations. In the Hebrew sports press, the term "ambassadors" is assigned only to Israelis playing on European teams, and are therefore perceived as representing Israel in the international arena. By defining the Arab players and teams as "ambassadors," the Arab press, in effect, affirms the limited dimension of integration: the Arab playing in the "Israeli" arena has the status of a guest; he is not an integral member.

Despite the hesitation, the desire and the demand for integration do appear, in one way or another, in all the Arab language papers. They are most pronounced in *al-Ittihad*, the main organ of the Communist Party. For example, in January 1999, in the framework of a friendly international tournament marking seventy years of the IFA, one of the tournament games (Norway versus Estonia) was played in the municipal stadium of Umm al-Fahm. The IFA labeled the event "a salute to the Arab sector," and the game was preceded by a ceremony in which trophies were awarded to outstanding Arab players of the past and present. Seven-thousand spectators watched the gala event (it appears that only the Islamic Movement is capable of bringing such a large number of people to this stadium). The following morning, *al-Ittihad* gave the event four full pages of coverage:

An historic day in Umm al-Fahm
For the first time in the history of the state, the Arab sector has won great and official recognition by the institutions of the IFA ... It is unfortunate that the international tourney did not include the Israeli national team, because then twice 7,000 would have attended ... We learned that everything is possible, and that nothing is impossible. Recognition of the Arab sector arrived (even though late) in order to give us some small portion of our rights – we are part of the state, and we have rights, not only obligations.[11]

"Nothing is impossible," writes the paper. In other words, the formal and informal restrictions imposed on the Arabs in the Jewish state are not insurmountable barriers and one must not lose hope that they will be removed – soccer can serve as an example. We, the Arabs, want to do our share as citizens of the state (therefore we are also interested in watching games of the Israeli national team), and we must not lose hope.

Another expression of the aspirations for integration which appear in the sports section of the paper is the attitude towards the Jewish reinforcement players. Even though *al-Ittihad* is critical of the massive investment in these players, the Jewish players are accepted favorably, and

---

[11] 'Izat Shala'ata, *al-Ittihad*, January 4, 1999.

when they score, they are received with joy. The wordplay on their names minted by the sportswriters relates to the Jewish–Arab connection and reveals a large measure of self-irony. For example, a Jewish player of Ittiḥad Abnaa Sakhnin, Oren Muharer, scored the winning goal against ha-Po'el Be'er Sheva'. The headline in the sports supplement of *al-Ittiḥad* the following day (September 26, 2000) read: "Oren Yuharer al-fawz al-awal li-Sakhnin" – in English, "Oren liberated the first victory for Sakhnin" (in Arabic Muharer means liberator). The year before, a Jewish player named Oren Dayan played for Sakhnin. He played an outstanding game against Maccabi 'Acca, scoring the tie goal. The head-line in *al-Ittiḥad* proclaimed: "General Dayan" – the allusion to the mythological figure of the IDF, General Moshe Dayan, being clear to every Arab. Oren Muharer is "the liberator" of Sakhnin, and "General Dayan" led the Arabs to victory over the Jewish team.

There is more to this Halloween-like fantasy than just the desire to capture the eye of the reader by a catchy headline. The combination of a favorable attitude towards the Jewish reinforcement players along with the ironic use of loaded names and concepts expresses a tendency towards intentional confusion of identities, to the blurring of national distinctions, and to the emphasis on the common denominator of Jews and Arabs. It is significant that this sort of wordplay appears only in *al-Ittiḥad* of the Communist Party, which holds a relatively integrationist political attitude.

The dilemmas created by Arabs playing on Jewish teams are nothing compared to the discomfort caused by the participation of Arab players on the Israeli national team. Theoretically, the appearance of Arab players in the Israeli national uniform should create a unique phenomenon in Israeli society – a symbol shared by Jewish and Arab citizens of the state. The Israeli national symbols are Jewish symbols, and, as such, they exclude the Arab citizens of the state (Kimmerling 1985). From the point of view of Arab citizens, active participation on the Israeli national team, which is a secular national symbol, presents an exceptional opportunity to identify with an Israeli national symbol. The national team, however, is not isolated from the other state symbols, and therefore, a televised inter-national soccer game becomes an arena in which the Arab citizen is faced with an array of symbols – some of which he interprets as inclusive, some as exclusive (a discussion of the fans' reactions appears in chapter 6).

In 1998 and 1999, two Arabs played for the national team, Najwan Ghrayeb from Nazareth and Walid Bdeir of Kafr Qasim. The combina-tion of Bdeir's family biography and some of his statements to the media presented a difficult challenge to those who seek to promote a distinct Arab national pride. Bdeir's grandfather was killed in the 1956 Kafr

Qasim massacre, without doubt the most traumatic incident in Jewish–Arab relations since the 1948 war. Asked about the incident by a reporter of the Hebrew daily, *Ma'ariv* (July 27, 1998), Bdeir replied that he prefers to forget about the past and to look ahead. He said that in the national team he does not feel like an Arab, but "like everyone." After playing with distinction in a game against Austria (September 5, 1998), in interviews to the Hebrew television and radio, he said that he is proud to be an Israeli, and that he is emotionally touched by the playing of the Israeli anthem. On the TV screen, his face (looking down, eyes often closed) indicated how much the Arab star was not at ease talking about his attitude to the anthem. The subject of our discussion, however, is not Walid Bdeir but the public reaction to his statements.

The interviews fueled angry reactions in all the Arab press. The severest reaction appeared in *Faṣl al-Maqal*, which printed in its opinion section (and not in its sports section) an article by the Jewish-Israeli historian, Amnon Raz, entitled, "The Israeli national team and the Kafr Qasim Massacre." His argument summarizes the paper's attitude towards Arab players' participation on the Israeli national team:

> Perhaps the game of soccer creates new possibilities, and Bdeir has a role in creating these possibilities. In realizing them, however, it is impossible to ignore identity or to forget the past. Whoever forgets the memory of his grandfather while standing on the pitch in Austria lives in a difficult and painful contradiction ...
>
> As on many occasions, matters are most sharply seen via the soccer field. This ball ostensibly creates equality, but it highlights the lack of equality in reality. By means of this, however, it is able to create aspirations for equality beyond the bounds of the field.[12]

In other words, although excellence in soccer opens opportunities for Arab citizens, it contains hidden dangers. One – on the tactical plane – is that success in soccer may veil the discrimination and deprivation in other fields. The positive aspect of integration in soccer lies primarily in its being an example of possible equality, but this equality must not be considered an achievement in itself. The second danger is that, in an excess of ambition to exploit the opportunity offered to the fullest, the Arab player might deny his Arab-Palestinian identity, subsequently also influencing his fans. *Faṣl al-Maqal* expresses a conscious attempt to avoid these dangers.

Along with the feeling of being threatened, the inclusion of an Arab player in the ranks of the national team is perceived as a complimenting public recognition of the minority's talents by the Jewish majority. On April 16,

---

[12] Amnon Raz, *Faṣl al-Maqal*, November 17, 1998.

1998, after an Israeli victory over Argentina,[13] the following appeared in the sports paper *al-Majala al-Riaḍiyya*: "How proud we were when we heard the broadcaster Yoram Arbel announcing the name of this Arab star ... Najwan's goal was, and still is, the subject of discussion in the Arab community, and I saw the joy in the eyes of all who spoke about this game, and I discerned the pride of the Arab public in this Arab star."

A year later, on the day of a home game of the Israeli national team against Austria at Ramat Gan (June 6, 1999), the sports section of *al-Ittiḥad* published pictures of Ghrayeb and Bdeir, the two Arab members of the team and wrote beneath the picture: "How much Sharf [the national team's coach] needs these two together in today's game!" The writer continues to lament the fact that "the human tank," Walid Bdeir, is unable to play because of two yellow cards. The next day, the news of Israel's victory (5:0) appeared on the front page of *al-Ittiḥad*.

The sports papers are also quick to defend the honor of Arab players when their standing in the national team is endangered. Maher 'Awawde, for instance, protested when the national coach, Shlomo Sharf, said that he intended to remove Walid Bdeir from the ranks of the national team:

It appears that even if the Arab player displays excellence again and again and again, he will be left on the side ... if Sharf removes Walid from the roster he will be punished for this step – punishment from the Master of the World. I heard a child says – if Walid does not play: "God, let *Nivheret Israel* [the Israeli national team in Hebrew] lose!"

'Awawde switches abruptly to a discussion of the Palestinian National Team, which was taking its first steps at that time. The attitude is generous, brimming over with solidarity, but the discourse is in the third person, i.e. from an external point of view: "They must solve all the problems facing the new baby, the Palestinian Team ... We hope that the brothers there in Palestine will deal with all the matters necessary to prepare them and afterwards they will declare the establishment of the national team and God will help them."

Despite 'Awawde's affinity for promoting Arab national pride through soccer, he feels that the Israeli national team is the team for which Arab citizens of Israel should play. The Palestinian team receives encouraging coverage, but this is the team of "the brothers" who are "there."

---

[13] On April 14, 1998, a friendly match between Argentina and Israel was held. Israel won 2:1. Two Arabs played. One of them, Najwan Ghrayeb, scored the first goal for Israel.

A semantic distinction developed in the Arab sports press: the Israel national team is called al-Muntakhab al-Qawmi, whereas the Palestinian team is called al-Muntakhab al-Waṭani. In modern Arabic, the term *qawmiyya* is used when relating to the wider Arab identity, while the term *waṭaniyya* refers to the particular nationality of different Arab countries. This different semantic distinction expresses the Arab sportswriters' decision not to concede even one of the two circles of reference. It also expresses the fact that the Israeli national team is perceived as also representing them. The exceptional skill of the Arab players wearing the Israeli uniform helps them reinforce their claim that they are worthy of integration. For example, in a friendly game between Israel and Russia, Walid Bdeir excelled. 'Awawde wrote:

The match between Russia and Israel was an object lesson for all those racists whose despicable cries poison the wells of sports and kill the sportive spirit. Despite the apathy of the Hebrew media and the attempt to erase Walid Bdeir's outstanding and decisive role from the beginning of the game, it was obvious that the giant Arab player was the star of the stars, and the crowning glory. The time has come to make a small change in the Hebrew language and say: [here 'Awawde switches over to Hebrew] "The Israeli national team is *Baderech hanechona*." [The usual Hebrew term for "on the correct path" is *baderech hanechona*; for the word *baderech*, however, 'Awawde substituted the similar sounding *Badeirech*, thus producing an ambiguous sentence which includes the star's name.]

Interpretation of soccer as a desirable path to integration into Israeli society is not rare in the Arab papers' sports sections, but it is accompanied by the constant fear of assimilation and loss of the Arab players' Arab identity. A tangible expression of this worry can be heard on the Arabic language sports broadcasts on the radio. The sports reporter (almost all radio sports reporters are also employed by the written media) will often correct a player who employs a Hebrew term, suggesting instead the appropriate Arabic term. These corrections symbolize the gaps between the reporters as an educated group with national consciousness, and the less educated players, who are not as concerned with national identity and tend to be easily influenced by the Hebrew language which reigns on the soccer field.

A comparative view: Arab soccer in the Hebrew press

In contrast to the Arab language sports press, which is predominantly characterized by a nationalistic line, with hesitant integrationist tones, the Hebrew press tends to stress the integrative dimension of soccer. In the sports sections of the most widely read Hebrew papers, *Yediot Aharonot* and *Ma'ariv*, soccer is presented as an ideal integrative channel for the Arab minority in Israel. Although martial metaphors are not alien to the Hebrew sports press, the use of concrete metaphors from the Israeli–Arab conflict is rare; excessive caution is exercised when dealing with a Jewish–Arab sporting meet. For the Hebrew press, the sports arena provides a relatively rare opportunity for self-flattery, for painting an egalitarian and tolerant Israeli society. Although the differences between the sports media in the two languages are consistent, on no occasion are they more sharply expressed than in the coverage of Sakhnin winning the State Cup in May 2004.

In the same week that Sakhnin won the cup the IDF conducted an assault on Rafaḥ in the Gaza Strip; over fifty Palestinians were killed and hundreds of families were left without a roof over their heads. The reportage of, and commentary on, that event and the Cup Final game competed for center stage and the limelight in every paper. The latter took place on Tuesday, May 18, but the two most widely read Arab papers, *al-Ṣinnara* and *Kul al-'Arab*, are not dailies, and when the papers were published on Friday, much more death and destruction had accumulated in Rafaḥ than was reported by the Hebrew press on Wednesday. Even so, it is difficult to ignore the fact that both in *Yediot Aharonot* and *Ma'ariv* the most prominent head-lines on the front page – including a photo blazoned across half the first page of both papers – related to Sakhnin's victory. In *Kul al-'Arab* and in *al-Ṣinnara*, the first page highlighted the attack on Rafaḥ; the extensive and enthusiastic coverage of the game appeared only on the sports pages.

On May 19, 2004, *Yediot* and *Ma'ariv* went out of their way to demon-strate good will, to participate in the joyous occasion and to embrace the players of Sakhnin and their fans. For the first time in the history of these papers, the main headlines appeared in the Arabic language (but in Hebrew letters). Inside the papers there even appeared Arabic phrases in Arabic script. In a rare gesture, the bylines of the main commentary carried Arab names. In *Ma'ariv*, beneath the patriotic headline regarding the Rafaḥ operation "Determined to go forward," a picture of 'Abbas Sawan (captain of Sakhnin), holding the cup, was prominently displayed; a large red title declared in Hebrew letters: "Sahteyn Sakhnin." *Sahteyn* is a common greet-ing in Arabic (which literally means health) that was absorbed into colloquial Hebrew. On the first page, the paper promised its readers a festive souvenir poster. The inside headlines radiated liberal optimism: "An achievement which will open doors," "This is how one creates coexistence," "Hopa – hopa – hopa, Sakhnin in Europa." The main headline in *Yediot* read:

Mabruk [Congratulations in Arabic – a word whose meaning most Jews would recognize – the title was written in giant red letters.] An historic achievement for the Arabs of Israel: Sakhnin defeated yesterday ha-Po'el Haifa 4:1 and won the State Soccer Cup * Arab Knesset Members: This is a holiday for coexistence, a dream come true * Prime Minister Sharon: "We will build a stadium in Sakhnin."

Beneath the headline appeared commentary by the Arab reporter and broadcaster Zuheir Bahlul:

There is hope
A new chapter in the cultural conflict between the Arab and Jewish citizens of the state was written yesterday. A chapter of conciliation. Sports has succeeded where others, for so many years, have failed. The educational system in Israel never learned to inculcate the values of coexistence … Behold! Sports overcame the historic obstacles, disposed of the stereotypes, and sowed pride and new hope in the Arab population.

The continuation of Bahlul's commentary is also saturated with optimistic pathos:

No more that same simplistic, supercilious, and arrogant view of him [the Arab]. Perhaps from today on, the attitude will be more respectful, more humane and decent.

Bahlul closes his article (the opening article of the most widespread Hebrew paper!) by wondering: "And, incidentally, perhaps this is a propitious time to consider amending *ha-Tikva* [the Israeli national anthem] with a few words relevant to shared life."

Other captions in the paper played the same theme: "Fraternity on the Turf"; "The Cup of the Brotherhood of Nations"; "We have not lost hope" (a phrase taken from the Israeli national anthem that was borrowed in this context to refer to Arab–Jewish relations); Sawan (captain of Sakhnin): "We are the team of the state"; Limor Livnat (Minister of Education, Culture, and Sports): "Championship for a team from the Arab sector – a certificate of honor for Israeli society." The commentator Uri Meliniak writes: "Yesterday, for one night, 20 percent of the state's citizens felt themselves to be equal, perhaps more than equal, while the other 80 percent felt free to relate generously to the Arab team without involving the question of the justice of our cause." The words of the Arab poet and editor of *Kul al-'Arab*, Samih al-Qasim, appeared on the front page of the *Yediot* sports supplement, declaring that Sakhnin presented "an excellent model for bridging gaps and promoting true brotherhood between the two nations."

Forty-eight hours later, however, the enthusiasm of *Kul al-'Arab*, Samih al-Qasim's newspaper, took on a different hue. Firstly, because of the additional killing of Palestinian civilians in Rafaḥ, Sakhnin's victory was not even mentioned on the first page of *Kul al-'Arab*. Instead, half the page carried a photograph of Rafaḥ victims covered with bloody shrouds. Other than advertisements congratulating Abnaa Sakhnin (paid for by commercial firms), the first mention of the game appeared only on page 12, which contained a commentary by the reporter and author Wadi' 'Awawde entitled: "An eye on Sakhnin and an eye on Rafaḥ." The writer expresses his joy at Sakhnin's victory but he also warns against "exploiting it for propaganda purposes by prettifying democracy's blemished image or by creating a gilded wrapping to decorate the ugliness of the discrimination against the Arab citizens."[14]

The sports section provided a stage for a non-Israeli Palestinian, Ihab al-Agha, a resident of Khan Yunis in the Gaza Strip, who called Sakhnin "a Palestinian Arab club," and connected the Palestinian struggle against the occupation with Sakhnin's success. Under the caption "From Rafaḥ to Jenin . . . Congratulations to the People of Sakhnin," al-Agha writes:

The siege of Rafaḥ, its destruction, the murder of its innocent sons in their homes, and the difficult situation in which the Palestinian people have lived for the last four years, did not prevent this nation from rejoicing and celebrating the achievement of Abnaa Sakhnin, the Bride of Galilee. The love of the masses of the Palestinian people from Rafaḥ which stands fast, to Jenin the great, through its leadership headed by its President, the symbol, Yasser Arafat, rose to the heavens, as they are proud of the dear victory which proved the ability of this people to realize wonders, regardless of their magnitude.[15]

The discourse in the Palestinian press in the West Bank was less enthusiastic. There was no explicit criticism of Sakhnin, but there was also none of the pathos which characterized al-Agha's article in *Kul al-'Arab*. This discrepancy may hint at the need of the Arab press in Israel to supply their readers with legitimacy for their joy, even as the TV stations broadcast pictures of the horror from Rafaḥ. This is also evident from the apologetic nationalistic tone of Hussein Suweiti's article, "Our right to rejoice," which appeared in *al-Ṣinnara* the same day: "Fifty-six years have passed, and we are in our place, weeping together, suffering together, unfortunate together,

---

[14] Wadi' 'Awawde, "An eye on Sakhnin and an eye on Rafah," *Kul al-'Arab*, May 21, 2004, p. 12.

[15] Ihab al-Agha, *Kul al-'Arab*, Sports Supplement, May 24, 2004, p. 11.

paining together. But this time, Sakhnin has given us the first opportunity to rejoice together. It is our right to rejoice in you."

The Arab press: the limits of its influence

The sports media in Arabic and Hebrew represent soccer in a very different way. The political implications of the prominent Arab presence in the soccer arena depend not only on the eye of the observer; but also on the ability of each social actor to create meanings and market them. At first blush, one might be tempted to conclude that we are discussing merely a metaphor for the power relationships in the "arena of meanings" of the Israeli public sphere. Actually, the extent to which Arab-Palestinian men in Israel are devoted to soccer turns the game into a thing unto itself – an arena in which the meanings created therein are liable to radiate beyond its boundaries and shape collective identifications in less dramatic – but wider – arenas.

In this context, the Arab language press is at a disadvantage compared with the Hebrew press, because the exposure of Arab fans to the Hebrew press in general, and to the Hebrew sports press in particular, is much wider than its exposure to the Arab press. In the nationwide survey I conducted in 2000, I asked: "Which paper do you usually read?" Fully 63 percent of those interviewed cited the name of a Hebrew paper; 32 percent cited the name of an Arab paper. In answer to the question: "What is the paper from which you draw most of your information about sports?" 53 percent named a Hebrew paper compared to 22 percent who named an Arab paper. The fact that there is only one Arabic-language daily (*al-Ittiḥad*) is not enough to explain these figures, for the overwhelming majority of interviewees who cited a Hebrew paper (87 percent for general reading and 91 percent for sports reading) also mentioned one paper (*Yediot Aharonot*). The picture becomes clearer when we add the question, "Do you also read the sports section of other papers?" The answers indicate that for 37 percent of those questioned, the Hebrew press is the sole sports press, 21 percent are informed by papers in both languages, and only for 15 percent is the Arabic-language sports press the only sports press. That is to say, Arab sports fans are more exposed to the integrative discourse dominant in the Hebrew sports papers than to the discourse of nationalistic pride that dominates the Arabic sports press.

The limits of the nationalistic discourse

Arab players in the Israeli national team are merely "ambassadors" in the Arab press, and the Palestinian national team represents the "brothers" not the Palestinians in Israel. This vocabulary, representing the dominant discourse in the Arabic sports press, reflects the double peripherality (Al-Haj 1993) of the Arab-Palestinian minority in Israel. In both spheres their inclusion is not self-evident but they are far from being completely excluded. The national identity promoted by this press is a specific Israeli version of Palestinian nationalism. This identity cannot avoid being subjected to constant struggles over its internal contradictions and tensions.

On the one hand, it is characterized by some of the classic elements of many modern national identities, including the use of imagery military battles as constitutive events and the construction of "naturalness" by the use of botanical metaphors. On the other hand, the supportive attitude towards the participation of Arab players on the Israeli national team, attests that at least on the practical level, Arab sports journalists do not crave any overlapping between the cultural boundaries and the political boundaries as suggested by the classical model of the nation-state. To a certain extent, they do perceive soccer to be a path to possible integration into the general Israeli arena, despite hidden threats in this integration. Despite their clear dissatisfaction with the state, they do not see a realistic alternative to the current political order. Therefore, they prefer to continue establishing their Palestinian-Arab nationalism within the existing political framework, while attempting to wrestle with their discrimination. The flexible interpretive space of the sports arena enables them to brave the various aspects of this complex identity.

6

"Maccabi Haifa is my flag": Arab fans of Jewish teams

> The crowd in the stadium is divided into two: enthusiastic fans of Maccabi, and supporters of the rival team. Both Jewish and Arab fans of Maccabi sit in the same bleachers. High iron gates separate them and the fans of the opposing club; two hard iron gates which create an atmosphere of common destiny, uniting those imprisoned together behind lock and key. An iron fence divides the people anew, granting them temporary definition, an open space where the Arab can for the moment fit in as if he were one of the guys. The soccer stadium is a space dealing with temporary reconstruction of identities. A temporary project that creates a temporary and provisional "we" . . .
>
> (Ra'if Zureik, "Through Arab Eyes," *Ha'aretz*, April 20, 1999)

The presence of Arab fans in the bleachers of Jewish teams is a highly significant phenomenon, wide in scope and long-term in duration. As mentioned in chapter 3, the Haifa teams were the first Premier League teams in which Arab players participated. With time, additional teams that included Arab players won considerable support among Arab soccer fans. For the Haifa teams, based close to Arab population centers in the north, the inclusion of an Arab star turned out to be a highly profitable financial move; thousands of fans traveled from the Arab towns and villages in the Galilee and the northern Triangle to watch the team.

Results of the nationwide survey from 2000 indicate that approximately two-thirds of Arab males between the ages of 18 and 50 consider themselves to be fans of at least one of the Premier League teams (see table 6.1). For the sake of comparison, table 6.2 presents the level of support for teams in the lower divisions; and it indicates that although support is given primarily to Arab teams, it is lower than support given to Premier League (PL) teams. It can be assumed that the support for the PL teams is underestimated, because the sampling

Table 6.1: *Do you consider yourself a fan*
of a team in the Premier League?

Team	%
Maccabi Haifa	35.0
ha-Po'el Haifa	13.6
ha-Po'el Tel Aviv	10.0
Maccabi Tel Aviv	4.5
Beitar Yerushalaim	2.0
Other teams	0.9
No team	33.9
Total	100.0

Table 6.2: *Do you consider yourself a fan of a team*
not in the Premier League?

Team	%
Team representing the respondent's town	26.4
Arab team from a different locality	31.5
A Jewish team	0.9
Fan of no team	43.1
Total	100.0

did not include residents of mixed cities, among them residents of Haifa and Jaffa.

About half of the supporters of the major teams (35 percent of all respondents), support Maccabi Haifa. Two additional teams enjoying relatively large support among the Arab public are ha-Po'el Haifa[1] and ha-Po'el Tel Aviv. The support for the latter team, while especially widespread in the southern Triangle, is an historic remnant of the dominant role played by the Histadrut in the Arab villages (ha-Po'el Tel Aviv was for years considered the "standard bearer" of the Histadrut). The team is also outstanding for its relatively large number of Arab stars, the first of whom was Rif'at Turk, who played in the late 1970s and early 1980s.

---

[1] The high support for ha-Po'el Haifa is certainly related to the fact that six months before the survey was conducted, the team won the championship (for the first and last time) while an Arab player, Najwan Ghrayeb, starred in its defense. The support for Maccabi Haifa, however, represents a more stable pattern.

In order to understand the secret of the "Jewish" teams' attraction for the Arab citizens, I offer two explanations. First, the apolitical image of soccer and its meritocratic aura have made it a preferred path to integration into Jewish-Israeli society. Second, the great similarity between the symbolic formations of national ceremonies and the experience of fandom in the soccer stadium makes soccer fandom an alternative practice for national identification. The concept of national identity, despite its vagueness and opaqueness, is both highly desired and extremely complicated to adopt by the Arab-Palestinians in Israel.

The bleachers as integrative space

In the middle of the 1983/4 season, Maccabi Haifa hired the star of Maccabi Shafa 'Amr, the Arab forward Zahi Armeli. At that point, Maccabi Haifa was far from the top and was not considered a realistic contender for the crown. But the addition of Armeli, who was in great form, gave Haifa tremendous impetus, which led to its first ever national championship. That season, in which an Arab player was the visible star and dominant factor in a Jewish team's winning the national championship, has become deeply engraved in the memory of the Arab soccer fans. The identification with Armeli was translated into support for his team among Arab fans, support that continued to exist even in those years when there were no Arab players on the team's roster.

Armeli's excellence alone, however, could not have brought about the widespread popularity of Maccabi Haifa. Nor can the fact that Maccabi Haifa has traditionally displayed an exciting playing style that has also won it many supporters among Jews outside Haifa explain such an impressive identification with a soccer team. A combination of social, geographical, and historical circumstances have magnified Armeli's success in Maccabi Haifa and loaded it with political meanings.

Haifa was a major Palestinian city that has been rapidly developing since the end of the nineteenth century. In 1947 it was the home of 80,000 Jews and 65,000 Arabs. During the 1948 war, the vast majority of the Arab population left the city before or during the attacks of the Zionist Haganah forces on the Arab quarters. While most of the Arab-Palestinians of Haifa became refugees, the remaining Arab population suddenly became a tiny minority of 4,000 people (Morris 2004: 186–211).

Despite this painful history, Arab–Jewish relations in Haifa have been characterized by relative tolerance and lower levels of mental separation and physical distancing in comparison with the pattern that developed in other mixed towns. It is possible to trace this relative tolerance to the class-based cooperation during the period of the British Mandate (Lockman 1996), even though this cooperation was an integral part of the inter-communal confrontation (Bernstein 2000). The well-known pro-Zionist argument that Arabs were asked by Jews to stay in their homes in 1948 is based mostly on the only place where such a plea was documented – Haifa (Morris 2004: 200–202).

One expression of the relative mental proximity between Arabs and Jews in Haifa can be observed in their joint support for local soccer teams. Despite the claims of discrimination and the agonizing memories of 1948 that have never disappeared, the Palestinians in Haifa found it easy to imagine the city as an extra-territorial island, a place driven by different social dynamics than those in force elsewhere in the country. Therefore the support for Haifa teams presents the opportunity to praise "the tolerance of Haifa," so different from the character of the state. The fact that Haifa teams have frequently included Arab players in their ranks adds an additional and decisive dimension.

These motifs are reflected in the following monologue of Suzanne, a Catholic-Palestinian resident of Haifa and a fan of Maccabi Haifa. When I met her in 1999 Suzanne was a lawyer in her early twenties. Pay attention to the complete separation she constructs between the Jewish-dominated state and the Jewish-dominated team:

I have never supported the national team. I always supported the opposing team. With Maccabi Haifa, I always went through fire and water till the end. With the national team – I had a problem, because in my family they have not liked the national team. My father did not like it, he was very happy when the national team conceded a goal. Even when Armeli played. For me, Zahi Armeli was Maccabi Haifa, a player of Maccabi Haifa, an Arab player. But with the national team it was different. I remember watching games of the national team with my uncles, and they were always for the team playing against Israel, and I took this for granted – Jews and Arabs – it doesn't work out, that's how it is. Even in soccer, that's how it is. But Haifa, Maccabi Haifa was legitimate, as it were. I wasn't afraid to say that I support Maccabi Haifa and that I have the flag and the song, and I encountered no opposition from my uncles, from my father, from my school-mates.

But the national team – this was unacceptable. There was a problem. When you grow up with this then it becomes a part of you. You begin to understand gradually why that is so, that even in sports this is so, it is the national team, it is the anthem, it is Israel. It is like Rana Raslan, [the Arab] Miss Israel, I have a problem with her, I have a problem with her representing Israel. Because to represent Israel is to represent all that Israel stands for, the anthem and everything ... I want Israel to lose, it does something for me, it makes me happy. I believe that in the Palestinian–Israeli conflict, Israel won a decisive victory. The very fact that there is a state for fifty years is a victory. So every time that Israel is defeated in any area, I feel good.

[T.S.: Maccabi Haifa is not Israel?]

No. Maccabi Haifa is Maccabi Haifa. As though Maccabi Haifa became my state. I am crazy about Haifa. I truly love this city, and I also want to be involved. I want to be here as a lawyer, and to work for the municipality and everything – if I remain in this country. It appears to me that this city has the potential of becoming a city of coexistence, because the people here are really nice, at least people I know, Jews and Arabs. Haifa has become, as it were, my little state which I want to change and can influence because it is a state small in size and there are Arabs, there are Jews and you can speak your voice here. Haifa is my little state and soccer is the only place in Israel where I can sense belonging.

Suzanne's local pride is not unrelated to the discourse of the nation-state. Haifa is her "little state," and she chooses to express her Haifa-ness in a competitive arena. "Haifa nationality" is an option reserved mainly for residents of Haifa, but even outside Haifa, the city has acquired a reputation as a city which accepts Arabs graciously. Furthermore, Haifa's geographical proximity to Arab concentrations in the Galilee and the northern Triangle contribute to the Arab fans' love for their team.

Walid, a student at the Hebrew University of Jerusalem, was born in Umm al-Faḥm. He studied in an Arab high school in Haifa, and it was there that he discovered Maccabi Haifa. His classmates took him to a Maccabi Haifa game, and the event left a deep impression upon him: "I enjoyed the atmosphere. Everyone around you is a fan of the same club. You feel a deeper identification. There is dynamism; you feel the competition in the air." Walid was captivated by the magic of the fraternity of the "green" fans and by the competition against the other fans. Furthermore, the support for Haifa is rationalized by linking support for soccer with the political character of the city:

On Maccabi Haifa there were also Arab players, and the very fact that this is Haifa, this is coexistence, if only all the . . . even in Jerusalem, even though the situation here is very difficult, if only there were a reality different from that which exists here [the interview was conducted in Jerusalem] – Arabs and Jews and so on. Even the mayor there is excellent[2] – always trying to help the Arab population, to advance it. For me, it's the perfect city. If the entire state would relate to the Arab population as we live in Haifa, the situation would be better.

The status of Haifa and its positive image are almost always mentioned in antithesis to other places in Israel. As we can see in the following monologue, this image is partly related to Haifa's location in the north. Ramez, an inhabitant of Sakhnin, is a young lawyer like Suzanne; I met

[2] Haifa's mayor at that time was 'Amram Mitzna, a former general who later became the chair of the Labor Party and its candidate for prime minister.

him a short while after his return from Italy, where he studied law. His sympathy for Haifa is based on the city's tolerant image and its geographical location. According to Ramez, these two qualities are related, and the character of the Jewish–Arab relationship is a result of Haifa's location on the map:

For me, in this country, I do not feel good with all the teams. Only Maccabi Haifa here in the north satisfies the Arab sector. Believe me, here nobody thinks about all the others. Maccabi Haifa, a few, ha-Po'el Haifa and that's it. For us all the rest – what is this? Who is this? Why? You know, there are problems of discrimination. It is impossible to ignore this. There are problems of discrimination for the Arab players who play in the national team, the way they relate to them. In Haifa you feel at home. Here everyone feels at home. But when you move south, to the center, it's not the same.

For residents of the Galilee, support for a Haifa team became an expression of northern regional patriotism. Similarly, in contrast to Jerusalem, the participation of Arab players fits in with the tolerant image of Haifa. Their emphasis upon "the northern" and "the Haifa (teams)" enables Arab fans to find common cause with Jewish citizens without confronting the issue of their problematic relations with the state.

The implied extension of Haifa's boundaries in Ramez's words is worth discussing. The interview was conducted in Sakhnin, but when he says, "In Haifa you feel at home, here all feel at home," he blurs the municipal borders of Haifa and actually sees it as a natural continuation of the Arab population that is concentrated in the Galilee. This identification with the Haifa soccer team makes possible the expression of local northern patriotism, and places an emphasis upon the contrast between the north and south, the "real" State of Israel, the source of the policy of discrimination and deprivation.

Attendance at Premier League games is correlated with the active use of Hebrew (table 3.f, in appendix 3), i.e. with the propensity to interact with Jews in general. This datum is reflected also in conversations I held with fans of Maccabi Haifa, most of whom work or worked in the past in Jewish localities, whose off-field meetings with Jews are frequent and whose Hebrew is fluent. From these tendencies, it appears that support for the Jewish soccer team is part of a general configuration of patterns of involvement in Jewish society.[3]

---

[3] There is even a correlation between attendance at Premier League games and the tendency to vote for Zionist parties in the elections, but this correlation is mediated by the variable, "active use of Hebrew," which indicates higher involvement in the Jewish society (see tables 3.e and 3.f in appendix 3).

The affinity between soccer fandom and integrative inclinations are reflected as well in the words of Bashar, owner of a café in downtown Haifa. The pictures and decorations on the wall of his café leave no doubt as to the subject of his loyalty – the "greens" of Maccabi Haifa. Bashar's family came to Haifa from the Christian Arab village of Bir'am, following an evacuation order "for 15 days" at the end of the 1948 war. Although the Supreme Court ruled that the residents should be allowed to return, the IDF blew up the village and destroyed it, and the state has never respected the court's decision (Kimmerling 1977). In our café discussion Bashar revealed his memories of the painful uprooting of his family. The conversation, conducted in the presence of a few of the café's regulars veered, at my initiative, between soccer and the political aspects of Arab–Jewish relations, with Bashar consistently trying to force a separation between the subjects:

You have to differentiate, you're not going to a political event – you're going to watch soccer. When I go to *Popolitika* [a major Israeli political talk show] or some other debate then I get into a discussion – everyone has his own different outlook. When we go to watch soccer it is purely for the game. How do you say, we leave the hard feelings at home . . . let's say there aren't any.

This is the essence of the stadium experience for many of the fans: "Come, let's say there are no hard feelings" – the frustrations and the protest are put on hold in order to make way for "pure soccer," he said. "You have to differentiate" between the political world outside and the neutral world which the fan intends to create within the stadium. That is to say, one has to insert wedges between various arenas in life and to guard rigorously the goals of each. This differentiation is essential to the survival of Arabs in Israel in the face of contradictory internal and external expectations.

A prevalent conception among both Jews and Arabs in Israel is that to be a "good citizen," the Palestinian in Israel must be "apolitical" (Sa'ar 1998). Amalia Sa'ar interprets the inclination of Arab Christians in Haifa to stress their Christian identity as an attempt to create an apolitical identity; because the emphasis of Arab or Palestinian identity is considered "political," the emphasis on identities that compete with national identity may improve the standing of the individual Arab as a "good citizen." In this context the clearly apolitical image of soccer amply fulfills this need. Affirmation of the individual's identity as "a fan of Maccabi Haifa" in the soccer stadium provides a safe arena of blessed "apolitical" identity.

The words of Suzanne – which follow – also show that the magic of the soccer field is tied to the possibility of marking it as an arena separate from political reality. Support for a team opens a door for the Arab citizen to be loyal to a flag without being perceived as a traitor or extremist by one side or the other, and enables the supporters to do so without perceiving themselves as people who respect Zionist symbols. In the following interview segment, Suzanne's stadium experience is described as a microcosm of an ideal and idyllic egalitarian society. There is no "security" and there are no "searches"; soccer is depicted as isolated from the political context:

And then I was fourteen years old, and there was the Intifada, and you see on the TV children my age throwing stones at soldiers, and in school I was educated to believe that a soldier is someone good, someone who guards the country. I remember how once I asked the history teacher why there is an Intifada. I was then thirteen or fourteen years old, and he gave me an idiotic answer which I remember till this day. He told me that there is an Intifada because of disturbed Palestinian Arab children, who throw rocks at soldiers and at Israelis, at Jews, hate Jews, and the soldiers simply want to protect us, to protect this country and they hit them back, and because of this there is an Intifada. This is how I was brought up – this is the definition of Intifada.

That's why I am angry, because at that time children my age struggled for a just cause. I was simply unaware. I grew up with the feeling that every time I speak Arabic, they certainly link me with those who throw stones, and because of that they don't trust me. With soccer it's different. In soccer there are no Arabs or Jews. That's what I thought in the beginning, and even today I attend games and really enjoy myself. There is no issue of Arab–Jew, no issue of "security," they don't search you as you enter the soccer field, they don't relate to you differently. And I have the flag; I have the song of Maccabi Haifa. If they score a goal, I am very happy, I am really happy. When Maccabi Haifa won the championship, I sang, we celebrated with everyone and with love! Soccer is the only subject that I discuss with a Jew, and I have no problem talking about it. Simply an intellectual conversation, a conversation about sports, without the "Arab–Jewish" . . .

Team support and Arab-Palestinian nationalism

The apolitical image of the stadium is certainly related to the findings of the national survey which indicate a negative correlation between unmediated consumption of soccer via stadium attendance and pride in Palestinian national identity (see tables 3.b, 3.c, 3.d in appendix 3). Although this finding holds true for both local and Premier League games, the relation is stronger for those attending Premier League games.

In the survey, interviewees were presented with nine possibilities of belonging and asked to choose the three identities that most inflate their pride. Among the respondents who chose the "Palestinian People" as their source of pride, only 15 percent attended a Premier League that season, as opposed to 23 percent among those who did not choose this identity. The greatest differences were among the "addicted" fans: among the seventeen fans who attended six or more games, only one chose the Palestinian identity as a source of pride. Furthermore, these findings are not mediated by background variables which were measured (education, level of religiosity, age, frequency of newspaper reading, level of fluency in Hebrew), and as a result it is difficult to argue that the correlations found indicate only that attendance at games is a form of class or status-group-related leisure activity of those who do not identify with the Palestinian cause. How, then, can we explain the "persistence" of this negative correlation?

Two explanations come to mind. First, the regression equation included the "active use of Hebrew" variable, but this variable does not overlap with the wide array of aspirations for integration. It may well be that people with aspirations for integration into Jewish society perceive their Palestinian identity as an obstacle to integration, and therefore they obscure it. Thus, the desire for integration is the variable responsible for differences in the frequency of game attendance and also for the tendency to refrain from demonstrating Palestinian national pride. This explanation harmonizes well with the fact that attendance at games is found to be a predictor of voting for Zionist parties in Knesset elections.

Another possible explanation is the capability of the soccer stadium to provide "a quasi-national" experience. Benedict Anderson argued that from the moment that national ideology took shape, it built up a self-generating vitality – capable of being transferred to numerous and varied social contexts – and attained causal autonomy with regard to social processes. Moreover, nationalism has reached a measure of "self-evident" status, as the national order is perceived as part of the world natural order, or, in the words of Anderson, "in the modern world everyone can, should, will 'have' a nationality, as he or she 'has' a gender" (Anderson 1991: 5). Even today, despite the transnational tendencies of the late twentieth century – globalization of consumption patterns, mass migration of labor, and decline in the power of the nation-state – the meta discourse of nationalism remains dominant and influential (Koopmans and Stathan 1999). Many world organizations, important sports competitions, and even many of the cable channels are built upon the foundation of the national unit. The absence of national identity is perceived as an anomaly; a man without national affiliation frequently feels like an imperfect being in this world. The "patchwork quilt" image that covers the world map still has power extending beyond concrete political demands. The foci of belonging that we choose are still influenced in large part by this discourse.

The prevalent view among scholars who follow developments among the Palestinian citizens of Israel has been that the strengthening of familial and religious identities is an attempt to compensate for the difficulty in crystallizing a national identity under the existing political circumstances (Bishara 1999; Ghanem 1998). 'Azmi Bishara links these processes to what he terms "latent Israelization." In his view, the "Israelization" process is not only instrumental (see chapter 1). Therefore, argues Bishara, adoption of cultural patterns and involvement in Israeli politics are not translated into a joint national pride along with the state's Jewish citizens. Because Palestinian identity is not consistent with the latent Israeli identity, other "non-nationalist" identities – religious or clan identities – are developed in order to satisfy the emotional need for pride and belonging.

In this sense, a soccer team may also be seen as a focus of belonging, fulfilling a similar role in resolving the dilemma of national identity. Support for a soccer team has an advantage over other foci of identification, in as much as it bears a degree of semblance to the nationalist experience. Like the ideal type of modern national identity, support for a team provides a special and binding relationship to key symbols, and is based upon an ideal of competition. In a situation in which adoption of any national identity is perceived as problematic, threatening, or loaded with inner contradictions – as in the case of the Arabs in Israel – *people will tend to seek an alternate identity which includes at least some of the characteristics of the national identity*. Soccer fandom, therefore, serves for the Palestinians in Israel as a "surrogate nationalism."

Scholars from various theoretical paradigms who study symbols tend to identify the classic national symbols, the flag and the anthem, as collective representations of society, in the sense formulated by Emil Durkheim. Since Bellah's article on "civic religion" (Bellah 1967), the flag (and sometimes the anthem) is viewed as the "totem" of the secular nation (Marvin and Ingle 1999), fulfilling exactly the same sociological function as does the cross for Christianity, or the statue of Buddha for Buddhism. Because of the functional similarity of the flags of national movements and nation-states to Durkheim's Aborigine "totem," this parallel is perceived as axiomatic in sociology.

However, national symbols hold essential characteristics, which set apart the modern form of national identity from other identities. The flag is not a simple totem but a "required totem." Despite the difference between the flags and anthems of different nations, all nations need the same "set" of symbols in order to prove their "nationhood." Durkheim describes the totem as "an object from the natural world which society defines as holy" (Durkheim 1969 [1915]: 124), but there are no additional concrete demands regarding the source of this totem; it may be an animal, a vegetable, or an inanimate thing.

Nationalist symbols, however, remain standard. A nation must have a capital city, its own stamps, and above all, a flag and an anthem, which are the heart of every national ceremony. Weitman (1973) points out that the overwhelming majority of nation-states in the world conform to standard patterns of flag design. Flag and nation are so bound up with each other that color combinations are linked associatively to nations. The anthem is a poem with melody, of limited length, which marks the opening and/or end of national ceremonies. Thanks to the standardization of the flag and anthem, their centrality to the national experience is not comparable to any symbol representing a religious community, voluntary organizations, or extended family. The symbols in the Jewish or Islamic religions, such as the Torah scroll, Sabbath candles and the Qur'an, are far from being perceived as the "essence" of Judaism or Islam; whereas the flag and anthem are perceived as metonyms of the nation. The two "totem" accessories are so central to the concept of "nationhood" that it is impossible to imagine the existence of a nation without them.

From this aspect, the symbolic alignment of soccer teams is built upon the standard nationalist logic. Every team must be identified with a specific set of colors and an identifying logo. These colors and symbols are worn by the players, decorate the bleachers, and are the focus of loyalty among team supporters. The allegiance of fans is not based upon primary *social* relations. This loyalty is not awarded to the players, who change teams with high frequency, nor to the management or to the coach. Support for a soccer team also lacks the universal moral principle upon which the monotheistic faiths are based. Allegiance is to the symbol of the team, and, through it, to the imagined community of tens of thousands of devotees of the chosen team – similar to the allegiance given to the national flag. The unilinear relationship between the nations and their flags also exists in soccer. Just as a national flag represents only one country, so the players in their uniforms – living symbols – can belong to only one team. This rule is true even when speaking of players hired from the outside (as is the case with soldiers of any nationality who join the Foreign Legion which "represents" France and French nationality).

It appears that the choice of the flag for a country's main symbol is embedded in the historical use of the flag by armies to indicate the location of their commanders in the melee of battle (Weitman 1973). In this respect, the flag connects to another element that is distinctive of the national experience: competition, the desire to win. Even though every collective identification is established through the overt contrasting of "us" with "them," the search for victory in tangible tests of power is most characteristic of modern national identities. Nationalistic feelings are aroused mainly through power struggles against another nation, and nations realize themselves mainly through competition and conflict with other communities (Lorenz 1966). National myths are almost always myths of war. Hence, some draw parallels between the national function fulfilled by wars and by sports competitions (Tomlinson 1994), and more specifically some scholars emphasize the similarity and the interpenetration of sports institutions and the military, sites of masculine competitiveness (Archetti 1994; Burstyn 1999).

Nir Toyb's empathetic film, *Mondial in Shefaram* (1998), dramatically illustrates the distress of Arabs in Israel at the constant demands by the national discourse to adopt a flag and an anthem. The film, which follows fans from the Shafa 'Amr town during the World Cup games of 1998, shows the town decorated with the Italian, Brazilian, German, and Argentinian flags, and portrays the intensity of the aficionados' identification with the different national teams. The scenes in Shafa 'Amr are no different from those in other Arab towns; when a world soccer championship tournament takes place every four years, flags of the participating nations wave over the inhabitants' homes – everyone with his or her own flag. When the anthems are played, the fans stand with emotion, and when a goal is scored, the air is full of fireworks and gunfire. 'Abud Malek, a fan of Italy and protagonist in the film, explains the meaning of his deep identification with the Italian anthem in front of the camera: "The Israeli [anthem] is for the Israelis, for the Jews, for the Jewish people, and everything is at the cost of my people . . . this is the reason, or one of the reasons. I have no anthem of my own. So I feel for the Italian one."

'Abud Malek rationalizes his adoption of the national symbols of Italy as a replacement for the anthem of the country he cannot adopt. But the World Cup, with all its excitement, comes only once every four years; and the experience is mediated by the TV and is therefore indirect. On the other hand, soccer teams play in Israel every week, and the excitement can be experienced on the field itself. They do not represent countries, but they also have colors and songs of their own, and they are able to provide similar experiences of identity. In my conversation with her, Suzanne – admitting to being an "addicted" fan of Maccabi Haifa – told me that:

What I do like in soccer is . . . For me as a Palestinian who lives in Israel – I don't have a flag. The Israeli flag doesn't represent me, and neither does the Palestinian

flag. If the Palestinian state were established now I would not go to live there ...
I have much more in common with a Jewish Israeli girl of my age than with a girl
from the West Bank. So I'm different. I am much more Israeli than Palestinian in
the sense of the Palestinian regime, of everything there. That's why I'm saying that
I simply don't have a flag. I don't have a national song ... I have the feeling of
belonging but I feel also that we got lost, that there are two different peoples – the
Palestinians beyond the green line, and the Palestinians who live in Israel. I have an
Israeli identity card, but I don't feel Israeli, I have a problem saying I am an Israeli –
but also saying I am an Arab ... I'm not ... it's difficult. So this is one of the reasons
that I feel I belong to the flag of Maccabi Haifa. I go to the games and I hold the flag
in my arms and I don't have any problem singing Haifa's song. There I can sing –
I have a song. I belong to a certain group with a certain song and a certain flag, you
can shout ... when you are in the field – you are with the flag and with the song. I'm
always saying – the Norwegians, the Americans – they have the American anthem –
I don't have one, I simply don't have one. The Palestinians in the West Bank have,
the Israeli Jews here have. I don't!

The words of Suzanne's monologue speak for themselves. As she con-
veyed in our conversation, while studying law at the university, she came
to realize how much she was discriminated against and deprived as an
Arab in the Jewish state. Consequently, the awareness of her being a
Palestinian-Arab was reinforced. Despite this, she still maintains that
"I have more in common with a Jewish girl my age, much more than with
a girl on the West Bank."[4] The love of Maccabi Haifa fans for the flags
and songs permits her, as an Arab citizen of the State of Israel – despite all
the contradictions and tensions in this concept – to participate in a kind
of nationalist experience. Her words indicate that the national order is
perceived by her to be the proper and natural order, and the absence of a
tangible flag with which she can identify is a void which must somehow be
filled. It is important to note that Suzanne speaks not only about feelings
of identity but also of the difficulty "saying I am an Israeli," "saying I am
an Arab." The declarative statement, the public declaration of belonging,
is a central component in the construction of an identity. The concretization
of national symbols includes a concrete demand for the individual "to
say" his or her belonging, to hold the flag, to sing the anthem. These
pressures produce a need to find an arena in which one can express one's
identification according to the same pattern.

---

[4] Suzanne's statement reflects a widespread trend. In Smooha's survey (Smooha 1999) it was
found that 69.8 percent of the Arabs in Israel feel that their daily life and style of living is
closer to Jewish Israelis than to Palestinians in the West Bank and Gaza Strip.

Threats to the definition of the situation and strategies for coping

The construction of a soccer game as an apolitical and non-national arena requires the exclusion of all explicit signs of political stands or national identification. This neutralization is not self-evident, and it requires investment of energy. In order to reveal the mechanisms that make such constructions possible, we shall discuss two types of events that are liable to undermine the event's apolitical definition: (1) anti-Arab cries by Jewish fans of Maccabi Haifa; (2) the playing of the Israeli anthem at international games of the team.

Maccabi Haifa's audience is very heterogeneous in terms of class, ethnicity, and political inclination. Racist slurs against Arab players of rival teams are not widespread, but occasionally are heard. These cries destabilize the non-national definition that the Arab fans attempt to attribute to the arena, and create anew the national dividing lines between the fans.

Salman was born in Umm al-Faḥm. He completed his studies at grade 9, and went to work in construction. When I met him in 2000, he was 31 years old, and had been working for a year in a restaurant in the Jewish city of Ra'anana. Since adolescence, he was active in the DFPE party,[5] and devoted much time and energy to political activity. Close to the 1999 elections, as a result of discord in the Umm al-Faḥm party headquarters, he withdrew from party activity. He claims that ever since he began to work in Ra'anana and as a consequence of many political discussions with new Jewish friends, he feels that the political positions of the Meretz[6] party are the closest to his own.

When he was 15 years old, Maccabi Haifa won its first championship, with Zahi Armeli in its ranks. Salman attended the game with friends, and fell in love with the team. Since Maccabi Haifa's 1994 championship season (and the birth of his first son that year), he tries not to miss a single match of Maccabi Haifa, taking with him his children, dressed from head to toe in Maccabi Haifa's colors, green and white. He gave his second son, born in 1996, a Hebrew name, Eyal, after Maccabi Haifa's Jewish star of the time, Eyal Berkowitz. Salman relates an incident that aroused his ire:

[5] The Democratic Front for Peace and Equality (DFPE) is a coalition of the Israeli Communist Party with other non-Zionist organizations. The party is formally defined as Arab–Jewish but gains the vast majority of its support from Arab citizens, and is therefore considered as an "Arab party."
[6] In 1999 the Meretz party represented the liberal edge of the Zionist political spectrum. The party gained 5 percent of the Arab votes.

During a game with ha-Po'el Tel Aviv, when we were sitting in the bleachers, someone began to curse Salim Tu'ama [an Arab player for ha-Po'el Tel Aviv] calling him a terrorist and an Arab. I told him to shut his mouth, and I spoke to him crudely. I told him – "half of your audience is Arab – the masses of young Arabs who follow Maccabi Haifa, how dare you?!" My Jewish friends shut him up. In the end, he came over to me and said he was sorry and embraced me, and the following week he sat next to me in the stadium.

The affronts to Tu'ama bring the Jewish–Arab conflict onto the soccer field, and threaten to sabotage the apolitical existence of support for Maccabi Haifa that the Arab fans attempt to create. The strategy chosen by Salman was not externalization of his anger, but immediate mobilization of his Jewish friends to minimize as much as possible the conspicuousness of the nationalist split which is under constant threat of surfacing. The denouement of the process is no less important – positive physical contact with the brother-fan who imperiled the preferred definition ("embraced me") and reinforcement of the fraternity with that fan at a later game.

Suzanne described a similar event that occurred in the bleachers. It may be that because of her double inferiority – an Arab among Jews, and a woman among men – she chose to contain her wrath, but this choice imposed a price:

There was one game in which I ... I simply ... someone called Walid Bdeir "Dirty Arab," and he was sitting next to me in the bleachers. Although I had a problem with this, I did not react. This lit a red light for me, and I promised myself that I would react another time, I'll just say something. Perhaps also the soccer stadium is not the atmosphere to enter into such an argument. But this burns, it pains. Until today I am hurt at not having reacted.

In this instance, Suzanne chose to remain silent, because she reckoned that a reaction on her part would extract a high price. On the other hand, when passive protest is a ready option, she chooses it:

There was a game between Milan [the prestigious Italian team that visited Israel] and Haifa. I know that ... OK, I have a problem standing when the anthem is played. I do not stand. Even at the graduation ceremony of my law studies I was the only one who did not stand. In the game with Milan, I was with my brother, and I did not stand. So my brother looked at me and did not rise ... I remember that everyone looked at me – incidentally, this was the first time that there was the anthem and I was in the group. So I did not stand, and all the fans looked at me, you know with the chain necklaces and the ... the really addicted fans who have no problem shouting obscenities, [those who eat] all those seeds. They looked at me, but not one said anything to me. One said – "Okay, she's probably an Italian and she's in the wrong section."

The anthem predicament described by Suzanne illustrates one method of dealing with a not-so-simple challenge to the definition of the arena as "purely sportive," one that is devoid of any political context related to Arab–Jewish relations. In the 1990s, Israeli teams began to play in the framework of European competitions. In addition, more friendly games were played between Israeli and European clubs. In the various European cup matches, the national anthems of the respective teams were not part of the protocol. Israeli teams, however, customarily open their games with the singing of *ha-Tikva*, the Israeli national anthem. Furthermore, probably due to the increasing television presence, the anthem is played at important league games. For Jewish supporters, the singing of the anthem provides another opportunity for the expression of national pride; for the Arab fans, it undermines the character of the territory as they have tried to define it: apolitical and non-Zionist, a space to feel common collective pride without becoming involved in the complexity of the Israel–Palestinian conflict. The fraternity of the white-and-green fans of Maccabi Haifa is in danger of disintegrating, and exceptional behavioral and cognitive strategies must be implemented in order to preserve it.

Salman remembers Maccabi Haifa's victories in the European Cup games as the peak events from the time he began to root for the team. He, too, was forced to cope with the anthem dilemma, but here, too, he chose a more active reaction:

I do not sing the anthem, because I do not know the words ... I know the ending – how you say, "land of Zion and Jerusalem." So I also sing the end along with all the others, but I say – "land of peace and Jerusalem," because I am not a Zionist. But I am for peace. I taught this to my Arab friends who support Maccabi Haifa, and this is what we sing.

The idea of amending the words of the anthem rises occasionally on the margins of the Israeli public debate and is mainly raised by Arab politi-cians or by post-Zionist Jews. But Salman's strategy is not a theoretical plan. He sings his alternative anthem and teaches his companions to do so. Thus he holds the rope at both ends – "sings along with everyone," not affecting the green-and-white brotherhood of Maccabi Haifa, but in actuality he sings a different, non-Zionist, anthem.

Cronin (1997) describes how, at national games of the Northern Irish national team, Catholic and Protestant supporters sing differ-ent anthems simultaneously. Maccabi Haifa Arab fans are not interested in using their team support to express their Palestinian national identity; they only want to dim the Zionist character of the international games – and to strengthen support for the team in itself. Therefore, some of them keep to themselves until the irritation subsides, and some offer an alternative anthem that is a variation on the existing one. Joint singing of the anthem by Jews and Arabs, each singing their own words, is a unique phenomenon, possible only on the soccer field. It is an offspring of the tension between the effort of the Jewish fans to express national Zionist pride in the stadium, and the Arabs' attempt to transform the support itself into a substitute of nationalism, free of existing national identities.

The various dimensions of identifications of fans are at the same time the product of circumstances and a resource for maneuver and survival in a complex social reality. In their interactions with Jews, many Arab fans prefer to emphasize their identity as supporters of Maccabi or ha-Po'el Haifa and to downplay their Arab or Palestinian identity. In a certain sense, the soccer arena is a refuge from the nationalist identity. Support for this can also be found in the distribution of answers to the question from the countrywide survey: "Do you have a dream in the sphere of sports, and if so, what is it?": 59.5 percent replied in the positive; 17.5 percent of the respondents tied their dreams to the local team representing their town; and 15.8 percent to a major Jewish team. Only 1.6 percent and 0.7 percent tied their dreams to the achievements of the national teams of Israel and Palestine respectively. Like 'Abud Malek from Shafa 'Amr, 33 percent of the respondents tied their dreams to a national soccer team of another country!

Even so, the structure of the national discourse endures within the soccer discourse. The term "surrogate nationalism" which I have chosen to employ reflects my view that the support of Arab citizens for Jewish teams is not part of the passage to a post-national identity. On the contrary, it is tied to the stable and powerful discourse of nationalism, and the Arab fans are only trying to find their place within this discourse.

Support in return for equality?

One of the interesting findings of the nationwide survey is the great popularity of the Israeli national team games. Fully 22 percent of those interviewed said they watched all of the Israeli national team's ten Euro 2000 qualifying games (the games were played between September 1998 and November 1999); 43 percent said they watched at least half of the games, and 77 percent reported watching at least one game. These findings deserve a special discussion because, in contrast to Maccabi Haifa or ha-Po'el Tel Aviv games, the games of the Israeli national team are marked by the ubiquitous presence of the national Zionist symbols which are liable to cause the Arab citizens discomfort. How does one explain the tremendous surge of interest in the Israeli national team? Can this be an attempt to penetrate a narrow opening to partake in an Israeli national symbol by the Arab citizens? Or perhaps, on the contrary, the great popularity of the team results from the Arab fans' anticipating a loss for the Israeli national team? The results of the survey and analysis of the in-depth interviews reveal that many of the Arab supporters do indeed consider the national team a symbolic entrance to and channel for integration into Jewish Israeli society. The presence of the Arab players brings them pride, and by supporting the team they also make a state-ment – it serves them as a certification of legitimacy when they come to demand civic equality. The contradictions and the tensions produced by their support are resolved by a variety of strategies.

The soccer national team as a national symbol

The establishment of the modern nation-state was accompanied every-where by the creation of a "set" of symbols. Control over the conscious-ness of the citizenry, more than physical control over the territory, necessitated a series of symbols, without which the nation-state could not exist. With time, an array of symbols – all essential for establishing the state in the public's consciousness – crystallized. As has been stated, the flag, the anthem, the stamps, as well as human figures that serve as personification of the state (king, queen, or president), are all part of the standard set of national symbols. During the twentieth century, another symbol of national sovereignty took shape and was added to the array. Athletes competing in the international arena have been almost univer-sally perceived as representing the nation with their bodies, enabling measurement of collective talents and abilities against those of other nations.

In most nation-states, the national soccer team won special status in this context. As Eric Hobsbawm eloquently put it: "The imagined com-munity of millions seems more real in the form of eleven named people" (Hobsbawm 1990: 143). A nation-state without a national team is like a nation-state without a flag, and a nation-state without a flag is not a nation-state. The disintegration of the Soviet Union and Yugoslavia at the beginning of the 1990s led almost immediately to the swelling of many international organizations that accepted the new nations. One of the most important signs of these nations' sovereignty was their joining FIFA, the international soccer association. As a national symbol, the national soccer team has important characteristics that set it apart from other symbols, intensifying its power as a recruiting symbol that arouses especially powerful emotions.

A national team is a symbol that may be compared to other symbols according to clear and universally recognized criteria. In earlier chapters, I discussed Ashworth's (1970) insight that sports enables individuals and groups to know themselves through a quasi-scientific comparison to others. Modern sports facilitates conducting controlled tests in which a certain social group can examine itself relative to another group. In contrast to human symbols like kingship or the presidency, the human make-up of a national sports team changes frequently and even in nation-states in which an ethnic code of citizenship is dominant (like Israel), tension between this code and the meritocratic sports ethic is often determined in favor of the sports ethic. Thus, the criteria for choosing the national squad, in most countries and in most periods, are influenced mainly by the players' professional competence and not by the degree in which they symbolize – by origin or biography – the hegemonic definition of the "nation." Thus, sectors which are not perceived as symbolically "representative," might actually represent the nation on the field.

If the national soccer team is a powerful national symbol, the appearance of an Arab player on the Israeli national team creates a rare phenomenon in Israeli society: the possibility, at least theoretical, of the existence of a national symbol shared by Jewish and Arab citizens of the state. All the national symbols of the state: the Star of David, the Menorah, *ha-Tikva*, are clearly Jewish symbols which exclude the non-Jewish public from the Israeli collective identity. The Israeli national team is a uniquely secular symbol, allowing identification also by the non-Jewish public. The willingness of Jewish fans to accept Arab players as their representatives, and the Arab players' decision to represent the State of Israel, are choices of belonging. For the sake of comparison, it is worthwhile recalling a famous historic event, that of Rashid Meklufi, a soccer player of Algerian origin who played on the French national team. In 1958, at the height of the Algerian rebellion, Meklufi deserted to the ranks of the FLN (the National Liberation Front which fought for the liberation of Algeria from the French occupation) at the head of a group of Algerian players from the French League, and, together with them, represented the FLN in a number of international games. Meklufi became a national hero in Algeria (Lanfranchi 1994). Such a phenomenon would seem fantastical in the reality of Arab soccer in Israel. True, there were Arab citizens of Israel, talented and influential, who left the state and joined the PLO (for example, the famous poet Mahmud

Darwish and the scholar Ṣabri Jiryis), but the soccer arena ties the player to the state with bonds of commitments, hopes, and aspirations which minimize the chance that a revolutionary national leader will ever come from the ranks of the ball kickers.

The Israeli national soccer team is a symbol of hope for the players and for many of the fans – the hope to be considered equals. While the Israeli collective identity is perceived to be a bipolar identity in which there is tension between the primordial "Jewish" code and the civic "Israeli" code (Kimmerling 1985), the Israeli national team is considered to be an obvious agent of creation of the second; the joint physical efforts of Jews and Arabs to overcome some "other" blurs primordial identities and creates a seemingly autonomous egalitarian arena.

The great popularity of the national team games, as reflected in the survey, raises the reasonable conjecture that most fans are not neutral, and that most of them are interested in either victory or loss for the national team. Amara and Kabaha, in their 1992 survey conducted in the Arab village of Barṭʻa found a high level of enmity for the Israeli national team among the Israeli citizens of the village. They point out that the victories of the team are perceived by their interviewees to be a provocation against Arabs, especially against Arab males (Amara and Kabaha 1996: 139–140). This study, however, was conducted during the first Intifada, in a village half of which is located in West Bank territory. In the study presented here (conducted in a relatively calm period), based on a representative sampling of the Arab young men in Israel, totally different results were found. Analysis of the distribution of the answers to the question, "When the Israeli national team plays against a European national team, whom do you tend to support?" shows that support for the Israeli team is very high (table 6.3). The question was asked in relation to two situations – when there is an Arab player on the national team and when there is none. When an Arab player participated, support reached 69 percent (a degree of support which the national team may not have among an equivalent Jewish public). Even when there was no Arab player in the line-up, 49 percent of those asked replied that they support the Israeli national team.

It seems reasonable to suspect that, because of the centrality of soccer in the interviewees' world, they consider this question to be a threatening but crucial loyalty test, and therefore many were inclined to declare their support for the national team despite their opposition to it. True, the support figures in the table may be inflated. This conjectured pheno-menon may contribute to explaining the figures, but its significance should not be overrated. After all, only 13 percent of those interviewed

Table 6.3: *When the Israeli national team plays against a European national team, whom do you choose to support?*

	When an Arab player plays on the Israeli team	When no Arab plays on the Israeli team
The Israeli national team	69%	49%
The other national team	17%	27%
Neither team	14%	24%

chose "The State of Israel" as a source of pride; 88 percent of them were willing to reveal their votes in the elections, and the distribution of their answers greatly resembled the distribution of actual voting among Arabs in the 1999 elections.

The following situation illustrates the validity of the figures. I watched the Euro 2000 play-off qualifying game of Israel against Denmark in October 1999, on television in a café in the center of the Arab village Furaydis, in the company of hundreds of the village's inhabitants who packed the café to the rafters. Israel was defeated 5:0. By the end of the first half (Denmark 2:0), it was evident that most of the audience was very disappointed. Accusations were exchanged between the fans of Maccabi Haifa and fans of ha-Po'el Haifa. The former accused the goalie, Dudu Awat (player for ha-Po'el); the latter blamed the Maccabi players on the team. In the middle of the second half, when defeat was certain, about two-thirds of the spectators left the café, expressing their disappointment at the team's way of playing. Among other causes, they blamed the defeat on the fact that Arab players were not included in the game. Furaydis is a village located on a major transportation artery. It is isolated from other Arab towns and villages and is therefore considered too "Israeli" and does not represent the general Arab public in Israel. Despite this, the protest walk-out by the spectators clearly indicates that identification with Israeli national teams exists even beyond the sociological questionnaire.

Did soccer fans who support the national team choose sources of pride different from those fans who are against the national team? Table 3.g in appendix 3 presents a cross-tabulation of pride in several identities and attitude towards the national team. The table shows, as anticipated, that among the minority desirous of the national team's defeat, the number of those who chose Palestinian identity was higher and the number of those choosing the Israeli identity was lower. Participation by Arab players on the team had a negligible effect on the interviewees' choices.

In addition, fans of the rival national team tended to choose male identity as a source of pride more than those supporting the Israeli national team and those indifferent.[7] Fully 20 percent of all participants in the survey chose male identity as a source of pride, but there is a clear difference between those who oppose the Israeli national team and the other participants. The survey revealed that 28 percent and 27 percent of those who opposed the Israeli national team (with or without an Arab player, respectively) chose male identity as a source of pride compared to only 18 percent and 17 percent (respectively) who supported the national team. The negative association between support for the national team and pride in male identity suggests that fans concerned about their male identity do indeed consider the international sports encounter an opportunity for shooting down the masculinity of the Jewish male. In other words, the threat to male identity is tied in a great degree to the sense of degradation on the national level, and the two dimensions, the gender and the national, maintain mutual relationships and each shapes the other.

The fans' dilemmas

Support for the national team is evidence that for the Arab citizen an exceptional opportunity for identification with an Israeli national symbol has been opened. Of course, this identification is far from being free of problems and restraints. The appearance of the team is not isolated from the other political symbols present on the field, on the sidelines, before, during, and after the game: the blue and white colors of the uniforms, the symbol of the Menorah on the shirt, and, of course, the anthem played before the game. The Hebrew sports press (which constitutes a primary source for soccer consumption by the Arab public – see chapter 5) occasionally asks the Arab players demanding questions, sometimes brutal in their straightforwardness, regarding their attitude to the flag and anthem and to their status as Arabs representing the State of Israel. The usual response of these players, whether they are actual or potential team members, emphasizes that they are

---

[7] Control for variables via logistic regression shows that these correlations are greatly mediated, but not totally, by education.

professional players and often, in order to placate the media, they also add an encouraging message regarding the state symbols, or, alternatively, declare their ignorance of the anthem's words (see the discussion below, on "strategies of ignorance").

The discourse which accompanies these newspaper interviews is intended, in my opinion, for internal Jewish needs; it is self-flattery by Israeli society which comes across as devoid of all favoritism and as providing equal opportunity. An extreme example of this may be found in an October 2000 issue of the Hebrew language newspaper *Ma'ariv*. A few days after thirteen Arab citizens of Israel were shot to death by the police, the Israeli national team played in Spain, and the presence of Walid Bdeir on the squad received special attention. The headlines in *Ma'ariv* dealing with game preparations reflected the tendency of reporters in the Hebrew media to demonstrate the integrative aspect of soccer: "Badir[8]: I have a goal, to win for all." In the article itself, the reporter, Ron Amikam, quotes the captain of the team, Tal Banin: "Walid is one of us, and he is no different from anyone else. For us to win this game, all the players have to be united." The reporter later adds: "Badir, by the way, does not understand what the entire hullabaloo is about. Yesterday, he even cynically asked: 'Tell me, why do you come with all these questions just now? You have never asked these questions before.'"[9] Thus, the overlapping interests of the Arab player on the national team (international exposure and prestige) and the Israeli media (liberal self-image) join together to portray the national team as an integrative arena.

Even though the primary target audience of this discourse is the Jewish public, the Arab citizens, too, are exposed to the Israeli national team as presented on television and in the Hebrew press, and they, too, are forced to cope with the prominent presence of the Zionist symbols. From in-depth interviews with soccer fans, one can detect diverse strategies for coping with this unique situation. One of these strategies, mentioned in the previous section, was employed by Salman, who changed the words of the anthem. Hereby, I would like to present three additional strategies: "the strategy of

---

[8] The pronunciation of Bdeir's name symbolized in a nutshell the relationship between him and the Hebrew media. The name was first distorted by some Jewish broadcasters who found it easier to pronounce it as "Badir," and then it was adopted by all the Hebrew sports media. Zuheir Bahlul, an Arab broadcaster who is dominant in the Hebrew media, alerted his Jewish colleagues to the mistake. These colleagues went to Bdeir and asked him how he prefers to be called. Bdeir answered without hesitation: "Badir" (based on my conversation with Zuheir Bahlul).

[9] *Ma'ariv*, October 11, 2000.

ignorance," "the strategy of differentiation," and the separation of the player from the national team. It is important to note that there is a tactical dimension to support for the national team. Those who supported the team wanted very much that I, as a Jew, should be aware of their position. It appears that they thought that this information could raise – in my eyes – their status as citizens with equal rights in the state.

The most common strategy for coping with the contradictions between support for the national team and the Zionist character of the game ceremonials is "the strategy of ignorance." This strategy is to be found mostly among the less educated fans, who exploit their lack of education as an alibi. Bilal, aged 45, a gardener by trade, is "King of the Fans" of Nazareth. A local joke tells that he has never seen his team scoring a goal, because his back is always to the field and his face to the audience – organizing the songs and cries of encouragement (accompanied by the "darbuka" drum held between his knees). When he described his attitude to the Israeli national team, it was fairly obvious that he hoped that his support for the team would advance his chances to win recognition as a citizen with equal rights. He tries to exploit his support for the team in order to receive my acquiescence and understanding of his demand for equal rights. The use of support of the team as a tool in the bargaining over rights intensifies the need to moderate the conflicts inherent in this support. The ignorance strategy is the simplest instrument for avoiding contradictions. In the following quote, Bilal describes the preparations in his home for the forthcoming game of the national team:

We are Israelis, sweetie. We are Israelis, this interests me – this national team is mine. I am not from Gaza. I am not from Jordan. I am Israeli. I, [Bilal] – am registered as Israeli. So I am interested in everything in Israel. I am also interested in receiving my necessary sustenance like the Jews. Why? Because I am Israeli, and really, I have it coming, you understand? All pray that today the national team will win, I am telling you the truth – and Najwan [Najwan Ghrayeb, an Arab player from Nazareth on the national team] will score a goal – this first of all . . .
[Question: At the beginning of the game, the two national teams stand and sing the anthem. What does that say to you?]
Look, the truth, I am not with them there. If I see . . . if I will be at this game I will stand and I will give respect as is necessary, but if I am at home, I remain silent until they finish. Why, because even when I wanted to learn these words and this song, I don't absorb it, it's a little difficult. But if I, for instance in . . . I was with Najwan at the Olympic team. When they played against Lithuania and against Romania, I was once in Ashdod and once in Kiryat Eliezer [a stadium in Haifa], I stood with all the others but I don't understand the song. That is to say, I wanted to sing but I don't know. But I paid respect.

The presence of Najwan Ghrayeb from Nazareth enables Bilal to root for the national team without deliberation, but it is very important for him to stress that he supports the team, and therefore he deserves all rights. Ignorance shields him from the need to confront the symbolic significance of the Israeli anthem: he "doesn't understand," "doesn't absorb." The ignorance plea is especially widespread when the Hebrew media interview the Arab players of the national team, and ask them about their attitude to the anthem. They usually point out that in school they were not taught the words of the anthem, thus freeing themselves of the discomforting question.

Another strategy, used by more educated fans, is that of "conceptual separation." Walid 'Ayub, poet, writer, and journalist, tells of his feelings during the playing of the anthem at a game of the national team:

I am also in the audience, standing with the others. I do not identify with the anthem, but I respect it. That is to say, just as I was in France and heard the French anthem and I heard the anthem of Brazil. I respect, but I do not identify. It tells me nothing. The anthem is the anthem of the state, it is not my anthem. It does not express my feelings or my opinions.
[Question: And the national team?]
The national team represents me, sure, that's natural. There is a difference. The Arab spectator stands during the anthem because he respects, but he does not identify, he cannot identify, with the anthem. The national anthem should express the . . . don't forget that Israel is a Jewish state, not a state of all its citizens. A state of all its citizens would . . . but the anthem is Jewish. It is a formal statement. The national team, however, is an Israeli national team which represents all the citizens of Israel, Arabs and Jews.

'Ayub's words, which epitomize the concept of the "integrative enclave," carry weight, because he is not just another fan. At the time of the interview, Walid 'Ayub was editor of the sports section of *Faṣl al-Maqal* (organ of the National Democratic Assembly party) which voiced the Arab nationalist line more clearly and decisively than any other newspaper in Israel. His wholehearted willingness to take advantage of the rare opportunity to identify with a general Israeli symbol shows how wide is the gap between the Arab citizen's aspiration to be an equal citizen in the Israeli public arena, and the willingness of the state and the Jewish majority to enable this. Because Arabs play on the national team, 'Ayub is certain that the national team represents him.

There is a third popular strategy of soccer fans opposing the national team. Basically, it is a distinction drawn between the player and the team. Qasim, a 26-year-old attorney, recalls the time when Armeli and Ṭurk played on the national team: "When I watched the national team play, I wanted the team to lose, but when the Arab players, Armeli and Ṭurk, were on the field, I was in a dilemma – I wanted the team to lose, but I wanted them to score and prove themselves."

Qasim's desire for the Jewish majority's recognition of Arab talents is pronounced. Despite his opposition to the team as a Zionist symbol, once the Arab players have the opportunity of integrating into the team, it is important that "they prove themselves." Amin, a Sakhnin grocer, describes a similar attitude: "When I watch Najwan Ghrayeb stand for the anthem, I feel sorry for him because he has to stand to attention for something that is meaningless for him. But when he plays, I am proud that he is representing me."

Once more we see the desire to participate in the general arena and to win recognition and representation. Amin's words reflect a feeling prevalent among soccer fans with whom I spoke – deep identification with the Arab player on the field, despite difficulty in identifying with the team. Throughout the study – in conversations, in interviews, and in the sports press – rarely did I hear or read criticism of the players for their willingness to represent the State of Israel in the international arena. I did find protest and even anger when speaking with people who are not soccer fans – a fact that reinforces the supposition that for those who take part, the soccer arena provides hope (or illusions); this is not the lot of the uninvolved.

The participation of Arab players on the Israel national soccer team, and the attitude of Arab soccer fans to this participation reveals the distress in which many Arab citizens of Israel find themselves: the strong desire to partake in the Israeli public arena and not remain on the sidelines, as against their continued marginalization by the Jewish majority. Despite their rejection on the practical level – from government office, from the faculty of institutions of higher education – and, on the symbolic level – from the national symbols – many refuse to give up. When a narrow breach is opened, even if it has only symbolic significance – such as the Israeli national team – they exploit the opportunity to its fullest, with identification and support.

This integrative orientation of soccer has provoked as well an isolationist reaction. The main institutional expression of this reaction is the creation of the Islamic Soccer League, discussed in the next chapter.

7

The Islamic Soccer League

Previous chapters focused on the contest over different potential interpretations of Arab success in Israeli soccer. This contest is based on a
consensus which legitimizes the participation itself: since the dismantling
of the independent Arab soccer teams in the 1960s the integration of
Arab teams and players in the Israeli soccer institutions has not been
seriously challenged. The exception to this rule is the separate and autonomous Islamic League, established by the Islamic Movement in Israel,
which offers a unique strategy for dealing with soccer. This uniqueness is
valid both in reference to the treatment of soccer by other Arab political
forces in Israel and in reference to the treatment of other "Western"
cultural formations by the Islamic Movement. This exceptionality
stems from the tension between the suspicion of soccer as a secularizing
sphere and recognition of its overwhelming popularity. This tension is
solved by containing the game and placing it under the strict supervision
of religious leaders.

Sports and religious fundamentalism

The Islamic Movement in Israel is part of a wider regional and global
phenomenon which is referred to in the academic literature as
"Islamism," "political Islam," "reformist movements," "Islamic revival-
ism," "integrisme" or "Islamic fundamentalism." The long and tedious
terminological debate cannot be discussed here. It is noteworthy, however, that whenever a comparative argument is required in this chapter I
will use the term "fundamentalism," since, although it is imperfect and
problematic (Benin and Stork 1996), most of the comparative studies of
Islamist movements and similar movements in other religions have used
this term. Fundamentalism, according to this body of literature, is a

religious reaction to the consequences of modernity and secularism which "manifests itself as a strategy, or set of strategies, by which beleaguered believers attempt to preserve their distinctive identity as a people" (Marty and Appleby 1993: 3). By "reacting" I do not mean "opposing" modernity, since fundamentalist movements are also a product and expression of modernity (Roy 1996: 50).

Unlike Christian and Jewish fundamentalism, the Islamic version of fundamentalism can also be seen as a reaction to colonialism and Western post-colonialist hegemony. Since modern sports games have long been used as representations of all these concepts – modernity, secularism, colonialism, and Western "cultural imperialism" – fundamentalist movements in the Muslim world have been very suspicious of these games.

For the purpose of this chapter it is crucial to distinguish between the suspicion of sports as an agent of secularism and decadence and the rejection of certain sports as a representation of the West and colonialism. This distinction is analytically valid, since, as I will show, there are noticeable common patterns in the ways sports is treated by fundamentalists from all three monotheistic religions (stemming from its secularist image) and some unique characteristics of Islamic rejectionist behavior (stemming from its association with Western colonialism).

The relations between sports and religion have occupied the minds of both sociologists of sports and sociologists of religion (in both cases, almost all the existing literature is about sports and Christianity). The central axis along which these issues have been discussed is the tension between the declared secularism of sports and the quasi-religious character of the configurations of its appearance, the functions it fulfills, and the discourse that takes place within it.

Guttmann (1978) notes that competitive bodily activity took place in the ancient world, but that there it constituted a part of religious ceremonials and was not an end in itself. He locates one of the major singular facets of modern sports in its secularity. Moreover, Guttmann, who takes a Weberian perspective in his analysis of sports, sees its modern appearance as an inseparable part of the process of "disenchantment" – that is, modern society's taking leave of the holy and the concealed.

At the same time, in a way that both complements and opposes modern sports' secular character, some scholars stress that the sporting experience has some of the features of a religious ceremony. The power of the emotions that sports can arouse and the community feeling that it generates have led many writers to compare it to religion (Hoffman 1992). The exceptional status given to sporting competitions in many people's everyday lives has brought researchers to term sporting events the equivalent of a "holy space" and "holy time" (Novak 1976). Followers of the Durkheimian tradition see sports as one of the ways for societies to achieve some level of "collective representation," similar to the way religion is seen by that same tradition (Coles 1975; Goodger 1985). Another parallel that has been drawn between sports and religions, particularly monotheistic ones, relates to the notion of justice: in religion, God is right. Sports is based on the belief "that the best man will win," and that, ultimately, justice will be done (Slusher 1993). Following these and other lines of comparison, there are those who have labeled sports as a "quasi-religious institution" (Edwards 1973).

As the most popular of global sports, soccer has received close scrutiny by European sociologists and anthropologists, who have drawn parallels between it and religious ceremonies, either in its functional aspects (Coles 1975) or symbolic structures (Bromberger 1995). Bromberger, however, also qualifies his claims and points out some essential differences. Soccer does not presume to give meaning and content to life, nor does it tell us where we came from and where we are going. Transcendent representations of the world, and elucidation of first causes, and ultimate purposes, are lacking from soccer, as are the notions of redemption and the promise of a better future.

These important distinctions return us to the strikingly secular face of sports and its dualism. On the one hand, sports is a secular site. On the other, it has the ability to fulfill functions parallel to religion and to create structures and forms of discourse similar to those of religion. This double-sided face gives sports the potential, under certain circumstances, to become an institution capable of *competing with religious ones*. It does not mean that religious organizations avoid the instrumentalization of sports games for their own purposes, and there are diverse examples of this phenomenon (Magdalinski and Chandler 2002). There are, however, two important qualifications for this instrumentalization. First, in contrast to secular nationalists whose positive attitude towards the mobilizing potential of sports is unequivocal, religious movements have developed a complex and ambiguous set of relations towards modern sports. Usually this complex attitude does not stem from the objection to physical activity but to the quasi-religious-but-secular excitement that sports might provoke. Second, even when sports become an important element in the social life of a religious community, it is more likely to happen in contexts where religious distinctions overlap with ethnic or ethno-national distinctions.

In the United States, the principal relationship between church and sports until the mid nineteenth century was one of restriction and probation.

Actually, most of the colonies passed laws against play and sports activity during the Sabbath. The Protestant objection to sports was the fear that it would detract attention away from spiritual matters, the concern that the resultant pleasure from play might become addictive, as well as worry over scenes of violence associated with the game. However, in the long term most churches recognized that this was a lost war, and gradually integrated sports into their program (Eitzen and Sage 1993).

Much research has been done describing the ways churches have used sports as a socialization apparatus, with the aim of increasing their attractiveness (Gems 1993; Willis and Wettan 1977). For some churches, these developments were too threatening and at the end of the nineteenth century, just as intercollegiate American football was establishing itself, Methodist and Evangelist leaders in the southern United States waged a furious war against the game (Doyle 1997; Sears 1993). In contemporary Canada, the suspicious attitude of Evangelists towards modern sports brought about the creation of an Evangelist church hockey league. Like the Islamic Soccer League, this league was also founded with the aim of providing an alternative sporting environment, one that would preserve Christian Evangelist values, which were perceived as contrary to the competitive and violent nature of the game as we know it (Stevenson and Dunn 1998).

In pre-Zionist and pre-modern Judaism, physical strength was not highly valued, and the Jews' increased proximity to sports was connected with two processes concerning secularization in Jewish society: integration into European and American society, and the crystallization of the Zionist movement (Eisen 1998). The only religious Zionist sporting organization (Elitzur) was established years after the secular ones were set up, and it has always remained a marginal feature on the map of Zionist sports. In Israel, the only big city (more than 150,000 residents) not represented by a soccer team in one of the top three divisions is the ultra-Orthodox Bnei Brak. In Jewish local authorities, a negative correlation (-0.34) exists between the relative number of Yeshiva students in the locality's population and the support given to sporting associations by the municipality.[1]

With the risk of over-generalization it can be argued that some features in Islamic traditions could have had the potential to make it more "sports-friendly" than Christianity and Judaism. First, the conception of time in Islam is based less on rigid distinctions between "sacred" and "regular" time periods, and thus, there is much more tolerance for a wide

---

[1] Based on the database described in appendix 5.

range of free-time activities than in Christianity and Judaism (Ibrahim 1982). Second, although the primacy of the soul over the body is evident in Islamic traditions (Chebel 1984), when compared with Christian traditions the tension between the two has been relatively minor. The early church's conception of the human body as an instrument of sin and its belief that bodily demands should be subordinated to the spiritual life had negative implications on the acceptance of physical entertainment until modern times (Eitzen and Sage 1993).

These differences might explain the relative tolerance of Muslim rulers to physical recreation in pre-modern times and the rich and diverse culture of physical entertainment developed in pre-modern Muslim societies (Al-Khuli 1995; Al-Taa'i 1999; Salamah 1983). Nevertheless, contemporary Islamic discourse on sports is characterized by suspicion about the legality of sports (Al-Khuli 1995: 23). In the modern Middle Eastern context, sports was promoted much more by secular nationalist leaders than by leaders of religious movements. Sports was extensively used by secular nationalist regimes as a "modernizing" agent and as a forger of modern national identities in Iran (Fozooni 2004), in Turkey (Yurdadon 2004), in Egypt (Di-Capua 2004), and in other Muslim countries. It has been used as well by the League of Arab Nations to promote Pan-Arab nationalism (Henry, Amara, and Al-Tauqi 2003).

At the same time, the Islamist streams reacted to sports in a way that closely resembled that of the Christian Puritans and Evangelists in the United States. Youcef Fatés argues that in Muslim countries sports, and especially soccer, became a "second religion" and therefore it was considered as a competitor with Islam, which might divert youth from Islamic socialization (Fatés 1994: 101). "For Islamists," claims Fatés, "sports is not considered as part of the natural framework of Muslim society. Rather, it is superfluous to the combat sports, which are very prestigious" (Fatés 1994: 118). That is, the Islamist reservations about sports are not related to its association with violence, as it is for some evangelical groups (Stevenson and Dunn 1998). The opposite is true – pro-sports Islamic writers who preach for the readoption of Islamic sports pay special attention to the non-popular, elitist, but bloody sports of hunting (Alawi 1947; Salamah 1983). The tangible threat for them is the extremely popular game of soccer and the emotion it might arouse.

When Islamists come to power, however, they have to face this popularity and adapt their approach. In Iran, after the revolution, the hardliners in the new regime argued that spectator sports, as a legacy of the Shah, should be replaced with participatory sports (Chehabi 2002). However, although spectator sports were not compatible with their

Islamist ideology, there was concern that any ban on soccer might lead to riots because of its popularity and lack of alternative entertainment options for young men (Gerhardt 2002). In subsequent years soccer has become a major sphere for expressing both Iranian patriotism and anti-conservative sentiments. A similar scenario occurred later in Afghanistan. As soon as the Taliban's mullahs took power in Afghanistan they banned soccer. This decision proved to be extremely unpopular and the Taliban reluctantly agreed to rescind the ban.[2]

In this regard, Islamism differs sharply from secular nationalism. Promoters of nationalist ideologies tend to rely on competitions, either through military struggles or on the sports field. Sports provides strict formal rules that are meant to neutralize elements unconnected with ability, and therefore it is seen as a mechanism that exposes "natural" differences between groups. Presenting sports as a locale in which the gaps of political, economic, and social power between the teams are suspended makes way for the claim that the differences revealed by the game are "real," a sort of primordialism, which is crucial for the construction of modern national identities (Eisenstadt and Giesen 1994).

Islamist groups, however, do not construct their boundaries as "natural" but as moral. They are less reliant on the ratification of identity via supervised and quantifying competition. What they do need, at least when they are not in power, is to fortify the moral boundaries of their community from cultural products that might "contaminate" it. This fear of moral contamination is what fueled the establishment of the Islamic League in Israel.

The birth of the Islamic Soccer League

The accelerated processes of urbanization and proletarianization challenged the traditional power base and the structure of the family among the Palestinians in Israel. The undermining of familial authority might explain the steep rise in crime and drug use, and subsequently the yearning for a new social order. The growing emphasis on religion in many spheres of life has been partly a result of this predicament. The Islamic awakening in Israel began in the 1970s and drew from the ideology of the Muslim Brotherhood, which demanded that religion be afforded a place in every part of social existence (Aburaiya 1991: 118). Islamic associations dedicated to educational and community activity – campaigns for eliminating alcohol, making collections and distributing money to needy

---

[2] "World Cup soccer returns to Kabul," http://www.cnn.com/2003/SPORT/football/11/23/soccer.afghanistan.ap/

families and students, and so on – began to appear in Arab villages and towns. These movements gained momentum through global and regional developments, including the Arab defeat in 1967 which undermined Pan-Arabism and the Islamist revolution in Iran in 1979. After a failed attempt to set up a quasi-military clandestine organization (which was discovered by the Security Service at an early stage), Islamist leaders chose to focus on educational, cultural, and welfare projects.

A loose network of organizations emerged throughout the country, collectively known as the Muslim Youth, whose leadership was based mainly among lower-middle-class graduates of Islamic seminaries in the West Bank (Rubin-Peled 2001: 131–132). In Umm al-Faḥm they set up a medical center that gave free medical services, a rehabilitation center for drug addicts, and an institution for Islamic studies (Aburaiya 1991: 132–136). In addition, committees were formed that organized social activities with an Islamic slant: art, festivals, and weddings (Aburaiya 1991: 108). A special emphasis was placed on the Da'wa – the call to the Islamic religion and the dissemination of its values. In 1983, for the first time, representatives of the Islamic Movement ran for office in the municipal election; one of its candidates was even elected as mayor. In 1989 the Movement's achievements were impressive – five mayors were elected, as well as weighty representation in all twelve of the Arab local councils and the two mixed cities in which the Movement flourished.

Islamist activists harshly criticize what they see as negative Western influences on their society. They strictly reject any kind of mixing of the sexes in the public sphere, and they are concerned with the liberal appearance of the female body in public. Women's beauty pageants, for example, have been the target of harsh attacks by the Movement's leaders. Among pious believers, Western-style clothing has been rejected in favor of traditional Islamic clothing, characterized by simplicity and modesty for both men and women. Other symbols of Western culture such as rock music and Western films have been decried by the Islamic Movement as corrupt and corrupting.

The decision to adopt or reject a certain institution or ideology, however, is also a function of power relations. When a cultural institution or ideology is too popular and deeply embedded in the social texture, it is safer for the Islamic Movement to adopt it and control its content rather than to avoid it altogether. Unlike rock music, the overwhelming popularity of soccer makes it too powerful an adversary to face head on.

The unique strategy taken by the Islamic Movement stems as well from its differential treatment of Jewish and Muslim publics in Israel. Towards the Muslim public, the Islamic Movement employs a reformist strategy. From its embryonic stages, the Islamic Movement activists have considered themselves as an integral part of the Muslim society and as a major agent of reforms within it. With regard to the state and the Jewish majority, the Islamic Movement has pursued mainly a separatist strategy, despite the variation that can be found between the different factions of the Movement.[3]

The major aim of a separatist strategy employed by fundamentalist movements is to avoid contamination (Tehranian 1993). The leaders of the Islamic Movement were concerned that, under conditions of high exposure to secular values and lifestyles, the religious foundation could be worn away. But since the Movement had a commitment to reform Muslim society, and since the game was popular, soccer was not banned.

Therefore, in 1986 the Islamic Movement founded the Islamic League as a separate and independent soccer league, with no organizational contact whatsoever with the Israeli Football Association. At first, a few teams were set up by the associations of Muslim Youth in the Triangle. Following a successful sports tournament held in Kafr Qasim, a group of leaders, headed by Sheikh Hashem 'Abd al-Raḥman from Umm al-Faḥm (who years later became the city's mayor), initiated the establishment of a permanent league to be run in the spirit of Islam.

The formation of the Islamic League was preceded by internal arguments within the Islamic Movement.[4] There were those who maintained that the Movement should be concentrating its energies within the framework of the religion, that is, in the Da'wa, the dissemination of Islam. The critics saw the release of urges as one of soccer's inherent characteristics, which they thought would corrupt the ranks of the Islamic Movement. Despite these objections, many of the leaders of the Movement were young and came from the generation that had already absorbed soccer as an inseparable part of its culture. The founder of the Islamic Movement himself, 'Abdallah Nimer Darwish, said once that "soccer is at least 10 percent of my life."[5] This affection for the game probably tipped the balance. During the first years of the League, the teams were run without organized funding and relied mainly on contributions. However, as soon as the Islamic Movement attained status among the municipalities, public funding started to flow towards the Islamic League's teams.

One of the ways the Islamic character of the League found expression was in the teams' names, some of which were based on Islamic myths. For

---

[3] In 1996, the Islamic Movement was split into two factions: a southern faction that participates in the elections and has closer ties with the Jewish public and a northern faction, which holds a more isolationist orientation.

[4] Interview with Sheikh Kamel Rayan, November 26, 1998.

[5] Haim Shadmi, "Mevukash Nasui o Talui," Ha'aretz, March, 26, 2006.

instance, Ḥitin recalls the battle of Ḥitin, in which Ṣallaḥ al-Din defeated the Crusaders, and al-Burak, the mythical creature which carried the Prophet in his nocturnal journey to heaven. The Islamic League is not professional, and all activity conducted within it is voluntary. Accordingly, its establishment did not presume to constitute an attractive professional alternative to the games run by the IFA. In fact, in many cases the teams in the Islamic League serve as reserve teams for those that play in the Israeli leagues, with players who have not been selected, yet who want to keep up their match fitness, turning up to play. Also, some of the players in the Islamic League were veterans of the Israeli League. This structure preserved the qualitative hierarchy between the two leagues.

The split in the Islamic Movement in 1996 had repercussions for the Islamic League, which was then divided into two leagues: the Islamic League, run by the southern faction, which in 1999 consisted of fourteen teams; and the General Islamic League, run by the northern faction, and consisting of nineteen teams in 1999 (the analysis in this chapter refers mainly to the larger league of the northern faction).

Formally, the General Islamic League is independently managed, but the Movement's leaders are highly involved. In the northern faction, the deputy head of the Islamic Movement, Sheikh Kamal Khatib, regularly participates in meetings, and the principles behind the League's functioning – principles that emphasize moral values above sporting achievement – are largely dictated or at least inspired by him.[6] Furthermore, he or another of the Movement's religious leaders opens important games, such as the Islamic League's cup final, with a speech.

The rhetoric of the Islamic sports press

The focus of my analysis is the sports section of the Islamic Movement's northern section's weekly newspaper, Ṣawt al-Ḥaq wal-Ḥurriyya (The Voice of Justice and Freedom) between January and August 2000. From March 2000, the sports section even began to appear as a separate supplement. The supplement's name – al-Riyaḍa wal-Akhlaq (Sports and Morals) – testifies to its pedagogic orientation. This stands in contrast to names such as "Sports Corner" or "A Week of Sports" that appear in the sports sections of other Arab newspapers (and all the more so with regard to the name of the column of the sports editor of Kul al-'Arab, "Cocktail," a name that could only be found in a declaredly

---

[6] Interview with Salim Awawde, editor of the sports section in Ṣawt al-Ḥaq wal-Ḥurriyya (September 22, 1999).

secular paper). While tension between the attempt to build Arab national pride and the desire to present soccer as a potential arena for integration can be felt in the secular Arab press, Islamic newspapers link soccer exclusively to the Islamic identity, without referring to the possibility of integration into Israeli society at all.

Additionally, the sports section in *Sawt al-Ḥaq wal-Ḥurriyya* and the Islamic League are virtually overlapping since almost all of the reports in this section are dedicated to the Islamic League. Every week, the supplement's front page carries an op-ed article, authored by a different writer each time. This writer is nearly always a religious leader and his signature, appearing at the start of the supplement, affords moral legitimacy for the Muslim faithful to read the rest of the supplement.

The analysis of the rhetoric used in the Islamic sports press reveals persistent tensions between the aspirations to promote identity based on a moral code and the instrumental use of a secular-oriented institution such as soccer. This rhetoric is based on two dimensions of dialectical tension that are mutually connected. In the first dimension, soccer is understood and described as a site that serves as an outlet for violent urges – as opposed to Islam, which is presented as a restraining force in this regard. Following this logic, the Islamic League is a locale in which Islam tames the wild and takes control of soccer. The other dimension of the dialectical tension is between accepting the dichotomy described above and rejecting it. In other words, from the moment the Islamic Movement decides to include soccer as one of its activities, two diametrically opposed modes – ideally speaking – of relating to it come into being: continuing to present soccer as a bastion of licentiousness, with Islam represented as an attempt to supervise it, or, alternatively, adopting soccer and representing it as directly stemming from Islam itself. This alternation could be done by selectively presenting and appropriately interpreting verses from the Qur'an and the Ḥadith. The religious leadership of the Islamic Movement swings back and forth between these two attitudes.

An institution of licentiousness or an Islamic tradition?

As a secular and originally Western institution, soccer is perceived as a threat by most writers in the Islamic newspaper's sports supplement. One can learn of the extent to which some Islamist leaders perceive soccer as destined for disaster, or as an impure institution, from the words of Sheikh Muhammad Ṣallaḥ Khatib, the Imam of the New Mosque in al-'Uzair. Using the rhetoric of "how much more so," he explains why it is so important to request forgiveness after a game:

Man is quick to forget and quick to sin, so I suggest to my soccer-loving brothers that they are strict in asking forgiveness – especially after each and every game. Who has a greater obligation to request pardon – the Prophet, or he who stands on the pitch, with God knowing his situation? God the blessed and lofty said to his emissary (peace be upon him) at the end of his days: "When comes the Help of God and the conquest, and you see that the people enter God's religion in crowds, so glorify the praises of your Lord, and ask for His forgiveness. Verily, He is the one who accepts the repentance and forgives."   [Qur'anic verses, Surah 110, verses 1–3]

In other words, if the Prophet was commanded to ask forgiveness, how much more so must one who has watched a soccer game and has been exposed to all the evils that necessarily attend to it. Following the same logic, Sheikh Khatib continues:

Also, who has a greater obligation to request forgiveness, the Hajj after the pilgrimage, or the soccer player on his soccer pitch? [God] the lofty said to the pilgrims after they had performed the pilgrimage and completed the Hajj, "Then pour out from where the people have poured out, and ask pardon from God; God is forgiving and compassionate" [Qur'anic verse, Surah 2, verse 195]. So who has a greater obligation to request pardon? The devotee who stood before his God, or he who spent hours at the soccer pitch and whose qualities were tested? God's Prophet (peace and blessings of God be upon him) taught the people that after each written prayer one must thrice request forgiveness from the Lord.

My brothers – how large are our crimes, and what is the extent of our sin at soccer pitches and other places. Never forget to request forgiveness, and the hand of God promised that he will never punish you if you ask pardon from him.[7]

"Crimes." "Sins." These are the terms the writer associates with soccer. Soccer's impurity requires all those who take part in it to request forgiveness after every game, even if the game took place under supervision and received the legitimacy of Islamic religious leaders.

Sometimes, the religious writers of the sports supplement's opening column explicitly disparage soccer, thus underscoring their instrumentalist – verging on cynical – approach to the Islamic League:

You who run after "a piece of leather" that is just a reason and a means, and not an aim – paradise is the only prize – "thus will the competitors compete" and it is the biggest victory of all, following the will of God. I say to the two teams, you must choose between cleanliness and impurity.[8]

This is not the only time that the derogatory term, "piece of leather," is used to refer to the soccer ball. Such explicit disparagement of soccer is

---

[7] *Al-Riyada wal-Akhlaq*, May, 31, 2000.
[8] Sheikh Hassan abu-Leil, *Al-Riyada wal-Akhlaq*, March, 10, 2000.

only possible in a sports supplement that declares from the outset that the game itself is of no importance.

Also, the dichotomous distinction between purity and impurity is fixed according to one's attitude towards the game. Those who treat the game as a means are pure, whereas those who see it as an end are sinners.

The dialectical position that stands in contrast to the formation of a soccer–Islam opposition is one that adopts soccer, and describes it as a direct continuation of Islamic tradition. In his writings, Sheikh Munir Abu al-Hija describes the two poles together, presenting sports as a direct continuation of Islamic tradition on the one hand, and on the other, expressing concern about the corrupting elements at its foundation. The joint appearance of both of these motifs reflects, to a large extent, the complex attitude of the Islamic Movement's leadership towards soccer:

It is neither strange nor difficult for he who traces the positions and sayings of the Prophet (peace and blessings of God be upon him) to discover dozens of sayings that deal with sports and strength. The Prophet (peace and blessings of God be upon him) said in the Ḥadith: "the strong believer is preferred and loved by God more than the weak believer." And we see that the Prophet struggled with an infidel named Rakanah and threw him down. He rode his horse in front of everyone, and advocated horse riding, shooting, and so on – yet despite this we can find him saying – "strength is not in the struggle, but he is strong who controls his anger." This is a clear and exact instruction from the prophets to all the sportsmen interested in morality and sports, and in improving their behavior while improving their body and strength ... We do not want sports to become a slippery slope away from remembering God, or a mere amusement [that distances us] from prayer, we do not desire the commercialization and licentiousness that the West wants, where man yearns for richness and fame, even at the expense of humanity ...

[A]long with our great love for you, for your sporting hobbies and skills, for the strength of your bodies and the health of your souls, we shall continue to love the integrity of your behavior and character, and the purity of your principles and aims. Not because of enthusiasm, nor courage, nor earthly gains. God does not look at the form of your bodies, but rather at your hearts and your actions.[9]

The verse that the writer quotes from the Ḥadith – "the strong believer is preferred and loved by God more than the weak believer" – is embedded within the discourse of Islamic sports activists, and is often referred to as physical strength, even though it could have other interpretations. Another sentence from the Ḥadith that is frequently quoted is: "Teach your children

[9] *Al-Riyaḍa wal-Akhlaq*, April, 21, 2000.

swimming, riding horses and throwing arrows."[10] The encouragement that appears in Islamic sources to busy oneself with swimming, horse riding, and shooting can also be interpreted as a practical need to promote fighting skills in a religious community that was born in conditions of war. A certain amount of interpretive acrobatics is required in order to construe it as promoting the quantified modern sports, which is not directed towards an external aim, such as preparedness for battle. Nonetheless, Sheikh Abu al-Hija's invention of tradition demands clarifications, such that no one would understand him to be giving indiscriminate legitimacy to all sports. Sports can also comprise a slippery slope, from the central peak of which (through the fulfillment of commandments) the believer can descend into distant and marginal territory located in the West, where sports are necessarily connected with commercialization and licentiousness, and not with godly labor.

Another example of this complex attitude can be found in the writings of Sheikh Jamal Sa'adi from Iksal:

The Lord forbids Muslims to have dealings with amusements and games, unless they take place within very clear boundaries agreed upon by the religion of God and the Islamic Shari'a. There is no disagreement that Islam approves of action, activity, and movement, and calls for its followers to exercise and care for their bodies by swimming, shooting, horse riding, soccer, running, and other permitted activities, and in the past it was said: a healthy soul in a healthy body. But having said that, and bearing in the mind the advances in our bodily health, we have no choice but to raise the level of our morality, whether we are players on the pitch or spectators. It is forbidden for a Muslim to get so angry that he loses his balance and discipline, which immediately leads to an inappropriate loosening of his tongue ... There are no winners or losers on the pitch – the defeated and humiliated is, with the help of God, Satan, and the winner and victor is good morality and true brotherhood. Make sports into an arena in which the competitors compete for obedience to God and for your place in paradise.[11]

In this text, the "invention of a tradition" is expanded. Sa'adi interweaves soccer – invented only 150 years ago – into a list of activities that are mentioned in Islamic sources, such as swimming and horse riding, and turns it into an Islamic injunction. At the same time, he adopts a certain degree of caution: sports can only be permitted after they are removed from the world of amusement and play and defined as a religious obligation.

---

[10] This quote used to appear on the head of the sports section of the Iranian newspaper, *Tehran Times.*
[11] *Al-Riyada wal-Akhlaq*, May 12, 2000.

Obedience, discipline, and temperance

As I mentioned in chapter 2, the original meaning of the Arabic word for sports, *riyaḍa*, means "discipline," but for Sa'adi, one of the central dangers latent in soccer is the loss of balance and discipline. In this context, it is worth saying a few words about the connection between sports, discipline, and temperance. Elias and Dunning (1986: 63–90) explain the appearance of modern sports as a side-effect of the ever-increasing restraints required by British society in the age of modernity. These restrictions led to the need for the creation of social enclaves in which moderated and permissible forms of excitement and enjoyment could be aroused and expressed – modern sports. Leaning on psychoanalytic logic, they claim that the creation of sports allowed the necessary release of violent urges in a framework both supervised and limited in terms of time and space.

A striking foundation of the Islamic Movement is its increasing supervision of public expressions of emotion and urges. The same ascetic basis of Islamism that demands that weddings be uprooted from traditional customs of happiness is that which can be seen trying to detach sports from its function as a safety valve for the release of violent urges. The crowd's swearing and cursing are an inseparable part of the desired "letting off of steam," but it is clear that that is not the purpose that the Islamic Movement assigned to soccer. On the contrary, temperance, restraint, and control over one's urges are of import in their own right, and the passing of a soccer match without such releases as discussed above becomes an end in itself. The Islamic values glorified by the organizers of the Islamic League are reflected in terms that are regularly found in the opening column of the sports section, underscored by terms such as patience, forbearance, conquering anger, obedience, balance, and discipline. Namely, if the Islamic League is the site at which the restraining force of Islam comes into conflict with the recalcitrant, rebellious nature of sports, and if the League's aim is to strengthen Islamic values, then only by moderating urges and violence in such a way as to differentiate it from other soccer environments can the League justify its existence.

The objective of restraint and obedience is given a two-directional expression in the way soccer is represented. On the one hand, because of the temptation to release one's urges, soccer is a test of self-restraint, and therefore also a test of faith. On the other hand, certain characteristics of a soccer match are represented as an idealistic metaphor representing the hierarchy of the religious organization, and the hierarchy between man and God. This is how Sheikh Kamel Rayan from Kafr Bara, one of the leaders of the Islamic Movement's southern faction, explains this idea: "Religious belief has influence over the game, and the game is a test of religious belief: can I really bear the discipline, the obedience? Also, everyone knows his place. There is a hierarchy – that is how the religion is built, too, and also the religious organization. It is not something liberal, where everyone can just do whatever he wants."[12]

The motif of obedience repeatedly appears in the sports supplement in different guises:

One of the most important factors in the success of a people, a nation, a movement, and a party is the principle of obedience to the ruler, obedience to the leader. In our religion, obeying the leader is an obligation which man must heartily imbibe, and he who transgresses will be accordingly blamed ... [At this point the writer presents a number of verses from the Qur'an and the Hadith that justify the importance he attributes to obedience. He also produces a number of historical examples of Islamic failures that followed a failure to obey the leader.] The player on the pitch must accept the instructions of his coach, for disobeying them will bring defeat upon his team, and he will have to pay the price of punishment, whatever that may be ... One of the most important characteristics that makes the youth playing in the Islamic League unique is his obedience to the referee and the sporting spirit, which emanates from him and influences his fellow brothers.[13]

The Islamic League's *raison d'être* can be clearly seen in the above text: to morally distinguish it from regular soccer, and to set an example for it. A player in the Islamic League has lofty values, of which obedience is a central one, and he is expected to influence those in his environment. The emphasis on obedience and temperance clashes with the widely accepted view of sports' functions. Competitive sports within the framework of leisure time falls into the category of what Elias and Dunning call "mimetic activities," which create excitement via the construction of tension but without the risk which might be found in other tense circumstances (Elias and Dunning 1986: 75). Excitement and tension find expression not only in obeying the laws of the game, but also in pushing them to their limits, or, as it is called in sports journalism, unsporting behavior: little pushes, even when the player does not have the ball; exaggerated pleadings to the referee; open displays of hostility to the opposing team's fans. The behavioral metamorphosis of hard-core fans in the stadiums includes a temporary adoption of improper behavior, and it is an important element in the ritualistic character of the game

---

[12] Interview with Sheikh Kamel Rayan, November 26, 1998.
[13] Sheikh Issam Hassan Dakhla, *al-Riyada wal-Akhlaq*, May 5, 2000.

(Bromberger 1995). On an individual level, the hard-core sports fan's experience is not complete if he cannot curse to his heart's content.

The Islamic League presumes to wipe out all of those elements from the game, to do away with swearing, to remove displays of hostility between the teams, yet nonetheless put on a soccer game and arouse interest in it. How can the contradiction be overcome? How can excitement and tension be created while canceling out all of its excesses, all emotional extremes, and the feeling that soccer is an end in itself? In order to deal with these difficulties, much effort is expended in making the soccer field an "Islamic space." Creating this defined Islamic space has value in and of itself in constructing Islamic identity, but it also serves to signify that the expectations of their behavior are entirely different from those regarding any other game of soccer. The Islamic nature of the game, thus finds expression in a number of elements:

1. The games start and finish with the two teams standing in the middle of the field and crying out "Allah akbar" (God is great). At certain times during the match, either before the game or at the half-time interval, the players, coaches, and managers join together in prayer. At the cup final (a game I attended), the gates were opened at the time of prayer so that the (400 or so) fans could also join in. At the end of the games, all the players meet together to hear a sermon.

2. The players play in long trousers, even on hot summer days (following soccer players in countries where the Shari'a dominates state laws – Saudi Arabia, Iran, and Afghanistan before 2002). The claim that bodily activity does not stand at the center of the game is strengthened by the players' covering up of their bodies, and the consequent lack of comfort fortifies the ascetic dimension of the Islamic experience.

3. If the Mu'adhin's call to prayer is heard from a nearby mosque, the game is halted for a few minutes. In this way, the mosque penetrates the soccer field. The only flags waved by the fans are the green flags, imprinted with Islamic verses – known as the flag of Islam.

4. In contrast to the chants heard at the Israeli leagues, which are mostly in Hebrew, the repertoire at Islamic League games is taken mainly from the Egyptian League or is based on variations of Islamic slogans. For instance, "There is no God apart from Allah, and Majd loved by Allah" – a chant shouted by the fans of the Majd al-Kurum team – is actually a paraphrase of the sentence: "There is no God apart from Allah, and Muhammad is his messenger."

5. There is a strict set of regulations regarding disciplinary transgressions. The utterance of offensive comments by players to one another

is forbidden by Islamic League regulations, and is punishable by expulsion from the League. Particularly serious offenses require permission from religious leaders before the recalcitrant player is allowed to play again.

6. The players' behavior is actively supervised by the crowd and the bureaucrats. When a player knocks over another player and emotions threaten to boil over, both teams' benches, as well as part of the crowd, immediately start enacting the compulsory script to be recited during occasions such as these, by crying, "Allah akbar wa-l'illah al-hamd!" (God is great, all praise to God), which reminds the players that they are currently in an Islamic space, and that they therefore must behave with restraint. Such events usually end with the players shaking hands, and not pushing each other or uttering swear words.

The Islamic definition of the situation is not always maintained. In the semi-final game between Majd al-Kurum and Bu'aina/'Uzair in May 2000, tension was running particularly high. More than once players tackled fiercely, which almost led to an outburst. The crowd duly and faithfully played its part. Instead of encouraging the players to be forceful, or even violent, as is usually the case at soccer matches, the fans cried out: "Wihda Islamiyya – Majdiyya – 'Uzairiyya," meaning, "Islamic unity – Majd (Al-Kurum) and 'Uzair." These cries were accompanied by chants of "Allah akbar" from the benches, and the tension was diffused.

Soccer in the service of the Da'wa

"Fundamentalists are boundary setters: they excel in marking themselves off from others by distinctive dress, customs, and conduct. But they are also eager to expand their borders by attracting outsiders who will honor fundamentalist norms by requiring that non-fundamentalists observe fundamentalist codes" (Marty and Appleby 1993: 4). Consistent with this assertion, the Islamic Movement's leaders do not see the Islamic League as an end in itself, but rather as a tool for advancing the Da'wa, and as a moral alternative to the extremely popular Israeli leagues.

Accordingly, an oft-repeated motif is that the players' attitude towards moral values is more important than their sporting skills. Sallah Lutfi from Umm al-Fahm is responsible for "Youth and Sports" in the Islamic Movement. For him, the relationship between the two spheres is taken for granted since sports has mainly a pedagogic function. "Soccer is just a way-station," says Lutfi. "Sports can help achieve Islamic educational aims." Lutfi is not only referring to the games of the Islamic League. In 1994, the Islamic Movement set up a soccer school in Umm Al-Faḥm. Before playing, the children read from the Qur'an and prayed. Lutfi explains: "There are children who don't pray, and we say that it will come with time, we don't force them."[14]

The Islamic League is open to all Muslims, regardless of their lifestyle off the soccer field, and, indeed, the gap between the religiosity of the leaders and officials and that of the players is remarkable. My impression (from discussions I had with players) is that many of them come to play soccer – and not to take part in a religious event – and that large numbers of them do not participate in the Movement's other activities. This discrepancy fits the leadership's perception that soccer can serve as a tool for disseminating Islam to people who would not otherwise be reached were it not for soccer.

Sheikh Kamal Khatib, deputy leader of the Islamic Movement (northern section), wrote a column in the first expanded sports supplement, published on March 3, 2000, in which he summarized his instrumentalist view of soccer:

We must say to our brothers, whatever their activity and position may be in relation to the *Da'wa*, that they must guard and defend those positions more than the goalkeeper guards his goal, that we will defend our *Da'wa*, we will support it and give it our backs to rest on with more skill than that of a defender. We will act to present our ideas and to bring our *Da'wa* to everybody with more enthusiasm and true will than those of an attacker running after the ball, trying to reach it so as to score a beautiful goal.

Your efforts will be blessed, brothers, as you strengthen the fortress of your *Da'wa*, along with your brothers and sisters. A blessing upon you, brothers of the General Islamic League, blessings upon *Ṣawt al-Ḥaq wal-Ḥurriyya*, blessings upon you all.[15]

In contrast to secular sports sections, in which political messages are hidden between the lines written by sports journalists, in the Islamic sports press the central commentaries and interpretations are written by politicians and religious leaders. While secular papers use political contexts as metaphors for describing a game of soccer, in the excerpt above we can see Sheikh Kamal Khatib using soccer as a metaphor for political-religious activity. This distinction nicely reflects soccer's relative place and intended role in each one of these streams. The attitude of the

[14] Interview with Saleh Lutfi, January 16, 1999.   [15] *Al-Riyaḍa wal-Akhlaq*, March 3, 2000.

Islamic Movement's leadership to soccer is declaredly instrumental, and no interest in the game itself is expressed:

> Our dealings with sports, and the existence of the Islamic League and the teams that comprise it, are part of our Islamic *Da'wa*, through which we call people to the religion of God, make it approachable for the people, and bring them closer to Islam. God revealed this means to us, and through it we cause youth to want Islam, and urge and encourage them to want to praise God.[16]

Through sports, claims the writer, Islamic Movement activists *make approachable*, *bring closer*, *urge*, and *encourage* – expressions that indicate an active missionary attitude, which is served by sports. Diya al-Din Abu Ahmad, the Imam of a mosque in Nazareth, speaks in similar terms. Under the headline, "This is our aim," he wrote in the sports supplement:

> Everybody knows that this is our aim – to make soccer a tool for desiring God, and winning a place in paradise – and not so that people will point at us and say that we are professionals and skilled on the soccer pitch. We want people to point to our morals, to our patience and temperance, to our conquering of anger, and to our joint responsibility, to our adherence and obedience, and also to our unity as one body, such that if one part is in pain, the rest of the body jumps to assistance to guard and protect it.[17]

It is important to pay attention to Abu Ahmad's outward-looking orientation. The Islamic League is not only meant to serve as an alternative model of morality, but also to be seen from the outside as a role model worthy of imitation: "We want people to point to our morals."

For those representing the Islamic League as a tool for the *Da'wa*, it is only one part of a larger educational project, but it is a particularly sensitive and dangerous part that demands special attention. In this regard, Sheikh Jalal al-Din Zu'abi, an Imam from Kafr Kana, writes:

> I have a number of hopes and desires regarding the Islamic League:
> 1. That the Islamic League's activity will include educational and spiritual themes – that it will not just remain in the sphere of soccer – and that there will be many lectures, clubs, lessons, hikes, and so on. 2. That the correct sporting spirit, mutual bonds, and true cooperation will reign between the players during competitions, without them becoming a source of hostility, mutual hatred, animosity, and lack of restraint. 3. That adherents of the Islamic religion – people who are committed to the principles of faith, the practices, the traditions, the morals, the

---

[16] Sheikh Ahmed Rashed, *al-Riyada wal-Akhlaq*, May 26, 2000.
[17] *Al-Riyada wal-Akhlaq*, April 28, 2000.

prayer, and the attitude of Islam – will be appointed to the leadership and management of the League's activities, and that they will plant love for goodness and fine morals in the souls of the young, and that they will make them keep the rules of the correct Islam, and distance themselves from all evil. 4. These educators must be of faith and good intention and must be able to bear the heavy responsibility placed on their shoulders. They must learn the ways of Mustapha [one of the Prophet's names], peace be upon him, and follow in his footsteps so that they will be able to bring the nation's young to the level of which they are worthy.[18]

These lines once more demonstrate the secondary place given to soccer. On the one hand, it is an educational tool (like the clubs and hikes), but on the other, there is a considerable concern with soccer's potential to become an arena for the release of urges. Therefore, strict supervision by carefully selected and authorized supervisory agents is required. After all, they must take care of a rampaging monster, and not everyone has the skills required to tame it. From this it follows that they must be "committed to Islam," and "able to bear the heavy responsibility placed on their shoulders." Apart from the latent criticism of some of the Islamic League's activists, whom the writer suspects are true soccer fans and not faithful enough to Islam, the writer's comments bring home the fear of a blurring of the boundaries, and of the danger that, in the heat of the game, the original purpose, the reason for which the League was set up, will be forgotten.

The emphasis placed on the players' morality is also reflected in the Islamic League's rulebook. Alongside the regular league table, which shows the teams' points according to the results of their games, one can always find a "table of morality" in which the teams are ranked by the fair play of their players. "Fair play tables" of this kind are found in many soccer leagues, but in the Islamic League the two tables are not independent. Having particularly low points in the morality table influences the team's points in the regular table. The supplement's headlines and articles treat this table with almost the same level of importance as they do the regular points table. The paper's editors even claim that sports supplements covering the Israeli League learned to present such fair play tables from them. This claim does not withstand the test of simple chronology, yet it tells us something about the way that Islamic Movement activists see themselves as offering a universalistic moral alternative. Furthermore, one could say that the attempt to quantify and measure moral values presents us with the essence of a synthesis borne of the dialectic between sports and religion.

---

[18] *Al-Riyaḍa wal-Akhlaq*, May 15, 2000.

Soccer and Islam in Israel

In their relation to sports, there is a basic difference between Islamist activists discussed in this chapter and the preachers of Arab and Palestinian nationalism discussed in chapter 5. The nationalist ideologies of Arabness, and even more so that of Palestinianness, assume the existence of an innate inherent identity. Language and consciousness are important elements in these identities, yet a Palestinian who denies his Palestinianness is seen by his environment as living in a state of false consciousness. On the other hand, there is no way of becoming a Palestinian for someone who was not born as Palestinian.

The imagined rigidity of the boundaries of these identities has implications for the attitude towards soccer by social agents who promote them. The sports sections of the secular Arab newspapers cover the Arab teams in the Israeli League and demand that the Arab teams preserve their Arab identity. At the same time, the newspapers *do not see the very encounter itself as threatening to Arab or Palestinian belongingness.*

For the Islamic Movement, however, the encounter constitutes a definite threat. Islamic identity, as it is interpreted by the Islamic Movement, has permeable boundaries: joining Islam is easy, and Islam has a strong proselytizing foundation. Diffuse boundaries are among the most outstanding characteristics of an identity based on a code of sacredness and universal moral values (Eisenstadt and Giesen 1994). The boundaries of Islamic identity are relatively permeable in both directions. Because Islam does not rely on an assumed internal essence (like Palestinian identity), exposure to a strong, hegemonic culture is seen as an existential threat. Therefore, while nationalists need competitive encounters against other nations in order to, seemingly, expose the "true" nature of the nation, the Islamic Movement's encounter with hegemonic Israeli society actually constitutes an existential threat. It is understood as an inter-cultural encounter with unequal starting conditions, such that it could lead to the negation of the Islamic identity of those taking part in it.

Due to soccer's overwhelming popularity, the Islamic Movement could not boycott it. Consequently, it incorporated soccer into its activities, and attempted to Islamicize the game and use it for its own purposes. The Islamic Movement's choice of incorporating soccer and turning it into a tool for proving the moral superiority of Islam inevitably produces various tensions. These tensions are inevitable because at least some of the features of soccer that elicited the initial antagonism have not simply disappeared after its adoption by the Islamic Movement.

Soccer is a quasi-religious institution that entails some very earthly orientations such as simple amusement. It also entails obvious materialistic orientations such as celebrating physical performances, serving as a model for professional success, and even supplying commercial opportunities – all considered by the Islamic Movement as corrupting if they stand as goals in and of themselves. By creating a separate league, the Islamic Movement has managed to eliminate the worship of professionalism and commercialism but not the pure amusement and the limited violence. These vital components of the sportive experience are crucial for seducing young players to join the league, but they remain subject to consistent criticism by the political-religious leaders.

A major source of tension stems from modern sports' capacity to supply an answer for people's "quest for excitement," to use the famous title of Elias and Dunning's (1986) book. Sports, they noted, serves as a social enclave that permits moderate, "civilized" forms of aggression. The regulation of emotions and the subjugation of aggression to a certain system of rules are essential to soccer itself, but the sporadic violations of these rules are necessary to reaffirm them. However, the Islamic League's managers even argue that they are able to eliminate these deviations, namely, any expression of aggression and anger.

At first glance, the excitement and aggression inherent in soccer confront the declared aspiration of the Islamic Movement to control emotions and discipline them. However, these very elements are those that enable the Islamic Movement to utilize the game by turning soccer into a challenge of self-control. In addition, the hierarchical structure of soccer and the necessity of obeying the coach enable it to be used as an exercise in obedience, simulating the relations between men and God. Hence, soccer is transformed into a tool of religious education, an ideal scene for practicing temperance and obedience.

Nevertheless, hesitation and ambiguities are present. They appear in the way the games are managed, and in the way the Movement's leaders try to represent the game to themselves and their followers. How should the game be represented? As a secular Western institution that poses a threat to the purity of Islamic morals, but which Islam nonetheless succeeds in controlling, or as the natural and logical progression of Islamic tradition? As a site that encourages the release of urges, or as a location in which to teach restraint, temperance, and obedience?

These unique tensions are very different from the tensions we encountered in other sites of the Arab soccer sphere in Israel. The Islamic League, therefore, is a minor enclave within the bigger integrative enclave.

8

Sakhnin – between soccer and martyrdom

On the evening of May 18, 2004, while Israeli troops stormed Palestinian refugee camps in the Gaza Strip in another attempt to crush the Palestinian uprising against the occupation, both Israeli Prime Minister Ariel Sharon and Palestinian President Yasser Arafat found time for phone calls concerning seemingly trivial issues. Sharon phoned the manager of an Israeli soccer team to congratulate him on winning the Israeli State Cup, which made it eligible to represent Israel in the EUFA cup. Prime Minister Sharon emphasized his confidence that the team would represent Israel in an honorable manner in Europe. That same evening, President Arafat called the director of an Arab soccer team to congratulate him on his team's victory, telling him that the team brought pride to the Arab nation.

What makes the co-occurrence of these two events remarkable is the fact that Sharon and Arafat had called the same director, Mazen Ghnayem, and referred to the same team – Ittiḥad Abnaa Sakhnin – after the team became the first Arab team to win the Israeli State Cup. This dual congratulation, while apparently paradoxical, was possible due to the peculiar and multifaceted image of Sakhnin among both Jewish Israeli and Arab Palestinian publics.

Since 1976 Sakhnin has gradually emerged as a visible juncture of two separate significant processes with far-reaching implications on the collective identity of the Arab-Palestinian minority in Israel and on local identity in Sakhnin. These two processes are the emergence of a local–national narrative of heroism and sacrifice, and the centrality of soccer in the negotiation of political belonging and allegiances. My main argument in this chapter concentrates on the complex ways that these two foci of collective identity interact, though rarely intersect. The heroic narrative leans towards Palestinian nationalism and political protest, underlining the historical continuity of Sakhnin as a bastion of struggle and the common fate of Sakhnin and the rest of the Palestinian people; and simultaneously, in the soccer sphere, Sakhninians are managing a dialogue with the Jewish-Israeli public in an attempt to achieve acceptance by the Jewish majority and create an *integrative enclave*.

Sakhnin's residents, local politicians and sports functionaries consistently manipulate the meaning of these spheres, alternately highlighting one and hiding the other, in order to navigate between different political expectations stemming from their subtle position as both Arab-Palestinians *and* Israeli citizens. Holding a shaky and marginal status in both Israeli and Palestinian social worlds, these social agents play with the meaning of soccer, martyrdom, and their local identity in order to employ a differential "impression management" towards distinct audiences in diverse contexts. The result is the creation of a "bi-focal" local pride based on a fragmented public space.

Irving Goffman noted that a "role conflict" might emerge when there is a potential contradiction between the expectations stemming from different roles. Therefore, individuals aspire to maintain a strict segregation between various spheres of life in order to separate different audiences. The case of Sakhnin illustrates that Goffman's insight, while originally referring to individuals, also applies to the collective level. Sakhnin demonstrates how in conditions of high tension between different dimensions of collective identification, social communities might compartmentalize their public space, dedicating separate social realms to distinct orientations of identification.

Bi-focal local pride in Sakhnin

Although local communities played an overriding role in defining Palestinian identity even before 1948 (Tamari 1999: 3–4), the new political circumstances in which the Palestinian minority in Israel was trapped have strengthened the status of local identity. Under the watchful eyes of military governors until 1966, Arabs in Israel faced difficulties in traveling from one town to another as well as in organizing a countrywide set of supra-local institutions. The state actively contributed to the fragmentation of the Arab minority along local lines, together with emphasizing ethnic, religious, and familial boundaries, as a means of control (Lustick 1980).

Even after the Military Government was removed, because of Arab public leaders' limited access to the state's political center, local politics became – by default – the main sphere in which these leaders could exert power (Rosenfeld and Al-Haj 1990). Most important, however, is the fact that unlike the Jewish majority in Israel, which controls the common space and landscape, the Palestinian minority has no Arab common space outside of the Arab towns and villages, and they also lack an autonomous urban center that is collectively recognized as a symbolic center or capital (Bishara 1998b). Therefore, almost every cultural production necessarily acquires a dominant local character that overshadows national connotations.

Beyond these structural constraints, localism is strategically used by Arabs in Israel in two different ways. In those towns that can demonstrate a history of struggle, resistance, and sacrifice, these themes allow residents to self-consciously promote a higher rank in the imagined hierarchy of Palestinian national mythology. Therefore, against the collapse of the urban centers and a large part of Palestinian villages in 1948, heroic local narratives have developed among the remaining villages that give meaning to their survival. People in these places formulated local myths of heroism that ascribe their non-expulsion to their unique steadfastness (Robinson 2003). This form of local pride is congruent with the hegemonic narrative of Palestinian nationalism, and it is projected towards an Arab-Palestinian audience.

The other pole of localism is oriented towards a Jewish-Israeli audience. Here, the emphasis on local identity aims to dull Palestinian national identity, which is frequently perceived as potentially dangerous to the Arabs' status as Israeli citizens. Hence, interactions with Jews tend to be accompanied by emphasizing institutions with a clear local character. The tremendous popularity of local Arab soccer teams and the local-patriotic rites which evolved around them stem in part from their potential to provide a warlike masculine and competitive pride that is non-nationalist and therefore does not contradict "Israeliness." What makes Sakhnin an especially interesting case is the dramatic and spectacular co-appearance of both kinds of local pride.

Sakhnin is a mainly Muslim town, with a small Christian minority of 6–10 percent,[1] situated in the heart of the Galilee. Although it gained formal recognition as a city by the Israeli government in 1995, according to its urban texture, the level of municipal services, and the self-image of its citizens, Sakhnin remains a large and very dense village. Also important is the fact that Sakhnin is flanked on three sides by Jewish settlements and military installations. Its efforts to expand its municipal

---

[1] The minimal 6 percent is taken from: *Demographic Characteristics of Population in Locations and Statistical Districts*, Jerusalem: Israel Bureau of Statistics, 1995. However, most local inhabitants of Sakhnin are convinced that this is an under-counting, and that a 10 percent Christian minority is closer to reality.

Table 8.1: *Percentage of interviewees who chose each identity as one of three identities of which they are proud to be part*

Sakhnin	77% (132)
Palestinian people	58% (99)
Arab nation	40% (69)
Muslims/Christians	38% (65)
Hamula (clan)	33% (57)
Men	32% (54)
The State of Israel	13% (22)
Galilee inhabitants	11% (18)

boundaries have consistently failed due to the demographic anxieties of Israeli governmental authorities which have employed a consistent policy of "Judaization of the Galilee" and considered any Arab expansion as contradicting this goal (Bashir 2004).

In 2004 Sakhnin was ranked by the Israeli Bureau of Statistics 33rd of 210 localities in Israel in an inverse ranking of socio-economic level.[2] It suffers from the lack of sources of income and a high unemployment rate,[3] a shaky infrastructure and the lack of necessary public services for a town of 24,000 people. Nevertheless, Sakhnin's collective self-image as well as its external reputation emphasizes a high level of local pride.

This image is supported by the pattern of reaction of interviewees in the local survey I conducted in March–April 1999 (see appendix 5 for methodological details), when they were asked to choose three circles of belonging of which they were most proud. As table 8.1 demonstrates, 77 percent of them chose the Sakhninian identity, more than any other identity. This finding stands in sharp contrast to the countrywide survey where local identity ranked only third after religious identity and the *hamula* (extended family or clan) while these two identities were ranked fourth and fifth in Sakhnin, respectively.

The most common combinations of two identities were the two local–national combinations: 43 percent chose both Sakhninian identity and Palestinian identity as a source of pride, and 26 percent chose Sakhninian

[2] "Local Councils and Municipalities, by Socio-Economic Index, Ranking and Cluster Membership," http://www.cbs.gov.il/hodaot2004/13_04_22t1.pdf
[3] In 2002 Sakhnin was ranked 209 out of 264 in the rate of unemployment benefits receivers among local and regional authorities in Israel: http://gis.cbs.gov.il/Website/Localities2002/Rashuyot_htm/tables/tab_2.htm

and Arab identities. These findings suggest that local pride might be co-produced with national pride. Two spheres are highly likely to serve as social sites for the production of this local–national patriotism: the commemoration of heroic struggles and the successful local soccer team.

"The martyrs' village": a narrative of struggle

Sakhnin is a town that has existed for thousands of years and is proud of the nationalism of its people. You know, we have given many martyrs, whether it was in October 2000, in 1976, or in 1948. Our entire history is a history of people who love their land, who always identify with the Palestinian people.

(Interview with Nidal, a political activist in Sakhnin, March 29, 2003)

After 1948, Sakhnin's population increased dramatically, from 3,000 to 6,100 in 1961, reaching 24,000 in 2004. At the same time, Sakhnin suffered from a continuous shrinking of its land due to a series of land confiscations. In 1961, 2,000 dunams of land belonging to Sakhnin and 'Arabeh, the neighboring Arab village, were expropriated to facilitate the digging of the national water-carrier. There was much bitterness, for in areas where the carrier passed through Jewish-owned land, an underground conduit was laid (Jiryis 1969). A few years later, 20,000 more dunams of the town's lands were proclaimed government areas and were expropriated. Despite this, under the Military Government substantial protest against this policy could not develop.

In 1976, however, a decade after the Military Government was removed, a striking change occurred. In February 1976, the Israeli government announced its intention to confiscate lands from their owners in Sakhnin and the neighboring Arab villages 'Arabeh and Deir Hana. This time the Palestinian citizens of Israel were able to organize themselves for a countrywide protest. The general strike and the large-scale demonstrations against the confiscation plan evolved into violent clashes between demonstrators and the border police troops who opened fire, killed six people, and wounded about seventy others throughout the country; three of the victims were from Sakhnin. The day on which the event occurred, March 30, was proclaimed "Land Day" – an annual day of memorial and protest by the entire Arab-Palestinian minority in Israel.

The Land Day martyrs dramatically changed the public image of Sakhnin among both Arabs and Jews in Israel. The event "marked" Sakhnin as the focus of Arab-Palestinian national protest within the borders of the State of Israel. The victims of Land Day became local martyrs symbolizing the bond of the people of Sakhnin to their land, and joins local pride with national pride. Overnight, Sakhnin turned from another medium-sized peripheral village in the Galilee into a symbol of national struggle. Following the fortieth day after Land Day (the end of the traditional Muslim mourning period), *al-Ittiḥad*, the Communist Party's mouthpiece and the only daily newspaper in Arabic at the time, wrote:

As early as before the setting of the sun on March 30, 1976, the name of Sakhnin and her sisters was known by all. Their fame spread across the horizon not as a victim of a natural catastrophe … but as weaponless villagers who defended their people's future and its destiny, relying on their right. The slogan that was heard from thousands of throats became real: "By blood, by spirit, we will redeem you, oh Galilee."[4]

The centrality of Sakhnin in the emerging Land Day myth was acknowledged by the Committee for Protecting Arab Land,[5] which decided to build the central commemorative monument for all six victims in the main cemetery in Sakhnin. This monument reflects a transitional phase and an historical juncture. It is the first attempt by Palestinians in Israel to carve out a symbol of national heroism and sacrifice in the public arena, linking it to a major Palestinian national theme: the land. The monument became an iconic symbol of Land Day and it serves as the final gathering point in annual Land Day ceremonies.

Since 1976, Land Day has been commemorated annually all over Arab localities in Israel through massive rallies and parades; in most years, the main rally has taken place in Sakhnin, signifying the centrality of the town in the event. For the generations who grew up after Land Day, the annual commemorations have become a natural anchor in the local and national calendar. Although the dilemmas and tensions characterizing the identity of Arabs in Israel repeatedly have been reflected in Land Day ceremonies, no other day in their collective calendar has been more intensively loaded with Palestinian national symbolism. This aspect became more visible after the Oslo accords in 1993, when Palestinian national flags were legalized. Since then Palestinian flags have dominated the rallies, together with slogans imported from Palestinian demonstrations in the West Bank and the Gaza Strip, and the singing of the Palestinian national anthem.

Sakhnin centrality in the national narrative of sacrifice was re-emphasized in October 2000 when thirteen Arab demonstrators inside Israel were killed by the police during the first days of the second Palestinian uprising in the

[4] *Al-Ittiḥad*, May 14, 1976, p. 5.
[5] A committee founded in 1975 to coordinate actions against land confiscation, it became one of the most important leadership institutions of the Arab-Palestinian minority in Israel.

West Bank and Gaza Strip. Two of the victims, Walid Abu Ṣallaḥ and Ahmad Ghnayem were from Sakhnin and they immediately gained the status of new local martyrs. Symbolically, they were buried as close as possible to the Land Day monument. These events further enhanced the salience of the linkage between national martyrdom and local pride, resulting in the birth of another annual day of commemoration, and another monument was constructed. This time its local orientation was even greater since the names of the two Sakhninian local victims were highlighted. In addition, October 2000 left the Sakhninians in shock and pain, but also confused and perplexed with regard to future relations with the state and the Jewish majority.

The sacrifices made by Sakhnin on Land Day and later in October 2000 serve also as an anchor for the construction of a glorified past for Sakhnin. Since 1999, during the month of March the local branch of the Islamic Movement has presented a photo exhibition of all Sakhninian national martyrs since the rebellion of 1936–1939. In *The Martyrs of Sakhnin*, a book published by the Movement following October 2000, the author, Mas'ud Ghnayem, emphasized the heroic role of Sakhnin villagers in 1948 in defending the other Arab villages in the area (Ghnayem 2000: 17–24). Based on memories of town elders, he portrayed an heroic narrative that posits Sakhnin at the top of the Palestinian national hierarchy among Arab villages: "after the fall of 'Acca and the neighboring villages, the people of Sakhnin took upon their shoulders the mission of protecting the villages located on its western side, such as Mi'ar, Kawkab, Sha'b, and al-Birwa, and attempted with their humble means to protect these villages."[6]

The Martyrs of Sakhnin positions Sakhnin high in the hierarchy of national Palestinian-Arab and Islamic importance. The book's cover features a picture of the Dome of the Rock, the most outstanding visual image of contemporary Palestinian nationalism. The advertisements published by the municipality in the wake of the events of October 2000 stress Sakhnin's Palestinian affiliation. On the fortieth day after the death of the October 2000 victims, the municipality publicized an invitation to participate in a memorial ceremony in which "Sakhnin and all the Arab masses will stress that our stand is one of honorable courage, for we rose up to protect al-Aqsa and al-Quds and to protect our existence and our national identity."

---

[6] Sakhnin's role in the 1948 war is controversial. Wasfi al-Tal, one of the commanders of the Arab Salvation Army, wrote in his memoirs that Sakhnin's people helped the Zionist forces in the battle.

It is noteworthy that publications of this kind are available only in Arabic. The success of Sakhnin's soccer team has given the people of Sakhnin frequent access to major Hebrew media and an abundance of opportunities to present themselves before a broader Jewish-Israeli audience. Yet in these presentations, the heroic narrative is mostly absent.

In the view of many of the residents, the belligerent image of Sakhnin as perceived in the eyes of the Jewish-Israeli public, presents a political, social, and economic threat to the town. Even under conditions of discrimination and injustice, the central government makes available to local Arab municipalities a variety of financial resources. The local Arab leadership actively seeks to provide its residents with the maximum – and therefore prefers an "apolitical" image. Furthermore, the Sakhninians come into daily contact with the Jewish majority: as hired workers in Haifa and its environs and in nearby Jewish settlements; as service providers and merchants in small businesses within Sakhnin along the main road; as consumers of services in the Jewish cities (mainly health services); and as citizens dealing with officials of the various authorities such as those of the National Insurance, Ministry of the Interior, and the courts. In many of these contacts, the identification of Sakhnin with nationalistic militancy is a dark cloud hovering above them, placing them in an apologetic and defensive position. Therefore, at such meetings the heroic narrative is downplayed.

This absence of a nationalist narrative has as well a specific economic incentive. Since the late 1990s, the municipality in Sakhnin has invested great efforts in cultivating a successful tourism industry. These efforts could be hampered not only by violent riots but also by an emphasis on Sakhnin's nationalist and wary image. In a tourist brochure published by the Sakhnin municipality (in Hebrew and Arabic), under the caption "Historic Background" and "Historic Sites," there is no reference to significant events in modern history that touch upon Palestinian nationalism. The 1936 rebellion, the war of 1948, and the events of Land Day are not part of Sakhnin "tourist" history.

What, then, is emphasized in the picture that Sakhnin presents to the Jewish-Israeli public? A number of "apolitical" aspects of Sakhnin are stressed in order to paint a non-threatening image. The tourist brochure mentioned above, for instance, highlights the grave of the saintly Rabbi Yehoshu'a of Sakhnin who, according to Jewish Talmudic tradition, was a member of the Sanhedrin, and was executed by the Romans and brought to Sakhnin for burial. The site, which was viewed as a holy place, became the locus of pilgrimages by Muslims and Jews alike, especially barren women seeking divine dispensations. Another institution emphasized by the municipality in its media publicity is the college that earned accreditation by the Council for Higher Education to grant an academic degree. Above all, however, the public prominence of the soccer team provides the people of Sakhnin with the rare opportunity of entwining local pride with aspirations for integration that are not perceived as threatening by Jews. Soccer is assigned the clear task of paving the way to integration into Israeli society.

Therefore, soccer is viewed by many as a major antidote for the potential negative implications of Sakhnin's nationalist image. For example, Hamid Ghnayem, head of the sports department in the Sakhnin municipality, was careful to schedule important sporting events close to Land Day (March 30). On March 29, 1999, a match was held in Sakhnin between the youths of Sakhnin and the Israel Youth National Team. In a conversation in his office he explained to me: "I intentionally scheduled it for the day before Land Day. I have to change the image of Sakhnin. The media presents Sakhnin as a hostile town, and this is not true."

It is also in this context that we should understand the statement made by a woman from Sakhnin – immediately after winning the State Cup – to a reporter from the Hebrew daily *Ha'aretz*: "Now they will speak of us not only in negative terms of Land Day and demonstrations. I believe this will change the perception. We are part of the state, we want to be part of it, to live together, but not always are we understood. Perhaps through soccer they will see our true face."[7]

The integrative face: soccer

As a small and peripheral village, relatively detached from the cultural transformations that occurred in the large Palestinian cities during the first half of the twentieth century, Sakhnin did not have a soccer team before 1948. However, some of the men who served in the British police were exposed to the game and brought it home. The Palestinian defeat in 1948 undermined many traditional institutions that were blamed for the destruction of Arab Palestine in the war. According to the same logic, some new cultural forms were intensively adopted, partly stemming from an urge to be "promoted" on an imagined scale of modernity. As discussed in chapter 3, the universality of soccer and the sportive ideology that celebrates achievements and "progress" made it a vivid representation of this modernity.

---

[7] Eli Ashkenazi, "Be-Sakhnin Hagegu im ha-Gavi'a," *Ha'aretz*, May 19, 2004.

According to memories of the town elders, in the early 1950s children already played soccer with a rag ball in the village's alleys. At the same time, in many of the Jewish settlements in the Galilee, the game was played with a "real ball," established goals, and formal leagues. Therefore, soccer was seen not only as one of several badges of modernity, but was also associated with the Jewish majority and the state, to create the politically significant triangle of state–sports–modernity. In the absence of the modern Palestinian cities that were destroyed in 1948, including their soccer infrastructure, Jewish settlements were considered the ultimate agents of this modernity.

The production of this cognitive association between soccer and Jews was intensified by the active involvement of the Israeli authorities in promoting soccer in Arab towns. From the 1950s officials invested efforts in order to channel the energies of young Arabs into a sphere that was considered both apolitical and under surveillance. In Sakhnin two soccer clubs were created in the 1960s. The first one, ha-Po'el Sakhnin, was founded in 1961 with the financial support of the Histadrut (see chapter 3). Five years later, a second club was founded in the village, this time by the rival Zionist sports organization, Maccabi.

The two teams attracted affiliates based mainly on overlapping familial, geographic, religious, class, and political lines. Ha-Po'el was traditionally considered as the established team, representing larger, stronger, and wealthier families who were politically closer to Mapai, the ruling Zionist party. Maccabi, established later, served as a default option for smaller families with less political influence in the internal politics of the village and fewer material resources; its supporters traditionally tended to vote more for the Communist Party and considered themselves to be more "nationalist" (for more on the nationalist orientation of Maccabi teams see chapter 3). In 1989, during the first Palestinian uprising in a party of Maccabi Sakhnin, the Palestinian national anthem, *Biladi, Biladi*, was sung. The master of ceremonies was arrested later and sentenced to two months in prison.[8] Both the Maccabi team and its nationalist orientation in the soccer sphere were soon to disappear.

In 1992 the two clubs, ha-Po'el and Maccabi, united in order to form a strong representative team: Ittihad Abnaa Sakhnin. Some of the most loyal fans of Maccabi are nostalgic about the days when they had their own team and are still somewhat bitter, especially because in the official documents of the IFA the team is named ha-Po'el. It seems, however, that for the vast majority of soccer fans in Sakhnin the transition was

---

[8] Interview with the MC, Wajih Abud, July 5, 2000.

relatively smooth. It is noteworthy that this merger was an exceptional and unprecedented step among Arab teams in Israel as well, since familial alliances within localities are strong enough usually to prevent this kind of unification. It is very likely that Sakhnin's uniqueness is related to the power of earlier local patriotism, which is in great part a result of Land Day mythology and the annual commemoration of shared sacrifice.

The merger in Sakhnin turned out to be a very successful one: first, in terms of popularity – 91 percent of the interviewees in my survey from 1999 defined themselves as fans of the united team – even before it climbed to the Premier League; second, in terms of achievement – in no less than four seasons the united club climbed its way from the fourth division up to the second division of the IFA. Within ten years of its unification, Sakhnin climbed to the Premier League, and the following year won the State Cup. Heavy media exposure and growing interaction between the Jewish public and other Arab towns, as well as the rapid professionalization and commercialization of the team, have drastically blurred the previous distinctions between Maccabi and ha-Po'el fans. Thus, the united team became a focus of local Sakhninian pride, rather than a sphere of inter-clan rivalry.

In early 1999, a few months after a heated municipal election, Khalil, a devoted fan of Sakhnin, told me: "This is what is good about soccer. The city has two separate parts, but in soccer everything is together. You should know, before the merger, we had many troubles, but since the merger in soccer, the Christians, the Muslims, the Communists, the Labor Party – everyone [comes] together in soccer, it is not like in the past when we had a coffee shop for ha-Po'el and a coffee shop for Maccabi."

Khalil ascribes to soccer the role of uniting the people of Sakhnin, and assumes that the unification of ha-Po'el and Maccabi made a great contribution to this unity. Whether he is right or whether local patriotism predated the merger (as the Land Day narrative might suggest), statistical evidence supports Khalil's implicit argument that local pride and soccer fandom are closely related. Table 8.2 illustrates that local pride is the only identity examined that has a positive correlation with game attendance.

The construction of local pride around the soccer team must be understood in the wider context of the Arab–Jewish relationship. Setting up soccer as a counterbalance to "Land Day" expresses the attempt of Sakhnin residents to preserve the delicate balance between the need for forceful protest and the fear that excessive protest will result in negative political repercussions. Soccer, therefore, is their space of normal

Table 8.2: *The relation between attendance in the local soccer stadium and the choice of various identities as source of pride*

Frequency of attendance at Sakhnin's soccer matches	Sakhnin (as 1st choice)	Sakhnin (as one of three choices)	The Palestinian people	The Arab nation	The State of Israel	Religion	Hamula (clan)	The Galilee	The men
0 to 2 games	26%	70%	54%	49%	10%	45%	34%	11%	27%
3 games or more	42%	80%	59%	35%	14%	31%	32%	10%	34%
χ^2	$p < 0.05$	$p < 0.1$		$p < 0.05$		$p < 0.1$			

citizenship. It is an area of integration *sans* hazards, in which they aspire to be considered "ordinary" Israeli citizens.

Jamal was a very devoted fan of Sakhnin when I met him in 1999 (later he became a member of the management). He owns a small private business on the main road of Sakhnin, which until October 2000 served many Jewish customers. In an interview with him he explained the importance of soccer, as he sees it: "What I want is that when a soccer team comes to Sakhnin, people will know that we are not violent. This is the image of Sakhnin in particular, and the image of the entire Arab sector. I want them to know that people here are not racist and want to live in dignity and peace."

Soccer provides the opportunity to perform the role of "good citizens." But how is this image actually constructed in the soccer sphere? Observation of soccer matches and public expressions by a diverse group of spectators and participants reveals several concrete practices: the exclusion of Palestinian national symbols, extensive use of Hebrew, an ungrudging attitude towards Jewish players, and selective and cautious reactions to provocations launched by opposing Jewish fans, aiming to define the conflict as "non-national."

The exclusion of Palestinian symbols

On the evening of May 30, 2003 I witnessed a strange spectacle in Sakhnin. Thousands of men crowded the square in the center of the village, and spontaneously celebrated the historical and unexpected climb of the local soccer team to the Premier League. Wedding feasts held that evening quickly were emptied of guests, and the sweating masses who streamed to an improvised celebration site became a single human cluster dancing in circles and chanting cheers of joy. Then, a heavy construction vehicle clumsily rumbled its way through the human swell. The operator stopped in the exact center of the joyful multitude, and began to raise on high a threatening thirty-foot steel arm. The meaning of this surrealistic scene quickly became clear – the machine had been brought by a resident of the village for a single purpose: to celebrate the ascent of Sakhnin to the Premier League by waving a flag. Exactly two months earlier, on March 30, the procession that passed this location proudly carried dozens of Palestinian flags. But for the soccer festivities only one flag was set aside, containing a picture of a horse on a background of red and white. This is the flag of Ittihad Abnaa Sakhnin which became as well the unofficial flag of Sakhnin the town. The Palestinian flag was not to be seen at these celebrations.

At all the soccer games I attended in Sakhnin, as well as at games played by other Arab teams, the Palestinian flag was never waved. Never did I hear Palestinian national slogans. Even at a game (to be described later in detail) in which there was nationalist tension, the fans refrained from mounting displays of Palestinian nationalism. Sakhnin residents are not alienated from their Palestinian belonging, as attested to by the Palestinian flags on Land Day, as well as by symbols and icons of Palestinian nationalism hanging from the internal walls of private homes in the town. In addition, the results of the survey I conducted indicate that second to the local identity, the Palestinian identity is the main subject of collective pride in Sakhnin (see table 8.2). Consistent with this, Arabs in Israel are careful to banish it from the soccer field; there it is liable to interfere with the integrative function that they assign to soccer. Instead, the soccer stands are marked by non-national local patriotism, which has no potential for threatening the Jewish majority.

This is also a reason why the visit by the Palestinian national soccer team to Sakhnin on November 25, 1999, and a match against Sakhnin, failed to attract more than a few hundred spectators (estimates place the number at between 300 and 1,000), despite the media hullabaloo conducted by Arab sports newspapers. For the sake of comparison, a regular league game during that season would attract about 2,000 supporters, and an especially important game, up to 4,000 fans.

Prior to the Oslo accords, expressions of Palestinian nationalism in Israel were considered to be illegal, and even today their legal status is not entirely clear. Beyond the legal issue, in the unwritten code of Arab–Jew relations in Israel, expressions of Palestinian nationalism in the public sphere are considered to be acts of Arab protest against Jews. Therefore, manifestations of Palestinian nationalism among Arabs in Israel are contained within private domains, whereas in public domains they are reserved for demonstrations and memorial days, such as "Land Day" and "Day of the Nakba." The joint agreement between Jews and Arabs about this meaning makes difficult the creation of social spaces that simultaneously contain tendencies of integration with expressions of Palestinian nationalism.

The transformation of the interior of the salon of Mazen Ghnayem, chairman of the Sakhnin soccer club, illustrates this point. On my first visit to his home in 1999, the team was in the second division and Mazen's exposure to the Hebrew media was relatively rare. The decoration on the walls of his salon included diverse forms of Palestinian national symbols, including trophies with the colors of the Palestinian flag and photos of

Yasser Arafat. Following the team's success and the intensive visits of Jewish public figures and journalists, his salon became a highly visible, soccer-related, quasi-public social space. On my visit to his house in August 2004, I noticed that all Palestinian signs had disappeared or were covered with a curtain.

The players participate as well in the de-Palestinization of the soccer sphere. It was not by chance that Samer Mi'ari, a former player and captain of Ittihad Abnaa Sakhnin, was included in the Israeli delegation to the ceremony launching the unofficial Geneva accords in December 2003 signed by Israeli and Palestinian peace activists. For the ceremony organizers, as a player of the multi-ethnic team of Sakhnin, he signified the ability of Jews and Arabs to live in harmony. Mi'ari's name echoes the village of origin of his family, Mi'ar, destroyed in 1948 and whose residents became "internal refugees" in Israel. This sensitive biographic fact has never been mentioned by him to the Hebrew media. On the contrary, Mi'ari, like other Arab soccer players, does the best he can to blur his national identity and avoid anything that has a connotation of the Palestinian national narrative. A reporter from the Hebrew daily *Yediot Aharonot*, who mistook him in Geneva for a member of the Palestinian side, was reprimanded: "I am Israeli exactly as you are ... an Arab-Israeli is not a Palestinian, understand?"

Extensive use of Hebrew

Most of the adult Arabs in Israel are bilingual, speaking both Arabic and Hebrew. Arabic is the spoken language in most Arab homes and in Arab schools. Hebrew is used for daily interactions with Jews and with most of the state's institutions. In addition, Arab citizens are consumers of the Hebrew media as a major source of information and entertainment. Many Hebrew words have also been integrated into the day-to-day language of the Arabs in Israel.

The level of Arabic use may be seen as an indicator of the speaker's frequency of interactions with Jews. In their study of the village of Bart'a, Amara and Kabaha pointed to the existence of a close tie between the tendency to incorporate Hebrew words into the language and the frequency of meeting with Jews (Amara and Kabaha 1996: 163–167). Although the adoption of Hebrew by Palestinian citizens undoubtedly stems from the power relations between Jews and Arabs in Israel, Arab citizens should not be conceived as merely passive actors in their linguistic behavior. Their bilingualism enables them to maneuver between different social spaces and to shape the character of these spheres. More specifically, the relative use of Arabic or Hebrew in a certain social interaction draws attention to the level of the integrationist orientation of the interaction.

As a national minority among a majority of non-Arabic speakers, the Arabic language has become central to the Palestinian national identity of Arabs in Israel (Suleiman and Beit-Hallahmi 1997). Meanwhile, Hebrew, which was first acquired in order to survive, has become a signifier of integration. For example, Arab Knesset members use Arabic in their addresses to the Knesset assembly only when they want to demonstrate an especially high degree of protest. By doing this, they remind the Israeli establishment of their latent separatist aspirations, culturally or even politically.[9] On the other hand, the choice of an author such as Anton Shammas to write in Hebrew was compatible with his desire, at least in the past, to be recognized as an Israeli. The extensive use of Hebrew by Sakhnin fans should be interpreted in this context.

The songs, cheers, and curses heard in Sakhnin games are largely taken from the verbal repertoire of Jewish-Israeli supporters as a whole, and very often they mostly lack a national-based uniqueness. The fans encourage the players with Hebrew expressions such as *ten lo* ("give it to him / hit him") and *hu gadol!* ("he is great!"). The curses are also in Hebrew: *zevel* ("garbage"), *titpater!* ("resign!"). An extreme example, even though not very frequent, is the adoption of anti-Arab racist cries. These curses, such as *'Aravi melukhlakh* ("dirty Arab") are shouted against Arab players who play on Jewish teams – a taunt mixed with a large measure of self-irony. In recent years, with the growing success of Sakhnin, and its emerging status as an Arab flagship team, the relative weight of Arabic slogans has been on the rise. It is interesting that these common Arabic slogans ("Ṣalu a-Nabi" – Pray to the Prophet, "Allah akbar" – God is great) are mainly religious-Islamic, and still do not include exclusive Palestinian nationalist slogans. In addition, the Arabic chants are still dominated by the Hebrew ones.

One could dismiss the extensive use of Hebrew by describing it only as a tool that enables the minority to communicate with the majority. It is true that engagement with soccer exposes the Arab citizens of Israel to enduring patterns of closer interaction with the Jewish majority. Every

[9] Member of Knesset Muhammad Mi'ari from the Progressive List for Peace was especially known for using Arabic in his parliamentary speeches.

week, thousands of Arab fans confront a Jewish soccer audience, in addition to the Jewish players on the Arab teams. Majority–minority relations dictate that the main influence of this interaction will be the adoption of the behavior and expression patterns of the Jewish audience by the Arab audience. And yet, inter-Arab public interactions in the soccer sphere are also immersed in Hebrew. An Arab referee is cursed in Hebrew, and even at intra-Arab games spectators exchange invectives in Hebrew. "Wine, wine, wine, Nazareth is on the prick" (the Hebrew words for wine and prick are *Yayin* and *Zayin*, which makes this slogan a perfect rhyme) is a common slogan chanted by Sakhnin fans against other teams, including the second main Arab team, al-Aakha al-Naṣira, from Nazareth. Sakhnin supporters even claim proprietary interests in the copyright to this Hebrew rhyme. Even the titles appearing on the red and white scarves worn by the fans are printed in Hebrew, and also the stickers which fans apply to their cars proclaim in Hebrew: "Sakhnin – with heart and soul."

A striking example of the status of Hebrew as the *lingua franca* of soccer is that Hebrew appeared during a game between the two most successful Arab teams from Sakhnin and Nazareth in the 1998/9 season. During the week prior to the game, the managers of Nazareth attacked Sakhnin's Arab coach, 'Azmi Naṣṣar, in the Arab media as a part of their long and complex relationship with him. Sakhnin's reaction was more than symbolic. Two large signs were set on the field, facing most of the audience and the television cameras, which stated in Hebrew: "'Azmi, ohavim otkha lanetzah" ("'Azmi, we love you forever"), "'Azmi, Hame'amen ha-bakhir bamigzar he-'arvi" ("'Azmi, the best coach in the Arab sector"). In this case, the writers are Arab, the readers are Arab, and the context is an internal Arab quarrel of which the Jewish fans are totally unaware.

As I have already pointed out, Hebrew is the "public language" for the Arabs in Israel that facilitates their communication with the state's institutions and the Jewish majority. But choosing Hebrew as a language for announcing messages regarding an internal conflict between Arab soccer fans indicates that there is something beyond Hebrew's status as a public language. In order to maintain the role of soccer as an integrative sphere, Hebrew has gained importance and prominence on the field and on the bleachers. Using Hebrew is a practice of "marking" the soccer arena, both inwardly and towards the Jewish community, as the area of integration. Unlike the games of the Islamic League (see chapter 6), in which the repertoire of encouragement, drawn from the Egyptian League, attests to an isolationist orientation, the general league games are assigned an integrative function and the language is chosen accordingly.

Jewish players in Sakhnin

With the growing professionalization of the club, the relative share of Arab players has declined. Only half of the players who won the State Cup were Arabs. The non-Arab players are Israeli Jews and foreign players from various countries, mostly East European. These changes have not impaired the status of the club as a focus of local pride (partly due to the fact that most of the Arab players are local), nor did it prevent Arab fans from outside Sakhnin from considering it as representing all Arabs in Israel. For the club's managers and local politicians, however, the multi-ethnic character of Abnaa Sakhnin was an important asset. It is a fact that they mention very frequently in their public declarations to the Hebrew media as proof of the tolerant nature and integrative tendencies of Sakhnin.

In my conversations with them, Sakhnin supporters repeatedly cited their great satisfaction with Sakhnin's Jewish players and praised their successful integration into the team. Some of the Jewish players received Arabicized nicknames – the Jewish player Tsabar Daniel, for instance, was called "Ṣabri" (an Arab name) by Sakhnin fans. The Jewish goalie from Bet She'an, Meir Cohen, who left Sakhnin in mid-season 1999–2000 for a more lucrative contract with a Premier League club (and returned later in 2004), received an emotional send-off by thousands of cheering fans at his last game: "Stay, stay," and his difficulty at leaving was clearly discernible. The supportive attitude towards Jews was honest, not contrived, but it does seem that Sakhnin fans also enjoy publicly demonstrating it, before me and before the Jewish public in general. Therefore, also in the interaction with hired Jewish players there is room for the establishment of a limited space of normal citizenship.

Non-national conflicts

On February 2, 1999, Ittiḥad Abnaa Sakhnin played in the final of the second division's Toto Trophy. The game took place in the national stadium in Ramat Gan, the most central site of Israeli soccer. Sakhnin played against ha-Koach Ramat Gan, but the attention and alertness of the fans was directed towards the encounters with fans of another team that was scheduled to play in the subsequent game.

This team was Beitar Yerushalaim (Jerusalem), a team whose fans have been traditionally identified as right-wingers, and racist anti-Arab slogans constitute an integral part of their repertoire. Past encounters of Beitar fans with another Arab team, ha-Po'el Ṭaibeh, ended up in a nationalist verbal confrontation (Ben-Porat 2001b).

Sakhnin and Beitar fans were located on opposing bleachers in the stadium. Beitar fans did not wait long before starting the provocations, shouting, "Death to the Arabs! Death to the Arabs!" At first Sakhnin fans, determined to shape the encounter as "purely sportive," rather than as a national confrontation, simply ignored them. When the game started, Sakhnin's fans began cheering their team with the regular repertoire, mainly Hebrew slogans such as, "Sakhnin, the first (goal) is on its way" and "The cup is ours!" Beitar fans tried again: "Death to the Arabs," "Haide Bibi" ("Way to go, Bibi," referring to the nickname of the right-wing prime minister at the time, Binyamin Netanyahu). Sakhnin's fans reacted again in Hebrew: "Zevel! Zevel!" ("Garbage! Garbage!") and "Yerushalaim 'al ha-Zayin" (literally translated – "Jerusalem on the prick"). One lone fan dared to violate the consistent attempt of his colleagues to avoid any expression that might produce an Arab–Jewish confrontation and cried, "Death to the Jews!" – but he was immediately silenced by other fans.

Beitar fans continued: "Haide Bibi!" At this point something happened that best illustrated the urge of Sakhnin's fans to paint the event as an internal Israeli dispute rather than an Arab–Jewish struggle. They shouted, "Bibi, son of a bitch!" and "Haide Barak!" referring to the opposition candidate for the prime minister's position at that time, Ehud Barak. Ignoring the "Death to the Arabs" cries and praising the opposition candidate was a strategic choice: "Haide Barak" was a slogan that, at that time, half of the Jewish public in Israel could identify with.

In time, tempers cooled. Beitar fans cheered ha-Koach Ramat Gan, but Sakhnin fans paid them no attention. To the great disappointment of their fans, the Sakhnin players demonstrated their sorriest play of the season, losing after an extension 2:0. Their disappointment was great, but interest remained high – the next game featured Beitar against Maccabi Tel Aviv, and the Sakhnin fans had an unmistakable preference. Barely a few minutes passed after the end of the Sakhnin game, and the fans began to cheer on Maccabi in a further attempt to erase any sign of an Arab–Jewish conflict.

But before the game began, the fans had to pass another test – the singing of the national anthem. It is not every day that a large Arab audience finds itself at an official ceremony where the national anthem of the State of Israel is sung. When the announcer announced the singing of ha-Tikva, the Israeli national anthem, an uneasy feeling came over the Sakhnin crowd. The song began and the fans looked at one another to see what to do. I, sitting among them and not wanting to demonstrate my being an exception, waited to see what they would do. From the nearby stands, supporters of the Jewish teams looked at the Sakhnin fans with curiosity: would they stand to attention? After a few seconds a few fans stood, and soon most of the Sakhnin crowd (about two-thirds) were on their feet. Despite this gesture, a group of fans located at the southern end of the stands, far from the Jewish fans, remained seated. The anthem ended, and it seemed like a silent sigh of relief rose from the rows of Sakhnin spectators. Five years later, on the occasion of the State Cup finals, the Sakhnin supporters were more experienced. They stood on their feet long before the anthem; when the anthem began they remained standing. Thus, in their own eyes, they did not rise for the anthem, but they were not perceived by the Jewish fans as having dishonored it.

In 2003, Sakhnin moved up to the Premier League, and on December 6, 2003 faced off against Beitar Yerushalaim in Teddy Stadium. Although this was not the first instance of an Arab team playing Beitar, Sakhnin's nationalistic image as perceived by the Jewish public turned the game in the eyes of many fans into the ultimate confrontation between Jews and Arabs. The Israeli police, realizing the explosive potential of the game, took pre-emptive steps and arrested twenty-three Beitar fans who had shouted "Death to the Arabs" even before entering the stadium. The management of Sakhnin did all in its power to minimize the nationalistic significance of the game. The team's spokesman addressed the media in Hebrew: "From the reactions of people I meet there is a kind of feeling that we are going to war or to return occupied territories, but such is not the case. We will arrive on Saturday at Teddy with the object of playing soccer, to enjoy ourselves, and return home with points. This is not a game of Jews against Arabs but a game between two Israeli teams."

A Sakhnin fan who wanted to visually illustrate for the Beitar fans the intention of the team spokesman brought an Israeli flag to the stadium. The irony of the scene was double, for the police had prevented Beitar fans from bringing the Israeli flag into the stadium. The only Israeli flag was to be found in the Sakhnin stands.

Since then, games between Sakhnin and Beitar have been tense and turbulent, if not on the grass, certainly on the stands. In one of these tense games, when the two camps of fans were cursing and throwing plastic bottles at each other, a fan of Sakhnin referred to the fans of Beitar in front of the camera, "They are not Jews, they are racists." Obviously, he did not question the Jewish identity of these fans. The significance of this sentence lies in its sub-text: our conflict with these fans has no ethno-national basis but a moral basis.

"We will beat the state"

The incidents in the Toto Trophy final illustrated the successful efforts made by Sakhnin's fans to maintain the definition of the situation as "purely sportive" even in the context of a clash with Jewish fans. It is noteworthy, however, that this definition is fragile and sensitive. Preservation of soccer as an "integrative enclave" necessitates a considerable investment of energy in the national supervision of the fans and the constant repair of breaches. Usually a non-conflictual definition of the situation, or at least non-nationalist, which suspends the Arab–Israeli conflict and overt political confrontations with the state, is preserved. However, under extreme circumstances, like when Sakhnin's fans feel they have been blatantly discriminated against by the referee, it might collapse. This kind of scenario constitutes a metaphor too close to the socio-political reality in which the Arabs in Israel live. The collapse of the "integrative enclave" is relatively rare, but when it happens, it crashes loudly.

On Saturday, March 3, 1999, in the twenty-first round (out of thirty) of the 1998/9 season, Sakhnin arrived to play against ha-Po'el Lod. The game took place in Kafr Kana, because of a punishment imposed on Sakhnin as a consequence of the disruption to the game by fans who threw bottles onto the field a few weeks before. Despite this, approximately 1,000 Sakhnin fans arrived at the field. Lod was considered to be a relatively weak club that was no match for Sakhnin; Sakhnin fans were optimistic.

Sakhnin began playing with their customary attacking style, putting great pressure on their rival. The crowd became encouraged, shouting as usual, in Hebrew: "Go on Sakhnin, first on the way!" But in the seventh minute the Sakhnin defense made a palpable error. 1:0 for Lod. Sakhnin's players continued to attack Lod's goal throughout the first half, but failed to score.

The second half began, and the scenario repeated itself. Sakhnin pressed, but after five minutes failed to block a fast-break goal. The Sakhnin spectators were convinced that there was an offside, and complaints were directed at the linesman, who was separated from the grandstand fence by less than two meters. The linesman was peppered with a hail of spitting and curses. At first the obscenities remained within the accepted repertoire of soccer games: "Son of a bitch," "Garbage," etc. At this stage the police intervened to shield the linesman. The appearance of uniformed men immediately created a change in the definition of the conflict. No longer a case of soccer fans embittered by a referee's call, it was now Jews versus Arabs, rulers versus the oppressed. The frustration of Sakhnin's fans was directed towards the policemen. Verbal exchanges proceeded apace: "Racist cops!" "You police Arabs, they send you only to Arab games!" "Go to Beitar, the state's team, Bibi's team!" "You are all on the prick, all of Israel is on the prick!" The shouts were accompanied by a shower of spit and refuse in the direction of the police. The game was halted for a few minutes. The chairman of the Sakhnin team, Mazen Ghnayem, tried to calm the crowd, and was partially successful. The game resumed but the protests did not cease. The fact that uniformed personnel had to come to the aid of the linesman emphasized his identity as a Jew, and the shouts of the Sakhnin fans related to this fact. They launched at him personal insults, relating directly to the Jewish–Arab conflict: "May the Hamas wait for you at home!" "May Ahmad Yassin [the leader of Hamas] send you someone to kill you!" "Go to Lebanon!" "May the Hizballah kill you and your brothers in Lebanon!" The linesman, his back already soaked with spittle, was careful not to react. The fact that I, as a Jew, sat among them did not deter the fans from shouting these curses. Those sitting near me were well aware of my presence and my identity.

Sakhnin continued to be superior on the field, and endured long stretches where they were unable to strike the goal. Towards the end of the game, it seemed that justice was about to reappear. In the 78th minute, Sakhnin scored. Three minutes later it equalized the score, 2:2. The Sakhnin crowd was wild with joy: "The third is on the way! The third is on the way!" But accounts with the state were not yet settled, and one of the fans called to the police: "*It won't help you, we will beat the cops, we will beat the referees, we will beat the state!*" His shout summarized the definition of the new situation – the police are the agents of the state, fulfilling their job against its Arab citizens. The game had become a head-on Arab–Jew confrontation.

Towards the end of the game, ha-Po'el Lod made a substitution, sending in Geraldo, the dark-skinned Brazilian who had played for Sakhnin in the first round and then transferred to Lod. The crowd did not take into account his earlier devoted service to the team. Whenever he touched the ball, sounds imitating monkey voices were heard, a racist taunt commonly used against dark-skinned players, even by some Arab fans. But the events of the game, which had already become – in the eyes of the fans – part of their conflict with the Jewish state, were also affecting the attitude towards Geraldo, and one of the spectators shouted (in Arabic, this time): "He's already become a Jew!"

Two minutes to go. A Sakhnin ball hit the top bar of Lod's goalpost. A minute passed. Again the spectators were pulling their hair as a Sakhnin forward missed from right in front of the goal. The final minute: in a fast break Lod scored again and the game ended 3:2 in Lod's favor. The shocked crowd dispersed in relative silence. The many policemen who had been waiting at the exit in anticipation of riots remained unemployed. One of the fans told them: "You came for nothing."

The incidents in the game against Lod were exceptions to the rule. The feelings of discrimination by the linesman and the rushing of uniformed personnel to protect him were a fairly accurate metaphor for the socio-political reality in which residents of Sakhnin live as Arab-Palestinians in Israel. The fragile maintenance of the soccer sphere as an arena unconnected to the Arab–Israeli conflict collapsed when the referee was perceived as having discriminated in a typical fashion, and when uniformed police forces stood at his side. This was the only occasion in all the games which I have witnessed that this apolitical definition was breached, but it seems that when it is broken its force is overwhelming. Before Sakhnin climbed to the Premier League punishment by away games has almost become a tradition with Sakhnin – every year the club management loses much money because games are played away from Sakhnin, sometimes without spectators, as a punitive measure.

Soccer and modernity

In Sakhnin, as in other Arab localities soccer has played an important role in representing the state as modern. The universality of soccer, its "biography" as a cultural product originating in Europe, and the ideology of sports which prizes talent, performance, and competition (Bromberger 1995), has made it a tangible and potent representation of "progress." The modernist discourse that presumes parallel linear development of certain values and technology is reflected in the attitude of fans towards soccer. Thus soccer not only nurtures the collective pride of the people of Sakhnin. It facilitates as well an improvement of their position on the imagined scale of modernity in the eyes of the Jews. Jamal, the same fan who told me, "I want them to know that people here are not racist" has some additional reasons to love soccer:

In my opinion, soccer is more modern and I love everything new. The people in Tel Aviv, the Jews, see us as second-class people, undeveloped. For example, on the soccer fields I see that when one curses his friend – what does he call him – "Arab" – that is to say we are not human beings. Soccer is modern – a person can develop his own intelligence – you go – a different atmosphere, people, crowd. But there is a stigma. There are people, especially in the center of the country, who think we are still in the 1960s. Today every house has a computer; almost every house has the internet ...

This is to say that successful soccer in Sakhnin is proof of a certain inner quality of Sakhnin. It is not a "backward village" located at the bottom of the continuum of modernity ("undeveloped") and chronologically retarded ("the 1960s"). It is a modern city with soccer and the internet.

The identification of the civic Israeli sphere with modernity and the distinction between the national and the civic arenas are often expressed in the terminology chosen to describe Sakhnin. Even though in 1995 Sakhnin obtained the formal status of a city, in terms of the poor condition of its infrastructure, and the historical memory of the inhabitants, Sakhnin is a village. But the use of the terms "city" and "village" also depends upon the political context in which Sakhnin is mentioned. In matters related to the Palestinian national arena, the term *balad* (Arabic for village) is the more widespread. The term *balad* has connotations of roots, of traditional folksiness, and primarily of the *fallah* (Arabic for peasant), a term that has a place of honor in Palestinian national mythology. When a text is addressed to Israeli Jews, and especially in the context of soccer, the term "city" is generally used. One reason for this is the importance that many residents attach to their position on the imagined tradition–modernity spectrum in the eyes of the Jews. A "city" is considered "more modern" than a village. Sakhnin is therefore both a "city of soccer" and a "martyrs' village."

Women may not enter

In most of the world, soccer is still considered a masculine sport, although during the past two decades there has seen dramatic change – women's soccer leagues have been established in many countries. Echoes of this global phenomenon have reached – but just barely – Israel; the approximation of a spirit of relative equality on the soccer field has been largely limited to the ethno-national conflicts, and remains almost totally absent within gender equality. In 1998, in order to comply with European regulations, the IFA hastily established a women's league. Until 2005, however, the lack of minimal funds impaired the league's regular activity.

At its inception, this league included one Arab team from Nazareth, *al-Aakha al-Naṣira* (since disbanded). Since 2003, only one Arab team plays, Barat Sakhnin (the "Daughters of Sakhnin"). In other Arab localities women demanded the establishment of women's teams, and the process is still underway, although their ability to compete with the men's teams for resources is very limited. In 2000, an Arab player, Diana 'Aweisat from Baqa al-Gharbiyya, was invited to join the Israeli national team, and Silvia Amsis of Ramleh soon joined her. Both received positive treatment from the Arab sports media.

The presence of women in the soccer stands has also become more widespread throughout the world. However, their presence in the Sakhnin stands during my field study (1998–2001) was rare. In all fourteen local games which I attended in Sakhnin, I never saw women (with the exception of very young girls accompanying their fathers). Male fans whom I interviewed attend games with their male friends or their children, but never in the company of a woman. The presence of women was tolerated only on an ad hoc basis, at rare and important games such as the State Cup Final.

The absence of women from the stadium at Sakhnin was not a simple derivative of their disbarment from the world of sports. Actually, the first athletes to win in national competitions and earn Sakhnin its first sporting prestige were girls from the Sakhnin high school athletic club in the late 1980s. These girls were even involved in a public scandal when they refused to carry the Israeli flag at an international competition where they were supposed to represent Israel (this confrontational approach is diametrically opposed to the appeasing attitude of most male soccer fans). In 2000, Shirin Zbeidat of Sakhnin won the Israel short distance championship. In the opening ceremony of the 1999–2000 soccer season held on the local pitch, Zbeidat sat on the stage among the honorees, and even received an appreciation cup from the mayor. Immediately after the ceremony, however, she returned home, not remaining to watch the game – further emphasizing the gap between the social acceptance of her sporting achievements and the uneasiness she probably felt in the soccer stadium.

During the period in which my study was made, the girls' team of Sakhnin won the Israel high school soccer championship and ironically received the honor to represent Israel in the Maccabiah Games (the "Jewish Olympics"). In 2000 Sakhnin joined the women's soccer league and in 2003 no less than four Sakhnin girls played on the Israeli national team for girls – an amazing proportion considering the size of Sakhnin. Among women in Sakhnin there is great interest in soccer in general and in the Sakhnin team in particular – but they do not feel comfortable in the local soccer bleachers.

The absence of women from the soccer bleachers reflects the wider absence of Arab women from the soccer stands. This absence is in contrast to their gradual entry into other public arenas, such as communications, law, and national politics (an Arab woman was elected as a member of the Knesset in 1999). In Sakhnin itself, despite the absence of women even from local politics, they are not absent from the political sphere, as evidenced by their large participation in the events of Land Day and other occasions of national protest. In contrast to the "integrative enclave" of soccer, there is no difficulty in including women in national protest events. In 2001, Sakhnin even hosted the "Conference of the Arab Woman," the first gathering of Palestinian feminist activists from Israel and the West Bank. Words spoken at the conference confirmed the effort to entwine the feminist discourse within a Palestinian nationalist discourse (Al-Zahara 2001).

The indirect barring of women from the soccer fields is not unique to Arab fans, but the need to establish an exclusively male public arena is rooted in the specific existential situation of Arab men in Israel. Maria Nelson wrote a book titled: *The Stronger Women Get the More Men Love Football* (1994), in which she argues that sports is a secure area for males who sense a threat to their masculinity. Among the Palestinian minority in Israel, the prevalent difficulties of earning a livelihood and of employment and occupational mobility have seriously damaged the image of the man as economic provider. Arab towns and villages are consistently among the localities with the highest levels of unemployment in Israel; and thus, making a living is difficult for many Arab men. In addition, the exposure to egalitarian patterns of gender relationships found among parts of the Jewish public threatens the masculinty of Arab men (Monterescu 1998; Shoked 1998). Alongside the desire to deepen their interaction with Jews in order to escape their marginality in Jewish society, there exists the fear among many that Arab women will demand for themselves the status enjoyed by Jewish women. Such a demand imperils both the dominance of the male and his identity as an Arab (Shoked 1998). Therefore there is added value to those areas where Jewish–Arab contact occurs on an exclusively male basis.

In secular Israel there exist two massive, exclusively male, competitive spheres – the military combat units (Sasson-Levy 2002) and the soccer field. The army is off-limits to most the Arab men but the soccer fields are highly available. Archetti (1994) claims that soccer in particular is necessary when there is no war. In this sense, the soccer field may provide Arab young men with an alternate arena for reinforcement of masculinity; Jewish youth has the army. This perception may contribute to an understanding of the great popularity of soccer among Arab males as compared with Jewish males.

From the previous discussion, it may be inferred that not only are women deterred from entering the stadium gates; women are also actively barred from the stadium by males. From among the 174 men interviewed in the Sakhnin survey, 58 percent expressed objection to the idea of their wives or sisters accompanying them to a soccer game; only 21 percent said that if requested, they would acquiesce. The prevalent reason given by the interviewees for their objection to the attendance of soccer matches by female members of their family was concern that the women would be exposed to curses and vulgar language. The main fear was of the sexual metaphors used by the fans in relating to members of the opposing team and its fans.

Khawla Abu Baker writes that gossip is a major weapon directed against women in Arab society in order to distance them from the public arena (Abu Baker 1999: 147–149). This phenomenon was reflected in my conversations with fans, which revealed that it is not so much the exposure itself that bothers them, but rather the image which will be assigned a girl who is willing to expose herself to this masculine discourse: "My father is an open-minded man, but not so much as to agree that my sisters could attend a soccer game. There are curses that I cannot even hear such a thing. If a girl comes, they will say – 'If she can listen to such things she must be a *sharmuta* [a prostitute]'" ('Amran, a Sakhnin supporter).

In 'Amran's words we can witness a particular segment of the vicious circle that denies women access to the soccer field. On the field one hears explicit and blatant sexual invective. The game is generally compared to a violent sexual act in which the favorite team fulfills the role of the active male, while the rival team fulfills the passive female role ("on the prick," "we'll fuck you"). Humiliation of the adversary through his feminization works indirectly to distance women from the stands. The use of aggressive sexual metaphors marks the field as male territory; a woman who enters male territory marked by sexual aggression attests to her surrender. Therefore a woman who is prepared to listen to these male expressions "must be a *sharmuta*" – a harlot. 'Amran is fearful of the stigma which may adhere to his family should his sister appear at the field, and therefore he objects to her coming. He unequivocally identifies the family as the rejecting agent. The male audience feels at ease to continue to employ sexual metaphors in its cries, secure that there are no women within hearing range, thus reinforcing their social distance from the activities of the soccer field.

Despite these prevailing tendencies, some of the people with whom I spoke expressed willingness to accompany a female family member to a game outside of Sakhnin, but not within Sakhnin. This trepidation is also mirrored in Jamal's explanations: "You understand, the tendency of soccer is masculine. There are lots of curses. It is not in keeping with our ideas. I would have no problem with my wife being at the field, but not alone. I would set up stands for them. You cannot be different from all the others."

Jamal would see no problem in having his wife watch the game if there were separate stands. The separate stand achieves a number of goals – it distances the daughter from the sexual idiom of the male stands, it saves the husband from being "different," and it preserves a male territory where one may continue "to curse." But the cause-and-effect relationships are not as clear as Jamal describes. In the Islamic League (see chapter 6) there is total prohibition against women entering the stadium. This is part of the separation between men and women customary in all areas, in keeping with the religious tenets of the Islamic Movement. But in the Islamic League, curses are rarely heard. This linguistic moderation declaratively derives from religious restraint and self-control, but it may also be linked to the fact that women's admission to the field is prevented at a very early stage, and there is no need to erect additional barriers.

Implicit in Jamal's phrase, "our ideas," is a contrast: "our ideas" as against "your ideas" directed at me, as a Jew. Such phrases as "our ways are different than your ways" in reference to the status of women were reiterated time and again in my conversations with men in Sakhnin. In the arena in which Jamal seeks to be accepted by the Jewish males he prefers to do so without the threatening presence of women. There is a double threat latent in the interaction with Jews in the company of a woman: the pattern of male–female relations among some of the Jews, as perceived by Jamal, which may threaten his identity as a man and as an Arab; and secondly, the patterns of relationships between him and his wife are liable to be perceived as "not modern" by the Jews, placing him on the slippery slope along the imagined spectrum of modernity, which is so important to Jamal, as witnessed earlier.

The neighbors

It should be noted that soccer is used as an integrative enclave not only by the residents of Sakhnin, but also by the Jewish public. Many residents of Jewish settlements near Sakhnin also joined the spontaneous festivities celebrating Sakhnin's ascent to the Premier League and later their winning the State Cup. True, the joy was for joy for its own sake, reinforcing equally shared Arab–Jewish pride originating from a sense of local geographic proximity. Still, under the surface lies serious tension flowing from the political goals which brought about the establishment of politically contested Jewish settlements very near to Sakhnin.

As stated earlier, Sakhnin is geographically choked from all sides, without any possibility of further enlargement and greater development. To the east is the village of 'Arabeh and on the west, an industrial area. To the southwest is an Israeli Defense Force base and a military research plant, which arouse suspicions among the residents of Sakhnin and rumors about possible health dangers. To the south is the hilly Yodfat ridge, upon which Jewish settlements were established as part of the "Judaization of Galilee" project. To the north of Sakhnin lies a former military outpost, set up as part of the same program, which in 1997 was converted into a civil settlement, Kibbutz Eshbal. In 2002, the kibbutz's outline plan[10] was approved by the National Council for Planning and Construction, thus, in effect, abolishing any possibility for Sakhnin to expand. This suffocating atmosphere, say many in Sakhnin, will lead sooner or later to additional eruption of violence.

On the heels of the Sakhnin's ascent to the Premier League, "The Circle of Sakhnin Supporters" which had been organized in Kibbutz Eshbal, organized a festive evening event to which the players and management of the team were invited. The members of Kibbutz Eshbal – secularists, middle class, self-proclaimed liberals – serve as a tool in the Israeli government's struggle against the Arab majority in the Galilee. Their attempts to come close to the residents of Sakhnin, and to organize joint activities, are received by residents of Sakhnin with suspicious politeness and with polite suspicion. Support for the team may also be understood as part of a strategic plan on the part of the members of Eshbal to bridge the gap between their self-image as liberals and peace-seekers and the oppressive political function for which their settlement was established.

Soccer as an integrative sphere – a statistical examination

Arguing that soccer is dedicated mainly to the integrative tendencies of Sakhnin means that individuals perform their integrative role in this sphere and save expressions of national political protest for other occasions. At the same time, however, another prediction stems from this argument. If the soccer sphere indeed has "integrative qualities," individuals who are involved in it would be expected to display a higher level of integrative tendencies than individuals who are not involved in it.

The local survey in Sakhnin was administered only a few weeks before the May 1999 elections. The timing of the survey was fortuitous since the forthcoming local elections facilitated inquiries into the voting intentions of those surveyed. In this regard, two indicators of political integration tendencies were measured. The first question asked whether or not the interviewee intended to vote in the upcoming election. This is a

[10] The Outline Plan is a zoning plan designed by the government which defines the boundaries of every locality.

conventional measure for probing political integration, although in this particular case a note of caution must be included. For Arabs in Israel, not voting has at least two possible different meanings: the demonstration of disinterest in politics, or an indication of an act of protest. Because of these contradictory meanings, a second indicator was considered; and it gauged whether or not the interviewee intended to vote for a Jewish-Zionist candidate. This indicator does not measure acceptance of Zionist ideology, as one would initially assume. Rather, since only Zionist candidates had a realistic chance to win in the election, voting outright for such candidates represents an active attempt to exert some influence in the Israeli political sphere. For the purposes of the present study, therefore, I consider it a valid indicator for the interviewee's aspirations of political integration.

At the time the survey was conducted, there were four candidates in the race: three Jewish-Zionists (Binyamin Netanyahu, Ehud Barak, and Yitzhak Mordechai) and one Arab candidate ('Azmi Bishara). It is noteworthy that in the direct election for prime minister (employed in Israel only between 1996 and 2001), the turn-out among Arab voters was considered crucial for the chances of the Labor Party candidate to win the election. In essence, the voters had several options. The first option was not voting. This strategy, as has been said, can be interpreted either as a form of protest[11] or as a reflection of the lack of political involvement. The second option was voting for the Arab candidate 'Azmi Bishara, whose political agenda emphasized Arab nationalism and the establishment of separate Arab institutions. Yet, since he didn't have any real chance of winning, voting for Bishara could have been considered a form of protest. Putting a blank note into the ballot box had exactly the same political effect and therefore I consider it to be of the same category for statistical purposes. The third option was voting for one of the Zionist candidates, which had greater potential for concrete influence on Israeli political alignments, and therefore it represented the highest integration tendencies.

The cross-tabulations of soccer involvement and voting are presented in tables 8.3 and 8.4. The results in table 8.3 indicate a strong association between the tendency to vote for a Zionist candidate and diverse indicators of involvement in the soccer sphere, e.g. attending games at the stadium, listening to live broadcasts of the game on the radio, opening the sports

---

[11] This was a widely adopted strategy later in 2001.

Table 8.3: *Involvement in soccer and voting intentions*

N =	Among voters for a Zionist candidate 79	Among those who do not intend to vote 30	Among those who intend to vote, but did not say/know for whom 25	Among voters for the Arab candidate 14
Attended at least one game of Sakhnin*	85%	70%	52%	50%
Listened to soccer live-radio broadcasts in Arabic*	76%	44%	55%	50%
Open the sports section in the newspaper first**	59%	32%	22%	17%
Watching the weekly TV program which covers Israeli soccer**	67%	36%	35%	50%

Chi-Square significance
** p < 0.001
* p < 0.01

section in the newspaper first, and watching the weekly television program that covers Israeli soccer. Moreover, the statistical association is strongest for the most direct form of involvement – attendance at soccer games in Sakhnin. Among those who intended to vote for a Zionist candidate, 85 percent had attended a Sakhnin match at least once during the season in which the survey took place, compared to 70 percent among those who did not intend to vote, and only half of those voting for Bishara.

The results in table 8.4 demonstrate a small, positive, and statistically insignificant association between attendance at the stadium and the tendency to vote in the 1999 election. At the same time, they testify to a strong, positive, and statistically significant association between attendance at the stadium and the tendency to vote for a Zionist candidate. The

Table 8.4: *Attendance at the local soccer stadium and voting intentions*

Stadium attendance frequency	No attendance	Low attendance (1–4 games)	High attendance (5 games or more)
N =	45	43	63
Voting in 1999 election	79%	86%	85%
Voting for a Zionist candidate*	27%	70%	60%

Chi-Square significance
* p < 0.01

frequency of attendance at the stadium was found to be less crucial than the question of whether or not the interviewee attended games in the stadium at all. Among those who did not attend the local soccer stadium at all, 27 percent intended to vote for a Zionist candidate, while among those who attended the stadium at least once, 64 percent intended to vote for a Zionist candidate.

Furthermore, this correlation holds even if we control potential variables that might predict political behavior: age, education, occupational status, and the level of religiosity. Tables 4.a and 4.b in appendix 4 show two sets of logistic regression models where the dependent variable is the intention to vote in the 1999 election (table 4.a) and the intention to vote for a Zionist candidate for prime minister (table 4.b). While the tendency to vote in the election is predicted mainly by academic education, involvement in soccer is found to be the *only* variable that significantly predicts voting for a Zionist candidate.

In 1999, Netanyahu was widely considered by the Arab public as responsible for halting the Israeli–Palestinian peace process, economic stagnation, and reversing the gains made by Arab municipalities in their struggle against discrimination under Rabin's government in 1993–1995. Voting for a Zionist candidate in 1999 represented a calculated and tangible political step to influence Israeli politics. Although they painfully regretted their choice later on, at the time, electing Barak was viewed by most of the Arab voters as fostering their collective goal. This perception was shared even by 'Azmi Bishara who withdrew from the race to ensure Barak's victory. And indeed, after Bishara withdrew, combined with the earlier withdrawal of Mordechai, Barak remained the only "anti-Netanyahu" candidate, and subsequently received 95 percent of the Arab votes.

It can therefore be said that soccer involvement is not correlated with general involvement in the Israeli political sphere but it is strongly correlated with practically oriented political behavior. This correlation and the lack of mediation by other potential predictors of political behavior further confirms and validates the argument that soccer in Sakhnin is a sphere in which strong integrative discourses are produced.

The case of soccer and heroic nationalist narrative in Sakhnin shows that localism might be a flexible strategy. Localism can be used alternately as an anchor of nationalist narrative *and* as an alternative to nationalism. The people of Sakhnin navigate between several self-presentations of their local identity: local–national heroism emphasized in the context of the Palestinian sphere; being "just Sakhninian"; and embracing localism as a safety net for their participation in the Jewish-dominated Israeli sphere.

It is noteworthy that both spheres, soccer and heroic patriotism, are not monolithic. Various social agents are involved in struggles over the level of integrative tendencies or nationalist orientations that both Land Day (Rabinowitz 2001; Sorek 2002; Yiftachel 2000) and soccer might represent. However, the dominant voice in each sphere is easy to identify. Soccer provides an opportunity to present an integrative form of civic behavior both for internal Sakhninian purposes and for the Jewish-Israeli public. The assumed "apolitical" nature of soccer and its potential to facilitate integration, has created a sphere in which the people of Sakhnin tend to emphasize their commonness with the Jewish citizens of Israel more than with their Palestinian compatriots. Hence, the spectators on the bleachers, as well as local players, managers, and local politicians, make noticeable efforts to abate national tensions and to use the soccer bleachers to carve out a distinctive territory promoting integration.

9

Conclusion

In the autumn of 2000, relations between Arabs and Jews in Israel reached a crisis point unprecedented since 1948. During the first days of the Palestinian uprising in the occupied territories, the Palestinians inside Israel went on stormy demonstrations which included rock throwing and blocking roads. In some localities the police reacted by shooting live ammunition into the demonstrators, resulting in the killing of thirteen Arab demonstrators. On one level, the uprising of the Arabs in Israel expressed solidarity with the struggle of Palestinians in the West Bank and the Gaza Strip; even more importantly, however, it reflected their frustration over failed attempts to be accepted as equals in a state which constantly proclaims that it is not theirs.

Soccer was, and still is, a major sphere through which many Arab citizens have sought acceptance. Thus, soccer was one of the institutions which suffered the most with the outbreak of violence. On the first Saturday of the riots, the Israeli police canceled soccer games throughout the country – with the exception of the two top divisions, in which only two Arab teams played (their games were postponed as well). The fact that almost all soccer players in Israel were forced to sit idle because of the tense relations between Arabs and Jews shows the degree to which the Arabs had become a prominent factor in Israeli soccer. Furthermore, it constituted a symbolic and tangible expression of the depth of the crisis.

In Sakhnin, two young residents were killed by the police, joining the growing list of the town's martyrs. Sakhnin's first game of that season was delayed for seven weeks, and when the games finally were renewed, bouquets of flowers awaited the first Jewish guest team, ha-Po'el Be'er Sheva. Although the pain and rage had not yet subsided, the collective effort of Sakhnin residents to use soccer as an arena for mollifying relations had not diminished after the traumatic events.

This strong integrative orientation of soccer is not self-evident. Studies of the role of sports in majority–minority relations show that the success of a national, racial, or ethnic minority has the *a priori* potential to contribute to integration or separation (Cronin 1997; MacClancy 1996; Sugden and Bairner 1993; Werbner 1996; Wiggins 1994). It can contribute to sustaining inequality, or, alternatively, it may serve as an arena of protest (Cheska 1988; Hartmann 1996; Hartmann 2000). The lack of national protest and the dominance of an integrative discourse in the soccer sphere in Israel are the result of specific historical dynamic and contemporary structural circumstances.

The integrative enclave and its construction

Historically, the pacifying image of soccer has deep roots in the first decades of the State of Israel. When Palestinian society was destroyed in 1948, soccer had not yet taken root as a popular sports in various social circles, especially those who were not uprooted during the war, and therefore the reconstruction of a sports infrastructure under Israeli rule was easily able to serve the needs of the state's institutions. Under Israeli rule, Arab sports in general and soccer in particular became a tool for diluting the Arab minority's nationalist identification while at the same time preventing political fermentation; soccer became one of the tools used by the state to strengthen its legitimacy among the Arab-Palestinian minority.

Thus, it was not by chance that Palestinian sports established during the Mandate completely disappeared from the collective memory of Arabs in Israel. Among all the journalists and fans with whom I met during the study, not a single person was aware of the existence of pre-1948 Palestinian Arab sports organizations. Even sportswriters imagined that Arab sports did not exist before the establishment of the state. When I was interviewed on this subject for an Arab cable TV station, the information was presented as an earth-shattering "scoop."

This collective amnesia might serve some immediate instrumental needs. Israeli political culture is characterized by a continuous incongruity between different powers and ideologies concerning Israeli collective identity, while the status of Arab citizens serves frequently as a main anchor of controversy. Peled (1992) has suggested the existence of competitive relations between liberal, republican, and ethno-national discourses of citizenship, discourses used in different ways by various groups in Israeli society. Both the republican discourse, which requires a commitment to the declared aims of Zionism, and the ethno-national discourse, which sets Jewish ethnicity as a criterion for inclusion, exclude the Arab minority. Blind to ethnic identity in its ideal form, the liberal discourse remains the only channel for Arabs in Israel to be accepted as citizens and gain access to resources. Therefore, negotiations over the relative importance of each discourse have significant implications for the status of Arab citizens, and social spheres in which the liberal discourse is dominant are highly attractive for them.

In the soccer stadium the ethnic-blind (though not gender-blind) liberal discourse is dominant, perhaps more so than in most other sub-spheres of Israeli cultural and political life. The growing commercialization of the game since the 1980s and the emergence of a capitalist market of players have further enhanced this ethnic-blind discourse. However, the weight of the liberal discourse in the soccer sphere is disproportional to its weight in most of the other public arenas in Israel. The existential predicament of Arabs in a Jewish nation-state and the dilemma of Zionist Jews, stemming from the tension between their self-perception as liberals and their commitment to the Zionist vision of a Jewish state (Rabinowitz 1997), have led to the construction of a fractured public sphere, where various discourses of citizenship are implemented differentially.

Both sides need a sub-sphere where they can implement a liberal-integrative discourse of citizenship without further commitment. On a very fundamental level, the Jewish majority has no interest in expanding the integrationist discourse from the stadium outward. Most of the Jewish public in Israel favors the liberal perception of equal opportunities for Arabs – but only as long as the majority does not risk its superior political status. The Arab minority, for its part, isolates the soccer sphere from any Palestinian nationalist tones. At the same time, Arab fans and players take advantage of some forms of discourse available in the sports field – such as equal opportunity and meritocracy – to supply their vital need for the implementation of the liberal discourse of citizenship.

Therefore, the construction of soccer as an "integrative enclave" is facilitated by the ad hoc interests of the Hebrew sports media and state institutions on the one hand, and the Arab soccer fans, players, and bureaucrats on the other. For years the latent power of soccer as an arena in which the Arab citizen can feel equal to the Jewish citizen has tempted the Hebrew media to argue – implicitly or explicitly – that sports proves that equality between Arabs and Jews in the State of Israel is possible. This discourse, steeped in self-flattery because of the opportunity for Jewish Israelis to view themselves as liberal and tolerant, is widespread in many sports-related fields, especially those related to the symbolic construction of Israeli national identity.

One anecdote, which illustrates this argument, can be found in the search for an Arab ambassador. In 1995, when the Foreign Ministry was looking for someone to serve as the first Arab ambassador, the Arab soccer broadcaster, Zuheir Bahlul, was suggested as a candidate. Bahlul had neither prior experience in diplomacy nor intimate familiarity with the target country (Finland). However, because he came from the soccer sphere and was famous for his virtuoso sports broadcasts in Hebrew, he was considered "Israeli enough" to represent the state abroad. Even more significant are the ways Arab citizens are represented in the formal national narratives. In the TV series *Tkuma* (Revival), produced as part of the fiftieth anniversary celebrations of the State of Israel in 1998, the episode dealing with the Arab citizens opened with an archive film showing Rif'at Turk, the first Arab player in the Israeli national team, scoring a goal. Furthermore, in a pavilion devoted to "The Arabs of Israel" in the Jubilee exhibition held in 1998, the presence of soccer players was very prominent.

Since external political struggles consistently reproduce and emphasize ethno-national identities, particular effort is invested by Arab fans and players in excluding elements that could undermine this discourse in the soccer field. The ability to insert wedges between different social arenas is certainly the lot of ethnic and national minorities throughout the world, but in conditions of intense tension between contradictory expectations that derive from different collective affiliations this compartmentalization becomes an existential necessity. The concept of "integrative enclave" may help in the analysis and understanding of ethno-national minority relations with the nation-state in other contexts as well. An enclave such as this is the combined product of the majority's interest in the preservation of the status quo, and the need of a discriminated-against national minority to maintain active protest while at the same time preserving proper relations with the majority society.

The sports arena is an ideal arena for the formation of an integrative enclave, but one can discern additional arenas, such as: theatre, where, as in the sports arena, role playing in combination with a professional discourse make possible the bridging of nationalist differences (Horowitz 1993); music, where Jewish and Arab composers and performers meet and maintain small integrative enclaves;[1] or the health system, in which Arab doctors sometimes treat Jewish patients, reversing the power relations which exist in day-to-day life (Rabinowitz 1992). A completely different, yet still similar, example is the underworld, where Arab and

---

[1] Noam Ben-Ze'ev, "To dream and to perform," *Ha'aretz*, November 12, 2003.

Jewish criminals maintain fruitful partnerships, as economic interests and a common enemy (the police) blur nationalist boundaries. The soccer arena differs from theatre and music, as well as from hospitals and the underworld, in its degree of popularity, in the wide audiences that participate, and in the competitive drama it generates – hence its centrality as an arena of integration.

The paradox of soccer as a political sphere

In terms of Arab fans and players, this book points to a series of findings which, when placed alongside each other, paint an ostensibly paradoxical picture. On the one hand, most of these fans devote effort to the construction of sports as an "apolitical" arena and to the fortification of the boundaries between it and the political arena. On the other hand, one discerns attempts by the Arab-Palestinian citizens of Israel to utilize their success in soccer as a tool in their demands for social equality. Furthermore, the positive correlation between attendance at the soccer stadium and the tendency to vote for Zionist parties and candidates alludes to the spilling over of the political meanings produced in the stadium beyond the sports arena. At the same time, since pride in Palestinian identity is negatively correlated with attendance at soccer games, and since Palestinian identity is considered as more "political" than other identities, it is possible as well to describe soccer as an agent of depoliticization of the Arab minority in Israel.

It seems that the key to understanding this complexity lies in a sensitive approach to the term "political" in ethnic conflicts. A survey held in the USA in 1975 showed that although the large majority of both blacks and whites believed that sports and politics should not be mixed, 57 percent of blacks and only 32 percent of whites justified the protest of black athletes in the 1968 Olympic Games. Hartmann (2003) explains that these findings might reflect the fact that for blacks, the struggle for equality is a moral issue, not a political one. Similarly, in Israel, any discussion of soccer as a political sphere should consider the meaning of the word "political." In Israel, as long as the Israeli–Palestinian conflict endures, the Palestinian identity of Arab citizens will remain an irritant to many Jewish Israelis, and will continue to be considered as "political." Therefore, an important element of the depoliticization of soccer is the exclusion of Palestinian identity from the field.

At the same time, because soccer is ostensibly apolitical, Arab fans assume that demanding equality from the soccer field outward might be less threatening and more acceptable to the Jewish majority than demanding it in other contexts. Namely, the "depoliticization" of soccer itself is part of the political game. For example, in the wake of Sakhnin's National Cup win in 2004, MP Tibi wrote that "the message sent from the field will perhaps open doors which were slammed shut and locked in the face of Sakhnin, Umm al-Fahm, Taibeh, Rahat, and Nazareth. These victories have their own dynamic."[2] The Arab broadcaster, Zuheir Bahlul, wrote in the same context and on the same day that "sports in particular overcomes historic obstacles, eradicating stereotypes and prejudices."[3]

Indeed, by their massive support for an Arab team who won the Israel State Cup and by their desire to represent Israel on the international level, Arab soccer fans presented the Jewish Israeli public with a dramatic proposal. Their consistent endeavors to articulate their success in Israeli, even patriotic terms, undermine the basic assumption of the hegemonic definition of Israeli identity. They offer, therefore, an Israeliness which is not necessarily Jewish, nor Zionist, and has nothing to do with the ethos of "security," so central to hegemonic Israeli identity. This Israeliness is bilingual, speaks both Arabic and Hebrew, vibrantly switching between or integrating the two. It is secular in its institutional form but tolerant of any religion, and can even tolerate Muslim prayer in the national sphere, like the collective prayer of Sakhnin's Muslim players right after their victory. It is based on active participation in the Israeli arena and on a dialogue between the various ethnic and religious groups within it. It is competitive and achievement-oriented without being predatory and manipulative.

Despite these aspirations of Arab soccer players and fans, and despite the peremptory optimism discerned in the remarks of politicians and journalists following Sakhnin's victory, there is no evidence yet that integration in the sphere of soccer contributes to the Arabs' acceptance by the Jewish majority as citizens with equal rights. This study has provided evidence for the political implications of soccer on Arab fans alone. There remains room, however, for an in-depth and systematic study to determine the ramifications of Jewish fans' exposure to Arab soccer. Only then will we be able to determine to what degree the efforts of Arab fans to shape soccer as a path to integration elicits an echo from the Jewish side.

Therefore, soccer seems to be operating as a latent producer of political power. Since soccer clubs were perceived by Israeli officials as a counterbalance to nationalist subversive tendencies, fans of conspiracy theories among us might welcome these findings. At first glance, they appear to offer an unmistakable confirmation of the "opium for the masses" theory regarding the function of sports in modern society.

[2] *Ma'ariv*, May 19, 2004, p. 13.   [3] *Yediot Aharonot*, May 19, 2004.

As neo-Marxist critics of sports have maintained, sports provides the optimistic promise of achievement while creating the illusion of the absence of structural limitations. Therefore, it has the potential for preserving the existing social order more than challenging it. Furthermore, "This justificatory function flows from sports's typically optimistic ideology of indefinite, linear progress. Progress can only lead to improvement, and hence any system which brings it about must be intrinsically good" (Brohm 1989 [1975]: 178).

Arabs in Israel face discrimination in matters of government budgets, employment opportunities, and prospects for development of their towns and villages. Deep involvement in the soccer arena, however, dulls the feelings of discrimination. As the Arab citizen's involvement in the soccer arena deepens, this egalitarian image receives more respectable weight in his world, and integration into Israeli society is seen to be a realistic possibility. Many fans also devote considerable efforts to preserving the egalitarian and apolitical character of the soccer field, ignoring those bits of political reality that threaten to invade the ideal bubble they have created.

True, soccer is frequently identified among the Arab-Palestinians in Israel with the state. The state, however, is certainly not considered "intrinsically good," as predicted by neo-Marxist scholars. In addition, Arab soccer fans are playing an active role in the construction of meanings in the soccer sphere and therefore there is nothing deterministic in the political significance of sports, and the hegemonic interpretations of soccer are constantly contested. At the same time, the state is still identified by many fans as an agent of some positive values; many of them are connected in one way or another to the elusive but powerful concept of "modernity," and soccer plays a significant role in producing this image of the state. One can give credit to the agency of soccer fans and reject the deterministic and mechanistic approach of Brohm but still admit that he identifies an important potential role that sports might play, and this potential for a politically conservative orientation came into being in the case of Arab–Jewish relations in Israel.

Finally, this study has also illustrated the importance of local identity in defining the boundaries between the "political" and the "apolitical" through its complex relations with national identity. Local pride in Sakhnin fulfills a double function: towards Arabs, the residents of Sakhnin highlight their pride in Sakhnin's status as a focus of struggle and protest against the state; towards Jews, local pride constitutes an apolitical refuge from nationalism, a means of bypassing the nationalistic pride that may threaten Jews, and it is this integrative meaning that is pronounced in the soccer arena.

In Haifa, on the other hand, local pride is related to Haifa's image as an absolute opposite of the discriminatory nature of the state in general. The construction of this contrast enables the Arab citizens of Haifa to simultaneously aspire to integration into Jewish-Israeli society when it is limited to Haifa's boundaries, while preserving their autonomy to express resentment against the broader Jewish public in Israel. This separation between the local and the national can be translated into tangible spatial practices through sympathy for a soccer team that represents the city.

Looking ahead

The integration of the Arab citizens of Israel into the soccer arena, as fans and as players, is a sad success story. During the period when this study was conducted, I became aware of the worldview of a society of which I am not a part. Even though I had earlier met and spoken with Arab-Palestinian citizens of Israel, the focused attention and frequent meetings enabled me to see and experience things much more deeply – and consequently, more empathetically – than before. I became conscious of the feelings of frustration and discrimination, and became witness to a process in which the willingness of the Arabs in Israel to continue to accept their inferior status, as individuals and as a collective, is dissipating. I watched this process take shape in the mayors' protest tent, in which I spent days and nights; in annual Land Day ceremonies in Sakhnin, where I was part of a large crowd tear-gassed for no valid reason – and in hundreds of conversations and fragments of conversation with soccer fans, university students, and people on the street. Surprisingly, this process is barely felt at the soccer games themselves. At games I attended in Sakhnin, Kafr Kana, Nazareth, and Taibeh, the fans tried, usually successfully, to preserve the definition of a "sportive" situation, and to ignore the national belonging which separates them from the Jewish players and fans.

In May 2003, following a victory in the penultimate round, al-Aakhaa al-Nasira, the team from Nazareth, ascended to the Premier League for the first time in history. 'Azmi Nassar, Nazareth's coach, could not contain his joy. He tore off his shirt and climbed the fence to conduct the chorus of supporters rejoicing in the bleachers. In a hoarse voice he spoke from the heart (in Hebrew) to the mass of reporters: "You see, this is how it should be – in soccer, as in life, on our team there are Muslims, Jews, Christians, Druze – there is no difference."

There was something touching in Nassar's cry, which was perhaps a wish, perhaps a reproof to the Jewish audience. In keeping with market economics which have gained control over Israeli soccer, players of different religions, ethnicities, and nationalities play in the ranks for al-Aakha al-Naṣira. Naṣṣar's desire to transform them into a model of interethnic relations in Israel recognizes that we are discussing an enclave of tolerance and integration, while at the same time, he aspires to convert it into a power for fueling change. Is such a change possible?

Despite the shock of both sides over the events of autumn 2000, the political and social factors that produced them have not disappeared. The discriminative mechanisms have remained as efficient as before, and the Israeli–Palestinian conflict in its totality is still far from resolution, threatening occasional escalation and influencing Arab–Jewish relations within the boundaries of the State of Israel.

The Arab-Palestinian minority in Israel is weary of its attempts to convince the Jewish majority of its right to civic equality, and is liable to give up ever finding cracks in the wall of discrimination. The soccer arena holds the potential for blurring the ethnic–national distinctions between Jews and Arabs in Israel, and, in a country where resources are divided in large part according to this distinction this is not an insignificant matter. Indeed, soccer can serve as an ideal model for equality between Jews and Arabs. The danger lies in transforming soccer into an enclave, delineated in time and space, in which equality exists, but whose symbolic power is exploited in order to distract attention from the deprivation and discrimination which rule in almost all other spheres of life.

Appendix 1: Interviews with functionaries

Mayors and heads of sports departments of the municipalities

Jaber Jaber – Mayor of Jaljulia (November 16, 1999)
Husein Heib – Mayor of Tuba Zanghariya (November 22, 1999)
Kamel Rayan – Former Mayor of Kafr Bara (November 26, 1998)
Mazen 'Adawi – Mayor of Ṭur'an (November 21, 1999)
Muhammad Shalabi – Mayor of Iksal (November 21, 1999)
Musa Abu Rumi – Mayor of Ṭamra (November 16, 1999)
Muhammad Abu al-Ful – Mayor of Jat (November 22, 1999)
Muhammas Kan'an – Mayor of Majd al-Kurum (November 22, 1999)
Muṣtafa Abu-Raya – Mayor of Sakhnin (October 24, 1999)
Nawaf Hajuj – Mayor of Kawkab (November 16, 1999)
Ṣaleh Suleiman – Mayor of Bueineh-Nujeidat (November 23, 1999)
Sami 'Issa – Mayor of Kafr Qasim (November 23, 1999)
'Omar Maṭar – Mayor of Nahaf (November 16, 1999)
Jum'a al-Qassassi – Deputy Mayor of Rahat (November 18, 1999)
Ibrahim Qaḍi – Deputy Mayor of Qalanswa (November 23, 1999)
Hamid Ghnayem – Head of Sports Department of Sakhnin municipality (March 13, 1999)
Ahmad Ḥilu – Head of Soccer Department of Nazareth municipality (May 10, 1999)

Club directors

Basem Suleiman – director of al-Aakha al-Naṣira (May 10, 1999)
Ahmad Hawashi – director of ha-Po'el Furaydis (September 24, 1999)
'Omar Yassin – formet director of Maccabi Ṭamra (September 30, 1999)
Shaker Abu al-Hija – former member on the board of ha-Po'el Bnei Ṭamra (September 15, 1999)
Mazen Ghnayem – Chair of Abnaa Sakhnin (January 7, 2000)
Abd Al-Qader Haj Yihia – Chair of ha-Po'el Ṭaibeh (July 15, 1998)

Abd Al-Rahman Haj Yihia – Director of ha-Po'el Ṭaibeh (July 8, 1998)
Fayṣal Khatib – Chair of ha-Po'el Kafr Kana (September 8, 1999)

Islamic Movement activists (without the four mayors from the Islamic Movement)

Hashem Abd al-Rahman (January 2, 1999)
Ṣaleh Luṭfi – director of Sports and Youth in the Islamic Movement (northern faction) (January 16, 1999)
Abd Al-Hakim – director of Al-I'itiṣam Kafr Kana (September 22, 1999)
Salim 'Awawde – editor of the sports section in *Ṣawt al-Ḥaq wal-Ḥurriyya* (September 22, 1999)
Nizam Biadsa – director of the Islamic League (northern section) (June 1, 2000)

Journalists

Jawdat 'Oda – Israeli Broadcast Authority reporter and later editor of the sports column in *al-Ittiḥad* (October 8, 1999)
Wajih 'Abud – former reporter for Kol Israel and director of Neptun – the local cable television station in Sakhnin (May 7, 2000)
As'ad Talhami – editor of the sports column in *al-Ittiḥad* (December 4, 1998)
Walid 'Ayub – editor of the sports column in *Faṣl al-Maqal* (July 1998)
Abd al-Salam Shalabi – editor of the sports column in *al-Ṣinnara* (March 12, 1999)
Yazid Dahamsha – reporter on Radio, 2000 and *Tevel* (July 4, 1998)
Maher 'Awawde – editor of the sports column of *Kul al-'Arab* (April 8, 1999)
Wail Hakrush – reporter of *Fasl al-Maqal* (May 21, 2000)

Functionaries in the 1960s

Victor Shaharabani – chair of the sports department of the Histadrut from 1962 to 1987 (March 2, 2000).
Shmuel Toledano – Adviser to the Prime Minister on Arab Affairs from 1966 to 1977 (April 3, 2000)
Na'im Zilkha – editor of the sports column in *al-Yawm* and *al-'Anbaa'*, Broadcaster on Kol Israel in Arabic, "emissary" of the Histadrut for disseminating sports in Arab villages (January 21, 2000).
Nawaf Muṣalha – player and director, ha-Po'el Kafr Qara', Foreign Minister Deputy 1999–2001 (February 23, 2000).
Ali Sa'd – player and director of ha-Po'el Jaljulia (December 24, 1999)

Appendix 2: Research design of the countrywide survey

Interviewees: 448 Arab men aged 18–50 who constitute a representative sample of this sub-population. The choice to interview only men aimed at ensuring an optimal variance in the independent variables (involvement in soccer) since preliminary fieldwork showed that the presence of Arab women in soccer stadiums is extremely rare. This is also the reason that the maximum age was restricted to 50. The interviews took place in January 2000 in the interviewees' homes.

Sampling: The interviewees were sampled by a two-step sampling. First, statistical areas (SA) were sampled by a proportional layer sampling. The sampling pool included statistical areas that contained at least 5,000 residents in a 1995 census held by the Israeli Central Bureau of Statistics, and statistical areas that contained at least 1,000 residents in localities that included more than one statistical area. The sampling was based on two dimensions: geographical area (the Galilee, the Triangle, the Negev), and education level, measured by the percentage of high-school graduate certificate-holders within the adult population in each area. The areas were distributed according to three educational categories, each one of them consisting of one-third of the areas: Low – less than 30 percent of high-school graduate certificate-holders; Medium – between 30 and 40 percent; and High – above 40 percent. According to these two dimensions a theoretical table of nine categories was composed. Practically, 141 of the 142 areas that were included in the sample were aggregated into seven categories; 15 percent of the SA were sampled from each category. Then, from each SA, 7 to 41 households were sampled. The sample did not include (a) statistical areas with a majority of Druze inhabitants, due to the exceptionality of the Druze case in Arab–Jewish relations; (b) statistical areas in the mixed Arab–Jewish cities, due to the heterogeneity of these areas that prevents the sampling of one representative area; and (c) the only statistical area in the Jerusalem region, the Abu Ghosh village, due to its geographical and social exceptionality. The second stage of the sampling was a "counting houses sampling" within each statistical area (in most of the Arab localities there are no numbers on the buildings).

194

Interviewers: 13 male and female Arab interviewers who were specifically trained for this research.

Questionnaire: the interviewers administered a closed questionnaire in Arabic. It was designed to take approximately 30 minutes and it included three groups of questions, as follows:

Independent variables: involvement in soccer. The interviewees were asked questions about the frequency of their involvement in the soccer sphere in several ways, including attendance at the stadium, watching TV, listening to the radio and reading a newspaper.

Dependent variables: The questionnaire, administered in January 2000, included the questions: "Did you vote in the Knesset elections of 1999?" and "For whom did you vote?" In addition, the interviewees were asked to choose three out of nine identities to which they were most proud to belong: the Palestinian people, the Arab nation, their religious group (Muslim or Christian), the citizens of Israel, their *hamula* (extended family), their town or village, their region (the Galilee, the Triangle, or the Negev), and their gender as men. The term "pride" was chosen to represent the emotional aspect of their identities and to distance the interviewees from "formal" elements of collective identity (such as the identities formally imposed by the authorities).

Controlled variables: (a) age; (b) education (number of school years); (c) active use of Hebrew, self-rated on a scale of 1 to 5, as an indirect indicator of interactions with Jewish citizens; (d) level of religiosity, self-rated on a scale of 1 to 5; and (e) the number of days in the week in which the interviewee reads the newspaper, as an indicator of involvement in the general public sphere.

Statistical procedures: the hypothesis regarding sports–politics relations was tested by a binary logistic regression. For the political vote I used three separate equations in order to measure the contribution of the soccer involvement variables to predict participation in the elections, both voting for Zionist parties and voting for Arab parties. For the pride dimension I used nine separate equations, in each one another identity served as a dichotomous dependent variable (if the identity was selected by the interviewee the value is 1, if not – the value is 0).

Methodological restrictions: The methodology used for this study is vulnerable to the common criticism against surveys in general and surveys among the Arab minority in Israel, including the use of an identity questionnaire in particular. Compared to the relatively high reliability that is attributed to surveys among Jews in Israel, there are many reservations regarding the reliability of surveys among Arabs. The main argument is that the Arab citizens are afraid to freely express their views when they are asked sensitive questions regarding their political identity. It is possible that a certain bias does exist among some of the interviewees, expressed in giving more "pro-establishment" answers. However, there is no need to over-estimate this bias. As Smooha (1998) writes, in surveys he has made since the mid 1970s, the high rate of support for the PLO (considered a terrorist organization by Israeli law until 1993) and a long list of anti-establishment attitudes indicate that collectively the Arabs in Israel are not a frightened public (although, apparently the threat is felt differentially by different segments of the population). Nevertheless, in order to deal with the possible bias I did not use a nominal sampling but used house counting. A nominal sampling employed by an Israeli public institution within the Arab population, especially when political questions are involved, is indeed likely to be threatening.

Appendix 3: Main findings from the countrywide survey

The statistical correlations between feelings of pride and the level of involvement in soccer were measured according to two dimensions of involvement. The first dimension relates to the distinction between the local–ethnic level and the general Israeli level. The second dimension relates to the distinction between immediate (physical attendance) and mediated involvement. These two dimensions produce four modes of involvement: attendance at local stadiums, attendance at the Premier League stadiums, consumption of soccer media in Arabic, and consumption of soccer media in Hebrew. Media consumption is composed of diverse practices and for this I performed a factor analysis that confirmed the existence of the above-mentioned categories (table 3.a).

The five elements of the mediated consumption in the general sphere were aggregated into one index by summation of the standardized score of each variable for each interviewee. This index has a high internal validity ($\alpha = 0.78$). The components of the mediated "Arab sphere" were aggregated the same way into one index. This index has a medium internal reliability ($\alpha = 0.48$).

Table 3.b introduces the correlations between involvements in soccer in the different spheres and different modes, and the pride in belonging to certain groups. The table shows 9 logistic regressions in which the dependent variable is pride (1 = the identity was chosen by the interviewer, 0 = the identity was not chosen). Namely, there is one equation for each identity.[1]

The main findings presented in table 3.b can be summarized as follows:

1. The mediated consumption of soccer in the Arab sphere is positively and significantly correlated with local identity.
2. There is a significant negative correlation between pride in Palestinian identity and attendance at soccer games, especially at the Premier League.

---

[1] The internal Pearson correlations between all of the independent variables, including the controlled variables, were calculated in order to eliminate the possibility of multi-colinearity. Since the highest correlation was 0.27, this possibility was eliminated.

Table 3.a: *Factor analysis of soccer consumption by the media*

	Factor 1: general sphere	Factor 2: Arab sphere
Explained variance (%)	**42**	**18**
Watching live broadcast of a PL game	.83	−.17
Watching the TV program that summarizes the PL game	.71	−.39
Listening to radio broadcast of soccer in Hebrew	.62	.30
Watching games of the Israeli national team	.79	−.22
Reading the sports section in the newspaper first	.64	−.18
Listening to radio broadcast of soccer in Hebrew	.48	.65
Watching the weekly sports TV program in Arabic on Israeli TV	.31	.70

3. Pride in masculine identity is positively correlated with attendance at PL games.
4. The study did not find any significant correlation between involvement in soccer in either mode and pride in belonging to the Arab nation, the State of Israel, the Arabs in Israel, the *hamula*, or the region.
5. The study did not find any significant correlation between mediated consumption in the general sphere and pride in belonging to any social group.
6. Beyond soccer, local pride is found to be positively correlated with reading newspapers and negatively correlated with their level of Hebrew speaking (most likely this reflects the negative correlation between local pride and working outside of one's own locality). Palestinian pride is positively correlated with education and age. Pride in belonging to the State of Israel is negatively correlated with education. Pride in being part of the "the Arabs in Israel" is positively correlated with age and negatively correlated with education.

Table 3.b: *The contribution of each variable to the probability of choosing each identity as a source of pride (standardized logistic coefficients)*

	The Palestinian people	The State of Israel	The Arab nation	The region	The family	The religious community	The interviewee's town/village	The Arabs in Israel	The men
Age	.21**	−.02	.00	.04	−.12	−.21*	−.13	.24**	.07
Education	.23**	−.60****	.24*	.10	.12	−.06	−.17	−.33**	.21
Level of religiosity	−.15	−.04	−.13	.13	−.15	.52****	.17	−.08	−.39***
Active use of Hebrew	.01	.55****	−.08	.05	.18*	−.07	−.43****	.12	.02
Reading newspapers	.14	.03	.06	.08	−.41****	−.08	.51****	−.03	−.29*
Mediated consumption in the general sphere	.07	.05	−.01	−.09	.09	−.10	−.09	.00	−.14
Mediated consumption in the Arab sphere	.03	.00	.07	.08	−.09	−.17	.36***	−.01	−.27*
Attendance at local games	−.27**	.10	−.07	−.04	.16	.10	.02	−.09	.12
Attendance at Premier League games	−.32**	−.07	.00	−.23	.11	−.11	.06	.08	.34***
Interviewer's gender									.50****
Constant	0.27***	−2.03****	−1.31****	−2.03****	.12	.64****	−.04	−1.33****	−1.55****
N =	426	422	422	426	426	423	422	423	422

*P < 0.1 **P < 0.05 ***P < 0.01 ****P < 0.001

Table 3.c: *Attendance at local games and pride in Palestinian identity*

Number of games attended	Number of respondents	Number of respondents who choose Palestinian identity	Average of standardized residual after logistic regression
0	268	131 (49%)	0.05
1 to 16	160	61 (38%)	−0.04
17 or more	15	2 (13%)	−0.52
		χ2 test: p < 0.01	ANOVA test: p < 0.1

Table 3.d: *Attendance at Premier League games and pride in Palestinian identity*

Number of games attended	Number of respondents	Number of respondents who choose Palestinian identity	Average of standardized residuals after logistic regression
0	356	165 (46%)	.04
1 to 5	70	28 (40%)	−.05
6 or more	17	1 (6%)	−.62
		χ2 test: p < 0.01	ANOVA test: p < 0.05

Explaining tables 3.c and 3.d: The right-hand column in each table presents the average of standardized residuals after calculating a logistic regression in which the dependent variable was pride in Palestinian identity, and the independent variable was frequency of attending official soccer competitions in the 1999/2000 season and the controlled variables were: age, level of religiosity, education, active use of Hebrew, and reading newspapers. Namely, the numbers in this column represent the residual contribution of attendance at soccer games to the probability of choosing Palestinian identity as a source of pride, after eliminating the contribution of the controlled variable.

Table 3.e: *Logistic regression model predicting participation, voting for Zionist parties, and voting for Arab parties in the 1999 parliamentary elections in Israel (coefficients are standardized)*

	Voting in the elections (β)	Voting for Zionist parties (β)	Voting for Arab parties (β)
Age	**.36	.13	.08
Education	−.03	−.18	.13
Level of religiosity	**−.30	−.03	−.15
Active use of Hebrew	.18	.57****	−.32***
Reading newspapers	**.34	−.18	.36***
Mediated consumption in the general sphere	.03	−.20	.16
Mediated consumption in the Arab sphere	−.06	−.06	.02
Attendance at local games	.18	.27**	−.12
Attendance at Premier League games	.26	.19	−.10
Constant	1.68****	−1.17****	.27**
N =	364	364	364

*p < 0.1 **p < 0.05 ***p < 0.01 ****p < 0.001

Table 3.f: *Variables predicting at least one attendance at an official soccer game (logistic regression, coefficients β are standardized)*

	Attendance at Premier League games	Attendance at local games
Age	−.45***	−.50****
Education	.04	−.22**
Level of religiosity	−.05	.20*
Active use of Hebrew	.30**	.13
Reading newspapers	.24*	.26**
	−1.53****	−.49****
	436	436

*p < 0.1 **p < 0.05 ***p < 0.01 ****P < 0.001

Table 3.g: *Percentages of interviewees who choose different identities as source of pride by attitude toward the Israeli national team of soccer*

	Palestinian people		The State of Israel		The Arabs in Israel		The men	
	When an Arab player is playing	When no Arab player is playing	When an Arab player is playing	When no Arab player is playing	When an Arab player is not playing	When no Arab player is playing	When an Arab player is playing	When no Arab player is playing
Supporting INT or indifferent	42	40	15	16	24	23	18	17
Supporting the other national team	55	53	6	8	8	16	28	27
$p\ (\chi 2)$	$p < 0.05$	$p < 0.05$	$p < 0.05$	$p < 0.05$	$p < 0.01$		$p < 0.05$	$p < 0.05$
Difference of standardized residual	−.22**	−.21**	.23*	.26*	.28**	.15	−.22*	−.23*

*$p < 0.1$ **$p < 0.05$

The last row presents the difference of standardized residual after calculation of logistic regression in which the dependent variable is the attitude toward the Israeli national team (Supporting INT or indifferent = 1, Supporting the other national team = 0), the main independent variable is choosing/not choosing each identity as a source of pride and the controlled variables are age, education, level of religiosity, and the level of active use of Hebrew. Namely, the number in each cell represents the correlation between the pride in each identity and the attitude towards the Israeli national team when all the other variables are controlled.

Table 3.h: *The differences between Maccabi and Ha-Po'el fans in Arab localities*

	N =	Pride in Palestinian identity	Pride in Israel identity	Average years of schooling
ha-Po'el fans	32	9 (28%)	8 (25%)	11.6
Maccabi fans	40	23 (58%)	2 (5%)	13.5
		$\chi^2 < 0.05$	$\chi^2 < 0.05$	

The legacy of the formative years of Arab soccer in Israel was still reflected in the attitudes of soccer fans in 2000. Compared with the fans of Maccabi teams, among fans of ha-Po'el teams that were considered as closer to the Zionist establishment, the pride in Palestinian identity is lower and the pride in their Israeli identity is higher. This table refers to 72 interviewees who participated in the countrywide survey, inhabitants of seven towns and villages where both ha-Po'el and Maccabi teams were active in 2000, and they identify themselves as fans of one of the two teams.

Appendix 4: Research design of the survey in Sakhnin

Sample: 174 male residents of Sakhnin aged 16 to 40 years were sampled by proportional geographical sampling (geographic borders in Sakhnin highly overlap with familial, class, and political divisions in the town (Rosenfeld and Al-Haj 1990). Sakhnin was divided into six sub-districts according to the division of statistical districts designed by the Israeli Central Bureau of Statistics based on the 1995 census. A proportional number of households were sampled in each district according to the absolute number of households within its boundaries. Interviewers were instructed to walk lengthways through the sub-district in pre-defined routes and to enter every 22nd house (Sakhnin had no street names or numbers in 1999). In each household they randomly selected one man in the appropriate age range (16–40). If there were two men within the appropriate age range in one household, interviewers were instructed to interview the elder the first time, the younger the second time, the elder the third time, and so on. In the case of three potential interviewees at a residence, interviewers were instructed likewise to select each time a different person in cyclical order of their age.

Data collection: The survey was conducted in April 1999. A structured face-to-face questionnaire-based interview was held with each one of the interviewees at their home. The two interviewers were male students from Sakhnin and the neighboring village of Deir Hana.

Dependent variables:
(1) **Voting intentions in the elections for prime minister planned for May 29, 1999 (open question)**
(2) **Pride in belonging to eight identities**: Sakhnin, the *hamula* (clan/extended family), the Palestinian people, the Arab people, the State of Israel, the religious group (Muslim or Christian), the Galilee region, and the men. Interviewers presented the interviewees with eight cards titled with these identities and asked them to choose the three cards of which they are most proud to be a part. These choices were used to create dichotomous variables for each respondent ("chose/did not choose" a certain identity).

204

Table 4.a: *Logistic regression model predicting participation in 1999 election in Sakhnin (coefficients β are standardized)*

	I	II	III
Attendance in local games	.27	.13	.13
Education (academic = 1)	.60**		.64*
Level of religiosity	−.10		
Occupational status		0.30	−15
Age		0.06	
N =	156	142	145
Constant	1.72	1.66	1.71

Table 4.b: *Logistic regression model predicting voting for a Zionist candidate in the 1999 election in Sakhnin (coefficients β are standardized)*

	I	II	III
Attendance in local games	.64***	.58***	.64***
Education (academic = 1)	.03		.31
Level of religiosity	−.21		
Occupational status		−19	−.39
Age		.14	
N =	156	142	145

*** $p < 0.01$
** $p < 0.05$
* $p < 0.1$

Independent variables: Involvement in the local and the Israeli soccer spheres. The questionnaire requested from the respondents to mention the frequency of their involvement in diverse practices of sports consumption, through media and by attending Sakhnin's soccer games. In another type of question the interviewees were asked to list the television and radio sports programs they watch or listen to.

Controlled variables: (1) *age*; (2) *education*: The interviewees were asked to state how many years of school they had completed; the variable was used later as a dichotomous variable: academic education (more than 12 years) vs. non-academic education. (3) *Occupational status*: the interviewees' occupation was coded according to the prestige index created by Kraus and Hodge (1990). (4) *Level of religiosity* was measured by self-ranking on a scale of 1 to 5.

Statistical procedures: In order to measure the correlation between voting intentions and involvement in the soccer sphere independent of demographic variables, I used a series of logistic regressions. Due to restrictions related to the sample size I did not include more than three independent variables in each equation.

Appendix 5: Explanations for chapter 4

On the databases for chapter 4

The calculation is based upon figures relating to the support of sports organizations by the municipalities, from publicly available information obtained from the Sports Authority (SA) of the Ministry of Education, Culture, and Sports. In order to establish standards for support of sports organizations based on the financial resources of the respective councils, I calculated the proportion of investment in sports clubs estimated from the overall general budget of each municipal council. Figures for the regular budgets were taken from the Report of Inspected Financial Figures of the Center for Local Government (FFCLG) for 1998. The Sports Authority provides figures only for plans, not for actual execution, and therefore in both instances the figures relate to the planned budget. My calculations are based exclusively upon the figures of municipalities which met two conditions: they were required to have a population of between 5,000 and 35,000 in 1998 (the logic behind the range: 5,000 is the minimal number for which the Central Bureau of Statistics has agreed-upon figures, while the Arab localities, Nazareth excepted, have no more than 35,000 residents); and relevant figures must have been available from both the SA and the FFCLG. The databases included, therefore, 72 Jewish municipalities and 65 Arab municipalities that met these conditions. Figures for the age pyramid, the Gini index, and the average wage are taken from the figures of the National Insurance Institute for 1997.

Table 5.a: *The ratio of support for local sports associations as predicted by various demographic attributes of localities (coefficients of linear regressions)*

	The ratio of support for sports associations from the total budget	The ratio of support for soccer from the general support for sports associations (calculated for 111 local authorities that support sports associations)
Ratio of high school diploma-holders	-.466**	-.156
Ratio of population under 17 years	-.182	.123
Gini index of income	.248*	-.064
Average wage	.185	-.436***
Nationality (Arab = 1)	.293*	-.110
	R = 0.402	R = 0.614

*p < 0.1 **p < 0.05 ***p < 0.01

Bibliography

Abu Baker, Khawla. 1999. *Bederekh Lo Slula*. Ra'anana: The Center for the Study of Arab Society in Israel (in Hebrew).

Abu-Ghazaleh, Adnan. 1972. "Arab Cultural Nationalism in Palestine during the British Mandate." *Journal of Palestine Studies* 1: 37–63.

Aburaiya, Issam. 1991. "Developmental Leadership: The Case of the Islamic Movement in Umm Al-Fahim, Israel." International Development and Social Change, Clark University, Worcester.

Alawi, Muhammad Kamel. 1947. *Al-Riyaḍa Al-Badaniyya 'Ind Al-'Arab*. Cairo: Maktabat al-Nahda al-Miṣriya.

Al-Haj, Majid. 1993. "The Impact of the Intifada on Arabs in Israel: The Case of Double Peripherality," pp. 64–75 in *Framing the Intifada, Media and People*, eds. A. Cohen and G. Wolfsfeld. Norwood: Albex Publishing.

Al-Khuli, Amin. 1995. *Al-Riyaḍa Wal-Ḥaḍara Al-Islamiyya*. Cairo: Dar al-Fiker al-'Arabi.

Allison, Lincoln. 1986. "Sport and Politics," pp. 1–25 in *The Politics of Sports*, ed. L. Allison. Manchester: Manchester University Press.

Al-Taa'i, 'Ali. 1999. *Al-Tarbiya Al-Badaniyya Fi Al-Turath Al-'Arabi Wal-Islami Khilal Al-'Aṣr Al-Abassi*. Amman: Dar al-Fakr.

Al-Zahara. 2001. *Mu'tamar Al-Mar'a Al-'Arabia Al-Awal*. Sakhnin: Al-Zhara (in Arabic).

Amara, Muhammad and Sufian Kabaha. 1996. *A Split Identity – Political Division and Social Reflections in a Divided Village*. Giv'at Haviva: The Institute for Peace Research (in Hebrew).

Amara, Muhammad and Izhak Schnell. 2004. "Identity Repertoires among Arabs in Israel." *Journal of Ethnic and Migration Studies* 30: 175–193.

Anderson, Benedict. 1991. *Imagined Communities: Reflections on the Origin and Spread of Nationalism*. New York: Verso.

Appadurai, Arjun. 1996. "Playing with Modernity: The Decolonization of Indian Cricket," pp. 89–112 in *Modernity at Large*, ed. A. Appadurai. Minneapolis: University of Minnesota Press.

Archetti, Eduardo. 1994. "Masculinity and Football: The Formation of National Identity in Argentina," pp. 225–244 in *Game without Frontiers: Football, Identity, and Modernity*, eds. R. Giulianotti and J. Williams. Aldershot: Arena.

Arian, Asher. 2003. *Israeli Public Opinion on National Security 2003*. Tel Aviv: Jaffee Center for Strategic Studies.

Ashworth, C. E. 1970. "Sport as Symbolic Dialog," pp. 40–46 in *The Sociology of Sport*, ed. E. Dunning. London: Frank Cass.

Badran, Nabil. 1969. *Al-Ta'alim Wal-Tahdith Fi-Lmujtam'a Al-'Arabi Al-Falastini (Al-Juz'a Al-Awal: 'Ahd Al-Intidab)*. Beirut: Palestinian Liberation Organization: The Research Center.

Bashir, Nabih. 2004. *Judaizing the Place: Misgav Regional Council in the Galilee*. Haifa: Mada – Al-Karmil (in Arabic).

Bauml, Yair. 2001. "The Attitude of the Israeli Establishment toward the Arabs in Israel: Policy, Principles, and Activities: The Second Decade, 1958–1968." Ph.D. Thesis, University of Haifa, Haifa (in Hebrew).

Bazzano, Carmelo. 1994. "The Italian-American Sporting Experience," pp. 103–116 in *Ethnicity and Sport in North American History and Society*, eds. G. Eisen and D. Wiggins. Westport: Praeger Publishers, 1994.

Beinin, Joel and Joe Stork, eds. 1997. *Political Islam: Essays from Middle East Report*. Berkeley and Los Angeles: University of California Press.

Bellah, Robert. 1967. "Civil Religion in America." *Dedalus*: 1–21.

Ben-Porat, Amir. 1998. "The Commodification of Football in Israel." *International Review for the Sociology of Sport* 33: 269–276.

2001a. *Biladi, Biladi*. Tel Aviv: Babel (in Hebrew).

2001b. "'Biladi, Biladi': Ethnic and Nationalist Conflict in the Soccer Stadium in Israel." *Soccer and Society* 2: 19–38.

2001c. " 'Linesmen, Referees and Arbitrators': Politics, Modernization and Soccer in Palestine," pp. 131–154 in *Europe, Sport, World: Shaping Global Societies*, ed. J. A. Mangan. London and Portland: Frank Cass.

2003. *Soccer and Nationalism*. Tel Aviv: Resling (in Hebrew).

Benziman, Uzi and Atallah Mansour. 1992. *Subtenants: Israeli Arabs, Their Status and the Policy towards Them*. Jerusalem: Keter.

Bernstein, Deborah. 2000. *Constructing Boundaries: Jewish and Arab Workers in Mandatory Palestine*. Albany: State University of New York Press.

Birrell, Susan and L. Cole Cheryl. 1994. *Women, Sport and Culture*. Champaign: Human Kinetics Publishers.

Bishara, Azmi. 1998a. "Israeli-Arabs: Reading a Fragmented Political Discourse." *Al-Ahram*, February 5–11, 1998.

1998b. *The Ruptured Political Discourse and Other Studies*. Ramallah: Muwatin (in Arabic).

1999. "The Arabs in Israel: Reading a Fragmented Political Discourse," in *Between the "Me" and the "Us*," ed. A. Bishara. Jerusalem: Van Leer Institute, Ha-Kibbutz ha-Meuchad (in Hebrew).

Bourdieu, Pierre. 1978. "Pratiques Sportives et Pratiques Sociales," pp. 17–37 in *7me Congrès international de l'Association internationale de l'histoire de l'éducation physique et du sport*. HISPA, Paris: National du Sport et de l'Education Physique.

1984. *Distinction: A Social Critique of the Judgement of Taste*. Cambridge: Harvard University Press.

1988. "Program for the Sociology of Sport." *Sociology of Sport Journal* 5: 153–161.

Bourdieu, Pierre and Jean-Claude Passeron. 1977. *Reproduction in Education, Society and Culture*. London and Beverly Hills: Sage Publications.

Boyle, Raymond. 1994. " 'We Are Celtic Supporters...': Questions of Football and Identity in Modern Scotland," pp. 73–101 in *Game without Frontiers: Football, Identity, and Modernity*, eds. R. Giulianotti and J. Williams. Hants: Arena, Ashgate.

Brohm, Jean-Marie. 1978. *Sport – A Prison of Measured Time*. London: Ink Links.

1989 [1975]. *Sport – A Prison of Measured Time*. London: Pluto Press.

Bromberger, Cristian. 1995. "Football as World-View and as Ritual." *French Cultural Studies* 6: 293–311.

Burstyn, Varda. 1999. *The Rites of Men: Manhood, Politics, and the Culture of Sport*. Toronto, Buffalo, and London: University of Toronto Press.

Caspi, Dan and Mustafa Kabaha. 2001. "From Holy Jerusalem to the Spring." *Panim* 16 (March).

Chebel, Malek. 1984. *Le Corps dans la Tradition au Maghreb*. Paris: Presses Universitaires de France.

Chehabi, Houchang E. 2002. "A Political History of Football in Iran." *Iranian Studies* 35: 371–402.

Cheska, Alyce Taylor. 1988. "Ethnicity, Identity, and Sport: The Persistence of Power." *International Review for the Sociology of Sport* 23: 85–95.

Cohen, Hillel. 2003. "Land, Memory, and Identity: The Palestinian Internal Refugees in Israel." *Refuge: Canada's Periodical on Refugees* 21: 6–13.

Coles, Robert. 1975. "Football as a Surrogate Religion?" pp. 61–77 in *A Sociological Yearbook of Religion in Britain*, ed. M. Hill. London: SCM Press.

Cronin, Mike. 1997. "Which Nation, Which Flag? Boxing and National Identities in Ireland." *International Review for the Sociology of Sport* 32: 131–146.

Curtis, James, John Loy, and Wally Karnilowicz. 1986. "A Comparison of Suicide-Dip Effects of Major Sport Events and Civil Holidays." *Sociology of Sport Journal* 3: 1–14.

Delanty, Gerard and Patrick O'Mahony. 2002. *Nationalism and Social Theory: Modernity and the Recalcitrance of the Nation*. London, Thousand Oaks, and New Delhi: Sage Publications.

Di-Capua, Yoav. 2004. "Sports, Society and Revolution: Egypt in the Early Nasserite Period," pp. 144–162 in *Rethinking Nasserism*, eds. E. Podeh and O. Winckler. Gainesville: University Press of Florida.

Dichter, Shalom and As'ad Ghanem. 2003. "The Sikkuy Report 2002–2003." http://www.sikkuy.org.il/2003/english03/en2003.html.

Doyle, Andrew. 1997. "Foolish and Useless Sport: The Southern Evangelical Crusade against Intercollegiate Football." *Journal of Sport History* 24: 317–340.

Durkheim, Emile. 1969 [1915]. *The Elementary Forms of Religious Life*. New York: Free Press.

Edwards, Harry. 1973. *Sociology of Sport*. Homewood, IL: Dorsey Press.

Eisen, George. 1998. "Jewish Sport History and the Ideology of Modern Sport: Approaches and Interpretations." *Journal of Sport History* 25: 482–531.

Eisenstadt, Shmuel Noah and Bernhard Giesen. 1994. "The Construction of Collective Identity." *Archives Européennes de Sociologie* 36: 72–102.

Eitzen, D. Stanley and George H. Sage. 1993. "Sport and Religion," pp. 79–117 in *Religion and Sport: The Meeting of Sacred and Profane*, ed. C. S. Prebish. Westport: Greenwood Press.

Elias, Norbert. 1978. *The Civilizing Process*. Oxford: Blackwell.

Elias, Norbert and Eric Dunning. 1986. *Quest for Excitement: Sport and Leisure in the Civilising Process*. Oxford: Blackwell.

Emmet, Chad F. 1995. *Beyond the Basilica: Christians and Muslims in Nazareth*. Chicago and London: University of Chicago Press.

Fatés, Youcef. 1994. *Sport et Tiers-Monde*. Paris: Presses Universitaires de France.

Finn, Gerry. 1991. "Racism, Religion and Social Prejudice. Irish Catholic Clubs, Soccer and Scottish Identity: The Roots of Prejudice." *International Journal of the History of Sport* 8: 370–397.

Fozooni, Babak. 2004. "Religion, Politics, and Class: Conflict and Contestation in the Development of Football in Iran." *Soccer and Society* 5: 356–370.

Frankenberg, Ronald. 1957. *Village on the Border*. London: Cohen & West.

Gallagher, T. 1997. "Ethnic and Religious Identity in Modern Scotland: Culture, Politics, and Football." *Ethnic and Racial Studies* 20: 422–423.

Gems, Gerald. 1993. "Sport, Religion and Americanization: Bishop Sheil and the Catholic Youth Organization." *International Journal of the History of Sport* 10: 233–241.

Gerhardt, Marcus. 2002. "Sport and Civil Society in Iran," pp. 36–55 in *Twenty Years of Islamic Revolution: Political and Social Transition in Iran*, ed. E. Hooglund. Syracuse: Syracuse University Press.

Ghanem, As'ad. 1995. "The Municipal Leadership of Arabs in Israel – Continuity and Change." *Ha-Mizrah ha-Hadash* 37: 151–165 (in Hebrew).

   1998. "Margins in a Marginal Society – the Uniqueness of the Bedouin Society," in *The Arabs in the Israeli Politic – Dilemmas of Identity*. Tel Aviv: Tel Aviv University – Moshe Dayan Center (in Hebrew).

Ghanem, As'ad and Sarah Ozacky-Lazar. 1999. "The Arab Vote to the Fifteenth Knesset." Giv'at Haviva: The Institute for Peace Research (in Hebrew, unpublished).

Ghnayem, Mas'ud. 2000. *Sakhnin – Arḍ Al-Buṭulat Wa-Mawṭan Al-Shuhada Min Thawrat 36 Hata Intifaḍat Al-Aqṣa*. Sakhnin: Al-Ḥaraka al-Islamiyya (in Arabic).

Goffman, Erving. 1959. *The Presentation of Self in Everyday Life*. Garden City: Doubleday.

Goodger, John. 1985. "Collective Representation in Sacred Sport." *International Review for the Sociology of Sport* 20: 179–187.

Gramsci, Antonio. 1971. *Selections from the Prison Notebooks of Antonio Gramsci*, eds. Q. Hoare and G. N. Smith. London: Lawrence & Wishart.

Gruneau, Richard. 1983. *Class, Sports and Social Development*. Amherst: University of Massachusetts Press.

   1993. "The Critique of Sport in Modernity," pp. 85–109 in *The Sports Process*, eds. E. G. Dunning, J. A. Maguire, and R. E. Pearton. Champaign: Human Kinetics Books.

Guttmann, Allen. 1978. *From Ritual to Record: The Nature of Modern Sports.* New York: Columbia University Press.

Hargreaves, Jennifer. 1994. *Sporting Females: Critical Issues in the Sociology and History of Women's Sports.* London and New York: Routledge.

Hargreaves, John. 1986. *Sport, Power and Culture.* Cambridge: Polity.

Hartmann, Douglas. 1996. "The Politics of Race and Sport: Resistence and Domination in the 1968 African American Olympic Protest Movement." *Ethnic and Racial Studies* 19: 548–566.

  2000. "Rethinking the Relations between Sports and Race in American Culture: Golden Ghettos and Contested Terrain." *Sociology of Sport Journal* 17: 229–253.

  2003. *Race, Culture, and the Revolt of the Black Athlete.* Chicago: University of Chicago Press.

Hawari, Areen. 2004. "Under the Military Regime." *Adalah's Review* 4.

Henry, Ian P., Mahfoud Amara, and Mansour Al-Tauqi. 2003. "Sport, Arab Nationalism and the Pan-Arab Games." *International Journal for the Sociology of Sport* 38: 295–310.

Hoberman, John. 1997. *Darwin's Athletes: How Sport has Damaged Black America and Preserved the Myth of Race.* Boston and New York: Houghton Mifflin Company.

Hobsbawm, Eric. 1990. *Nations and Nationalism since 1780.* Cambridge: Cambridge University Press.

Hoch, Paul. 1972. *Rip Off the Big Game: The Exploitation of Sports by Power Elite.* Garden City: Anchor Books.

Hoffman, Shirl. 1992. "Sport as Religion," pp. 1–12 in *Sport and Religion,* ed. S. Hoffman. Champaign: Human Kinetics Books.

Horowitz, Dani. 1993. *Kmo Gesher Taku'a.* The Center for the Study of Arab Society in Israel, Beit Berl (in Hebrew).

Ibrahim, Hilmi. 1982. "Leisure and Islam." *Leisure Studies* 1: 197–210.

Jacob, Wilson C. 2005. "Working out Egypt: Masculinity and Subject Formation between Colonial Modernity and Nationalism, 1870–1940." PhD thesis, New York University, New York.

Jiryis, Sabri. 1969. *The Arabs in Israel.* Translated by M. Dobson. Beirut: The Institute for Palestine Studies.

Kabaha, Mustafa. 1996. "The Role of the Press and its Discourse in the Arab-Palestinian National Struggle." Ph.D. Thesis, Tel Aviv University, Tel Aviv (in Hebrew).

Katz, Sheila Hannah. 1996. "Adam and Adama, 'Ird and Ard': Engendering Political Conflict and Identity in Early Jewish and Palestinian

Nationalisms," pp. 85–101 in *Gendering the Middle East: Emerging Perspectives*, ed. D. Kandiyoti. New York: Syracuse University Press.

Kaufman, Haim. 1993. " 'Ha-Po'el' in the Mandate Period." Ph.D. Thesis, Haifa Univeristy, Haifa (in Hebrew).

1998. "The Zionist Sports Association: From National Sport to Political Sport." *Zmanim* 63: 81–90 (in Hebrew).

Khalaf, Issa. 1991. *Politics in Palestine: Arab Factionalism and Social Disintegration, 1939–1948*. Albany: State University of New York Press.

Khalidi, Rashid. 1997. "The Formation of Palestinian Identity: The Critical Years, 1917–1923," pp. 171–190 in *Rethinking Nationalism in the Arab Middle East*, eds. I. Gershoni and J. Jankowski. New York: Columbia University Press.

Khalifeh, Suha Maher. 1986. *The History of Organized Sports in Jordan*. Coral Gables: University of Miami.

Kimmerling, Baruch. 1977. "Sovereignty, Ownwership and 'Presence' in the Jewish–Arab Territorial Conflict: The Case of Bir'im and Ikrit." *Comparative Political Studies* 10: 155–176.

1985. "Between the Primordial and the Civil Definitions of the Collective Identity," pp. 262–283 in *Comparative Social Dynamics*, eds. E. Cohen, M. Lissak, and U. Almagor. Boulder: Westview.

Kimmerling, Baruch and Joel Migdal. 1993. *Palestinians: The Making of a People*. New York: Free Press.

Koopmans, Ruud and Paul Stathan. 1999. "Challenging the Liberal Nation-State? Postnationalism, Multiculturalism, and the Collective Claims Making of Migrants and Ethnic Minorities in Britain and Germany." *American Journal of Sociology* 105: 652–696.

Kraus, Vered and Robert W. Hodge. 1990. *Promises in the Promised Land: Mobility and Inequality in Israel*. New York: Greenwood Press.

Lanfranchi, Pierre. 1994. "Mekloufi, Un Footballeur Français dans la Guerre D'algerie." *Actes de la Recherche en Sciences Sociales*: 70–74.

Lenskyj, Helen. 1986. *Out of Bounds: Women, Sport, and Sexuality*. Toronto: Women's Press.

Levenberg, Haim. 1993. *Military Preparations of the Arab Community in Palestine 1945–1948*. London: Frank Cass.

Lockman, Zachary. 1996. *Comrades and Enemies: Arab and Jewish Workers in Palestine*. Berkeley: University of California Press.

Long, Jonahan and Ian Sanderson. 2001. "The Social Benefits of Sport: Where's the Proof," pp. 187–203 in *Sport and the City: The Role of Sport in Economic and Social Regeneration*, ed. C. Gratton and I. Henry. London and New York: Routledge.

Lorenz, Konard. 1966. *On Aggression*. New York: Harcourt, Brace, and World.

Lustick, Ian. 1980. *Arabs in the Jewish State*. Austin: University of Texas Press.

MacClancy, Jeremy. 1996. "Nationalism at Play: The Basques of Vizcaya and Athletic Club de Bilbao," pp. 181–199 in *Sport, Identity and Ethnicity*, ed. J. MacClancy. Oxford: Berg.

Magdalinski, Tara and Timothy J. Chandler, eds. 2002. *With God on their Side: Sport in the Service of Religion*. London and New York: Routledge.

Mahlmann, Peter. 1988. "Sport as a Weapon of Colonialism in Kenya: A Review of the Literature." *Transafrican Journal of History* 17: 152–171.

Malkki, Lisa. 1992. "National Geographic: The Rooting of Peoples and the Territorialization of National Identity among Scholars and Refugees." *Cultural Anthropology* 7: 24–44.

Mandle, W. F. 1979. "Sport as Politics: The Gaelic Athletic Association 1884–1916," pp. 99–123 in *Sport in History*, eds. R. Cashman and M. McKernan. St. Lucia: University of Queensland Press.

Mangan, James A. 2001. "Soccer as Moral Training: Missionary Intentions and Imperial Legacies." *Soccer and Society* 2: 41–56.

Markovits, Andrei S. and Steven L. Hellerman. 2001. *Offside: Soccer and American Exceptionalism in Sport*. Princeton: Princeton University Press.

Marty, Martin E. and R. Scott Appleby. 1993. "Introduction: A Sacred Cosmos, Scandalous Code, Defiant Society," pp. 1–19 in *Fundamentalism and Society: Reclaiming the Sciences, the Family and Education, The Fundamentlism Project*, eds. M. E. Marty and R. S. Appleby. Chicago and London: University of Chicago Press.

Marvin, Carolyn and David W. Ingle. 1999. *Blood Sacrifice and the Nation: Totem Rituals and the American Flag*. Cambridge and New York: Cambridge University Press.

Mason, Tony. 1995. *Passion of the People? Football in South America*. London and New York: Verso.

McKay, Jim. 1991. *No Pain, No Gain?: Sports and Australian Culture*. Brunswick: Prentice Hall.

Messner, Michael A. 1988. "Sports and Male Domination: The Female Athlete as Contested Ideological Terrain." *Sociology of Sport Journal* 5: 197–211.

Messner, Michael A. and Donald F. Sabo. 1990. *Sport, Men, and the Gender Order: Critical Feminist Perspectives*. Champaign: Human Kinetics Books.

Mitchell, Timothy. 2000. "The Stage of Modernity," pp. 1–34 in *Questions of Modernity*. Minneapolis: University of Minnesota Press.

Monterescu, Daniel. 1998. "The Cultural Construction of Arab Manhood in Jaffa." Tel Aviv University, Tel Aviv.

Morris, Benny. 1987. *The Birth of the Palestinian Refugee Problem: 1947–1949*. Cambridge: Cambridge University Press.

2004. *The Birth of the Palestinian Refugee Problem Revisited*. Cambridge: Cambridge University Press.

Mosse, George L. 1985. *Nationalism and Sexuality: Respectability and Abnormal Sexuality in Modern Europe*. New York: Howard Ferting.

Nauright, John. 1997. *Sport, Cultures and Identities in South Africa*. London and Washington: Leicester University Press.

Nelson, Mariah B. 1994. *The Stronger Women Get, the More Men Love Football: Sexism and Culture in Sport*. London: Women's Press.

Nelson, M. R. 1998. "Basketball as Cultural Capital: The Original Celtics in Early Twentieth-Century New York City." *Immigrants & Minorities* 17: 67–81.

Neuberger, Binyamin. 1996. "Trends in the Political Organization of the Arabs in Israel," pp. 27–40 in *Arab Politics in Israel at a Crossroads*, ed. E. Rekhess. Tel Aviv: The Moshe Dayan Center for Middle Eastern and African Studies, Tel Aviv University.

Novak, Michael. 1976. *The Joy of Sports*. New York: Basic Books.

Okay, Cunayd. 2002. "The Introduction, Early Development and Historiography of Soccer in Turkey: 1890–1914." *Soccer and Society* 3: 1–10.

Paz, Reuven. 1990. "The Islamic Movement in Israel and the Municipal Election of 1989." *Jerusalem Quarterly* 53: 3–26.

Peled, Yoav. 1992. "Ethnic Democracy and the Legal Construction of Citizenship: Arab Citizens of the Jewish State." *American Political Science Review* 86: 432–443.

Peres, Yochanan and Nira Yuval-Davis. 1969. "Some Observations on the National Identity of the Israeli Arabs." *Human Relations* 22: 219–233.

Plaut, Pnina O. and Steven E. Plaut. 2002. "Income Inequality in Israel." *Israel Affairs* 8: 47–68.

Rabinowitz, Dan. 1992. "Trust and the Attribution of Rationality – Inverted Roles amongst Palestinian Arabs and Jews in Israel." *Man* 27: 517–537.

1997. *Overlooking Nazareth – The Ethnography of Exclusion in Galilee*. Cambridge: Cambridge University Press.

2001. "The Palestinian Citizens of Israel, the Concept of Trapped Minority and the Discourse of Transnationalism in Anthropology." *Ethnic and Racial Studies* 24: 64–85.

Reshef, Nurit and Jeremy Paltiel. 1989. "Partisanship and Sport: The Unique Case of Politics and Sport in Israel." *Sociology of Sport Journal* 6: 305–318.

Robinson, Shira. 2003. "Local Struggle, National Struggle: Palestinian Responses to the Kafr Qasim Massacre and its Aftermath, 1956–1966." *International Journal of Middle East Studies* 35: 393–416.

2005. "Occupied Citizens in a Liberal State: Palestinians under Military Rule and the Colonial Formation of Israeli Society, 1948–1966." Ph.D. Thesis, Stanford University, Stanford.

Rosenfeld, Henry and Majid Al-Haj. 1990. *Arab Local Government in Israel*. London: Westview Press.

Rosenhek, Zeev. 1995. "The Origins and Development of a Dualistic Welfare State: The Arab Population in the Israeli Welfare State." Ph.D. Thesis, Hebrew University of Jerusalem, Jerusalem.

Rosenthal, Ruvik (ed.). 2000. *Kafr Kassem*. Tel Aviv: Ha-Kibbutz ha-Meuchad.

Rouhana, Nadim. 1988. "The Civic and National Subidentities of the Arabs in Israel: A Psycho-Political Approach," pp. 154–174 in *Arab-Jewish Relations in Israel: A Quest in Human Understanding*, ed. J. Hofman. Bristol: Windham Hall Press.

Roy, Olivier. 1996. *The Failure of Political Islam*. Cambridge: Harvard University Press.

Rubin-Peled, Alisa. 2001. *Debating Islam in the Jewish State: The Development of Policy toward Islamic Institutions in Israel*. Albany: State University of New York Press.

Sa'ar, Amalia. 1998. "Carefully on the Margins: Christian Palestinians in Haifa between Nation and State." *American Ethnologist* 25: 215–239.

Sage, George. 1998. *Power and Ideology in American Sport: A Critical Perspective*. Champaign: Human Kinetics Books.

Sakakini, Khalil. 1943. *Ma Tayassar*. Jerusalem: Franciscan Fathers.

Salamah, Abd al-Hamid. 1983. *Al-Riyadah al-Badaniyah ind al-'Arab*. Tripoli: Al-Dar al-Arabiya lil-Kutab.

Sasson-Levy, Orna. 2002. "Constructing Identities at the Margins: Masculinities and Citizenship in the Israeli Army." *Sociological Quarterly* 43: 357–383.

Schaeygh, Cyrus. 2002. "Sport, Health, and the Iranian Middle Class in the 1920s and 1930s." *Iranian Studies* 35: 341–369.

Sears, Hal. 1993. "The Moral Threat of Intercollegiate Sports: An 1893 Poll of Ten College Presidents, and the End of 'the Champion Football Team of the Great West.'" *Journal of Sport History* 19: 211–230.

Semyonov, Moshe. 1986. "Occupational Mobility through Sport: The Case of Israeli Soccer." *International Review for the Sociology of Sport* 21: 23–33.

Semyonov, Moshe and Ephraim Yuchtman-Yaar. 1992. "Ethnicity, Education, and Occupational Inequality: Jews and Arabs in Israel." *International Perspectives on Education and Society* 2: 215–224.

Shohat, Ella. 1989. *Israeli Cinema: East/West and the Politics of Representation*. Austin: University of Texas Press.

Shoked, Moshe. 1998. "Ethnic Identity and the Status of Arab Women in Israel," pp. 225–243 in *The Intercultural Experience – A Reader in Anthropology*, eds. M. Shoked and S. Deshen. Jerusalem and Tel Aviv (in Hebrew).

Silverstein, Paul A. 2002. "Stadium Politics: Sport, Islam, and Amazigh Consciousness in France and North Africa," pp. 37–55 in *With God on their Side: Sport in the Service of Religion*, eds. T. Magdalinski and T. J. Chandler. London and New York: Routledge.

Slusher, Howard. 1993. "Sport and the Religious," pp. 173–195 in *Religion and Sport: The Meeting of Sacred and Profane*, ed. C. Prebish. Westport: Greenwood Press.

Smooha, Sammy. 1998. "Suvreys among the Arab Population in Israel." *Emet Veseker*, vol. 173–198, ed. K. Fux and S. Bar Lev. Haifa: Ha-Kibbutz ha-Meuhad.

   1999. "The Advances and Limits of the Israelization of Israel's Palestinian Citizens," pp. 9–33 in *Israeli and Palestinian Identities in History and Literature*, ed. K. Abdel-Malek and D. C. Jacobson. New York: St. Martin's Press.

Sorek, Tamir. 2002. "Memory and Identity: The Land Day Monument." *ISIM Newsletter*: 17.

   2003. "Arab Football in Israel as an 'Integrative Enclave.'" *Ethnic and Racial Studies* 26: 422–450.

Soto, Helene and Maxime Travert. 1997. "La Rencontre des Footballs dans un Quartier Populaire Marseillais." *Sociétés* 55: 51–56.

Stevenson, Christopher and Robert Dunn. 1998. "The Paradox of the Church Hockey League." *International Review for the Sociology of Sport* 33: 131–141.

Stevenson, Thomas and Abdul-Karim Alaug. 1997. "Football in Yemen: Rituals of Resistance, Integration and Identity." *International Review for the Sociology of Sport* 32: 251–265.

Stuart, Ossie. 1996. "Players, Workers, Protestors: Social Change and Soccer in Colonial Zimbabwe," pp. 167–180 in *Sport, Identity and Ethnicity*. Oxford: Berg.

Sugden, John and Alan Bairner. 1993. *Sport, Sectarianism and Society in a Divided Ireland*. Leicester: Leicester University Press.

Suleiman, Ramzi. 2002. "Minority Self-Categorization: The Case of the Palestinians in Israel." *Peace & Conflict* 8: 31–46.

Suleiman, Ramzi and Benjamin Beit-Hallahmi. 1997. "National and Civic Identities of Palestinians in Israel." *Journal of Social Psychology* 137: 219–228.

Tamari, Salim. 1999. "The Local and the National in Palestinian Identity," pp. 3–8 in *Israeli and Palestinian Identities in History and Literature*, eds. K. Abdel-Malek and D.C. Jacobson. New York: St. Martin's Press.

Tehranian, Majid. 1993. "Fundamentalist Impact on Education and the Media: An Overview," pp. 313–340 in *Fundamentalism and Society: Reclaiming the Sciences, the Family and Education*, eds. M.E. Marty and R.S. Appleby. Chicago and London: University of Chicago Press.

Theberge, Nancy. 1995. "Gender, Sport, and the Construction of Community: A Case Study from Women's Ice Hockey." *Sociology of Sport Journal* 12: 389–402.

Tidhar, David. 1961. *Be-Sherut ha-Moledet*. Tel Aviv: Yedidim.

Tomlinson, Allan. 1994. "Fifa and the World Cup," pp. 13–23 in *Hosts and Champions*, eds. J. Sugden and A. Tomlinson. Aldershot: Arena.

Tuastad, Dag. 1997. "The Political Role of Football for Palestinians in Jordan," pp. 123–140 in *Entering the Field – New Perspectives on World Football*, ed. G. Armstrong and R. Giulianotti. Oxford: Berg.

Vinnai, Gerhard. 1973. *Football Mania*. London: Ocean Books.

Wagg, Stephen. 1995. "Mr. Drains Go Home: Football in the Societies of the Middle East," pp. 163–178 in *Giving the Game Away – Football, Politics and Culture on Five Continents*, ed. S. Wagg. London and New York: Leicester University Press.

Walvin, James. 1978. *Leisure and Society 1830–1950*. London: Longman.

Weitman, Sasha. 1973. "National Flags: A Sociological Overview." *Semiotica* 8: 328–367.

Werbner, Pnina. 1996. "On Identity and Social Empowerment among British Pakistanis." *Theory, Culture and Society* 13: 53–79.

White, Philip and Brian Wilson. 1999. "Distinctions in the Stands: An Investigation of Bourdieu's 'Habitus,' Socioeconomic Status and Sport Spectatorship in Canada." *International Review for the Sociology of Sport* 34: 245–264.

Wiggins, David K. 1994. *Glory Bound: Black Athletes in a White America.* New York: Syracuse University Press.

Wilcox, Ralph C. 1994. "The Shamrock and the Eagle: Irish Americans and Sport in the Nineteenth Century," pp. 55–74 in *Ethnicity and Sport in North American History and Culture,* ed. G. Eisen and D. Wiggins. Westport: Praeger Publishers, 1994.

Willis, Joe and Richard Wettan. 1977. "Religion and Sport in America: The Case for the Sports Bay in the Cathedral Church of Saint John the Divine." *Journal of Sport History* 4: 189–207.

Wilson, Thomas. 2002. "The Paradox of Social Class and Sport Involvement: The Roles of Cultural and Economic Capital." *International Review for the Sociology of Sport* 37: 5–16.

Yiftachel, Oren. 2000. "Minority Protest and the Emergence of Ethnic Regionalism: Palestinian-Arabs in the Israeli 'Ethnocracy,'" pp. 145–180 in *Ethnic Challenges to the Modern Nation State,* ed. S. Ben-Ami, Y. Peled, and A. Spectorowski. London and New York: Macmillan and St. Martin's Press.

Yurdadon, Ergun. 2004. "Sport in Turkey: the Post-Islamic Republican Period." http://www.thesportjournal.Org/2004journal/Vol7-No1/ Yurdadon.Asp.

Zureik, Elia. 1979. *The Palestinians in Israel – A Study in Internal Colonialism.* London, Boston, and Henley: Routledge & Kegan Paul.

Index